MS-DOS MASTERCLASS

Rex Last

SIGMA PRESS – *Wilmslow, United Kingdom*

CW01481082

First published in 1994 by

Sigma Press, 1 South Oak Lane, Wilmslow, Cheshire SK9 6AR, England.

British Library Cataloguing in Publication Data

A CIP catalogue record for this book is available from the British Library.

ISBN: 1-85058-322-6

Typesetting and design by

Sigma Press, Wilmslow

Cover design by

Design House

Distributed by

John Wiley & Sons Ltd., Baffins Lane, Chichester, West Sussex, England.

Acknowledgement of copyright names

Within this book, various proprietary trade names and names protected by copyright are mentioned for descriptive purposes. Full acknowledgment is hereby made of all such protection.

Preface

Thank you for acquiring this book, or at least for picking it up from the overcrowded shelves of the computer section in your local bookshop to see if it is "just another" allegedly indispensable guide to MS-DOS, which really does little more than rearrange the manual. If you want that kind of thing, look elsewhere. This is a book for tinkerers and enthusiasts, who like to rise to the challenge of making the operating system "go that extra mile", as a politician once put it, to stretch its capabilities in order to make your life as a programmer and general user just that little bit easier. And, at the same time, it is also designed for those of you fascinated by what makes your computer work on the software side, and who like to try something out just for the fun of it.

To make full use of many of the programs and batch files in this book, you will need Version 5 or 6 of MS-DOS, but much can run under any Version from 3.2 upwards.

This is not in any sense a sequel to my previous book, *MS-DOS Revealed*, and there is no assumption that you have read your way through it first. This is a separate book in its own right, although there is nothing to prevent you from going out and buying *MS-DOS Revealed*, with which it has one thing in common: it's designed to help and encourage enthusiasts who like to lift the veil a little and explore behind the scenes of MS-DOS, pushing the system to the limit and discovering all kinds of new tricks it can perform. In addition, it's for those of you with plenty of curiosity, who don't just accept, for example, that colours appear on the screen. You want to know how and why and what you can do about them. Or you want to know how to make your files secure from prying eyes, what the best way of finding out which of your files has that quote from Shakespeare in it without having to load the lot of them and put them through a wordprocessor.

Those questions and many others will be answered in these pages. In addition, I shall be sharing with you some of the many hints and tips about MS-DOS which I have accumulated over years of writing about the PC's favourite operating system in a variety of computing magazines.

We begin by looking at the commands of the operating system itself, then I shall gradually stir in a little QBASIC, and later on, some assembler, but you do not have to be an expert programmer to make sense of what is happening. All I assume is a little knowledge of BASIC.

You do not need to have a technical background to follow what's going on in these pages. Where the going gets difficult, I'll explain everything in terms that I can understand, and if I can follow it, believe me, you can. There are appendices to help you on your way with assembler, DEBUG, and other advanced topics. Some of the material in the appendices borrows from *MS-DOS Revealed*, but the information has been expanded and extended. The same applies to the Bibliography.

One comment about jargon. I prefer to use the term *filetype* for the letters appearing after the dot in filenames, but extension is a synonym for it. MS-DOS also tends to refer to directories, but I prefer the term subdirectories for all directories except the root directory itself. I find that a little clearer, even if the word is a bit of a mouthful.

Rex Last

CONVENIENCE DISK

For those of you who find it a tiresome and error-prone business to type in programs, there is a disk accompanying to book, which contains all the main listings in these pages together with a few extra programs thrown in for good measure.

To obtain a copy, send a cheque for £6.50 made out to LocheeSoft, Oak Villa, New Alyth, Perthshire PH11 8NN, clearly stating that you require the MS-DOS Masterclass disk and also whether you require a 3.5 inch or 5.25 inch disk. Please allow up to 28 days for delivery.

CONTENTS

1

Getting under way

Let me begin by telling you what this book is not about. You will, I hope, be relieved to know that it isn't just another introduction and tutorial guide to MS-DOS 6. Heaven knows that there are more than enough of these weighty and expensive tomes on the market, and I have no intention of adding to their number.

Nor is it absolutely essential to own MS-DOS 6.2 before you can read and enjoy the contents of this book. Quite a few of the programs listed in these pages will actually run on earlier versions of MS-DOS, although some require features only found in Version 5 and later.

If you are considering moving up to this version of Microsoft's operating system for the PC, you will find quite a few compelling reasons to do so. To this extent, you can use this book as a shop window for MS-DOS 5 and 6, although I shall have nothing to say about the new shell, the menu-driven interface which you can run the system from if you really must.

In fact, the first thing I did when I obtained MS-DOS 5 was to remove the line:

SHELL

– from the AUTOEXEC.BAT file. This, as you will know, is the batch file which – if it is found – is run at power-up time, and which sets up various defaults, such as what path is to be selected and various other bits and pieces. The best way of removing SHELL is to type:

EDIT AUTOEXEC.BAT

Then, if you were not aware of it already, you would discover that – at last – MS-DOS 5 (and 6) has a half-decent screen editor, which will enable you to prevent SHELL from being executed by adding the command REM:

REM SHELL

It is always wise to leave a line in place rather than just delete it, in case you need it at a future date. When you have left edit (by pressing Alt+F followed by X and Enter), you should consider setting up an archive of old versions of AUTO-EXEC.BAT and CONFIG.SYS (the other file run at power-up time, which helps set up the system and install device drivers).

This is best achieved by creating a subdirectory:

MD ARCHIVE

– and then copying the BAK version to it. It is unwise to leave BAK versions of AUTOEXEC.BAT or CONFIG.SYS sitting around in the root directory, for one very good reason.

If you install an applications package, like a word-processor or a spreadsheet, it will do all kinds of things with those two files, probably creating its own BAK and OLD versions of them.

In fact, it is useful to examine your AUTOEXEC.BAT file in particular whenever you have installed such a package. I noticed, for example, with Word for Windows, that the PATH command had been changed so that MS-DOS looked first in one of the directories set up by Word, and only then at the /DOS subdirectory where all MS-DOS external commands are stored.

Tweaking the PATH

A bit of tweaking soon ensured that a more reasonable pecking order was restored, saving a bit of unnecessary twitching of the hard disk head whenever I wanted to work from the prompt.

This can be a great advantage in a variety of different circumstances. Here are just two examples. If you are developing an assembler program (which you will be doing later on – but don't worry, it will all be spelled out in simple terms for you) it may be useful to work from a RAM drive rather than a physical drive. In other words, you can set up an area of memory which behaves just like a disk drive, except that it is a great deal faster and doesn't involve physically moving disk heads around.

The RAM drive is set up from the CONFIG.SYS file from a command line which will look something like this:

```
C:\DOS\RAMDRIVE.SYS 4096 /A
```

Of course, the contents of the RAM drive disappear when you switch off or reboot the computer, so you have to build in a strategy to make back-ups of actual programs under development, but the resultant savings in wear and tear and, above all, time, are considerable. However, if you have a RAM drive loaded and then want to run a BASIC compiler which grabs all the memory, you will probably find that it won't work with a RAM drive taking up some of the space, so it would be nice to have two different versions – at least – of CONFIG.SYS, one containing the command setting up the RAM drive, the other with it duly omitted.

Incidentally, do check that your CONFIG.SYS file contains the line:

```
DEVICE=C:\DOS\ANSI.SYS
```

This screen driver should be present, otherwise some of the programs in this book won't work.

Another alternative use of options within AUTOEXEC.BAT is with a CD-ROM drive, which requires a different device driver setting up and possibly different path settings, too. I run the CD-ROM for a while and then load LocoScript which – despite protestations from friends with 'power' word-processors like WordStar and WordPerfect – is still my favourite word-processor after Trendtext, which, in my version at least, won't run under MS-DOS 5 or 6 even with the SETVER command seeking to pretend to it that it isn't really MS-DOS 5 (or 6) at all.

What does LocoScript do at that point? It insists on looking at Drive L, the drive letter allocated to the CD-ROM, and sits there sulking unless you switch the drive on and insert a CD. So it is better to have a customised set-up procedure for each major different use of the computer.

In fact, too few people recognise that their PC isn't just one computer – it is used for a whole variety of sometimes incompatible applications, and is in fact several machines in one. The 386 on my desk is a word-processor, a BASIC and assembler program developer, a DTP machine with a scanner attached, a CD-ROM reader, and so it goes on. One day it will have so many bells and whistles hung on to it that it will become like one of those old Russian generals, who don't die, they simply collapse under the weight of medals pinned on to them.

Under MS-DOS 6, you can in fact incorporate options within your CONFIG.SYS file, and under 6.2, you can also be selective with the AUTOEXEC.BAT as they run at start-up time, but personally I prefer to switch the computer on first thing in the morning and wander off to let it sort itself out and warm up without my having to stand over it. In addition, it is only relatively infrequently that I need the CD-ROM or the RAM drive, so I prefer to boot up with different start-up procedures for those options.

As you might gather, I am an inveterate tinkerer with operating systems, and far prefer to work from the prompt, which may be less friendly but gives you far greater control over the machine than a customised shell which only lets you do what it wants you to do.

A new HELP system

At least, under MS-DOS 5 a half-decent help system emerged. Now, under 6.2 as HELP and FASTHELP, this gives you about as close as a manual on a screen as you are likely to get. That, in my view, is one more reason why these huge guides to MS-DOS are becoming almost entirely obsolete.

I have tried to present in this book what the manual doesn't offer, additional features and new insights, rather than tiredly restating the help screens. Areas I have avoided – because manuals and HELP cover them effectively – include virus protection, disk compression, and memory management.

Those are run-of-the-mill housekeeping matters which really hold little of interest. I am much more fascinated by stretching the operating system to make it do things it didn't know that it could, and to bring added benefits and insights to myself as a user. First, though, we ought to look at Versions 5, 6, and 6.2 to examine just how radical the changes are that have been brought about in the operating system of your PC, what can be done that could not previously be achieved, and what enhancements we can add to make it even better.

2

The newer versions of MS-DOS

Why MS-DOS? There are 60 million reasons, the number of machines which Microsoft claims have MS-DOS in one Version or another loaded on to them.

The original version 1.0 ran in 8K of RAM, but Version 5 requires 2.8 Mb of hard disk space or so, not that this is a matter for concern in times when memory of all kinds is cheap. If MS-DOS 5 put the shareware add-on merchants out of business, MS-DOS 6 is threatening to do the same with commercial suppliers of packages like file compressors and virus checkers.

One really surprising feature of MS-DOS is its conservatism, its apparent reluctance to move as fast as users want it to. That's why so many little programs sprang up to fill in the odd gaps here and there, and people have made a good living in the past writing books with disks stuck on them containing improvements to this or that feature of MS-DOS.

Only now, for example, do we have a CHOICE command which allows us to interact properly with batch files, and a DOSKEY command which gives us a history of commands keyed in from the prompt and the opportunity to edit the command line without having to remember prehistoric function key options. And only with Version 6.2 has DISKCOPY really been brought up to speed.

Even more surprisingly, only now do we have an equivalent to that good old workhorse add-on program WHEREIS, which would sniff out files for you wherever they happened to be buried in the remotest subdirectory. DIR with the /S switch does it all for you.

Above all, only now do we have a really top quality HELP facility which gives full information on all aspects of the system at the touch of a button (or two). So now let us survey what Versions 5, 6 and 6.2 have to offer us.

The need to upgrade

The real question for most users now is that, if they have a reasonable version of MS-DOS, say 3.2, 3.3 or 4.1, is it really worth the time and effort of upgrading? What have the newer versions got that your version hasn't and which you might need to improve the performance of your system?

The simplest answer is that if you use your machine simply to run applications programs like word-processors, DTP, spreadsheets and the like, it may well be better to stick with the Version you know, not least because many packages will not work with the newer Versions (see the command SETVER as a means of deluding a package into thinking it's running under an earlier Version).

However, if you like to explore the system and benefit from the latest improvements – in other words, if you are a typical reader of this book – then the answer is a resounding Yes. But do check with your software suppliers that packages which ran under Version 3 or 4 will run under the latest Version, and if not, whether SETVER will do the trick.

Benefits of the new Versions

So what are the benefits? The most apparent in Version 5 is that you can use the system in one of two basic ways, either from a "shell" or in the familiar way from the command line prompt. Over its various versions, MS-DOS has been struggling away from the old CP/M operating system more and more in the direction of a WIMP-type environment (windows, icons, mice and pull-down menus, in case you were wondering).

The shell allows you to use either the keyboard or mouse, if you have one, to interact with dialogue boxes and so forth. However, the advantages of DOSSHELL appear not to have penetrated into the user base, because from Version 6.2 DOSSHELL is no longer available, although it can continue to be used if you wish.

Wiping it all out

Accidental file erasure has come in for a great deal of scrutiny in Versions 5 and following. When you delete a file under MS-DOS, you don't actually delete it. All that happens is that the directory entry is marked as free and the space which the file occupies is equally marked as available for writing over.

The actual contents of the file are still there on the disk. The only problem in the past has been that there has been no way of reassembling the bits of a deleted file, which may be scattered all over a disk in non-contiguous sectors, since the system has had no good reason for keeping a record of where all the bits of a deleted file were.

This means that, if the facility existed, it might be possible to retrieve an undeleted file provided that you haven't in the mean time created a new file which has used up some or all of the space which the deleted file occupied.

In the MIRROR

The best way of optimising your chances of retrieving a lost file under 5.0 is to use the MIRROR utility. What this does is to keep track of the files which have been deleted. It's a TSR (terminate and stay resident – in the memory, that is) program which takes up around 6.4K and which you invoke like this:

MIRROR /TA /TC

In that example, you have told MIRROR to keep a track of deletions on drives A and C, and bless its heart, MS-DOS comes up with a nice inconsistency here, just to keep consistent with its other inconsistencies, if you get my drift. You must not put the colon after the drive letter, which is rather like the notice which states: Do not throw stones at this notice.

You are warned by the manual not to use MIRROR with JOIN and SUBST, and to be careful if you are using ASSIGN not to use MIRROR first. In my view, those three commands should only be available on prescription anyway.

When you delete a file, PCTRACK.DEL is updated, and the system has a default value for the number of deleted files it keeps records on and the consequent size of the tracking file. This ranges from 25 entries on a 360K disk, which involves a tracking file of 5K to a whopping 300 on a 32Mb plus hard disk which cranks PCTRACK.DEL up to 55K.

To override the default number of files to be tracked, you have to employ this format:

MIRROR /TC-200

– which keeps track of up to 200 files on drive C.

Of course, if you are deleting large numbers of files, MIRROR will slow your system down. The most obvious way to install the program if you feel the need for it is to put the appropriate MIRROR command in your AUTOEXEC.BAT file.

To try and recover a lost file, you use UNDELETE. The golden rule is to try and recover a file as soon as possible after it has been deleted and certainly before running other programs or saving or creating more files.

If you type plain:

UNDELETE

– it will try and recover all the files it can. Otherwise specify a particular file or use wildcards to try and recover groups of files. If you haven't got MIRROR installed, it is still possible that you can undelete a deleted file or files.

Of the other switches available with UNDELETE, the most useful is this one:

UNDELETE /LIST

– which lists the files which are able to be recovered, without actually doing any recovery work. This can be very useful in helping you to recall which files you have recently erased.

Useful though the utility is, it doesn't perform miracles, so don't expect it to be able to restore a deleted directory or files from a directory which has been deleted. It may, however, be possible by using another command, UNFORMAT.

Among other benefits of Version 5 are DOSKEY and improvements to DIR, both of which we shall be considering in some detail in this book.

Version 6.0

When I first started working on this book, MS-DOS 6 was still nothing more than a vague promise, a twinkle in the programmer's eye. Its predecessor, MS-DOS 5, had settled down well in the market place, with very reasonable reviews and a great deal of gratitude that at long last Microsoft had filled in the many gaps in the operating system which had long been lamented by the many and leaped on by the few who promptly designed routines and whole packages to make up for the deficiencies.

Some of these alleged deficiencies were more apparent than real. Take, for example, the much lamented absence of a MOVE command to shift a file from one disk, drive and directory to somewhere else in the system. From MS-DOS, this is hardly a problem, requiring just a few keystrokes. Now MOVE comes into being in its own right.

So, of course, it was possible to achieve a great deal with earlier MS-DOS versions, but it required knowledge and time which most people did not possess. Two examples among many of what was missing were the ability to find a file anywhere on a disk or drive and the ability to make quick and efficient back-ups of data files.

It should be pointed out that there are occasions when the operating system is not necessarily the best means of carrying out certain tasks, like tagging a subset of files in a directory and copying them to a back-up disk. You may well find that your word-processor, spreadsheet or other major pieces of software will contain just those facilities you want.

The argument about the deficiencies, real or apparent, of MS-DOS has shifted dramatically in MS-DOS 6 to a quite different area, that of what the role of an operating system is. Where does it stop and where do the proper boundaries lie?

Is it appropriate, to cite one example where a lot of software companies have a big stake, to incorporate antivirus software? Or a disk fragmenter or file compressor? Areas which had long been thought to be the territory of third-party software houses have now been taken over wholesale by Microsoft.

Or, with all those excellent help files, is it threatening to put people like me out of business! Now under Version 6, there is a comprehensive HELP facility based on the EDIT program, and a FASTHELP utility, which gives a screenful of help based on Version 5's HELP program.

Perhaps in a strange way this is a recognition of the fact that, at last, MS-DOS has matured to the point at which it's getting difficult to see what else you could possibly add to it to improve it, as a traditional command driven operating system.

A big change comes with the manual, which apart from winning first prize in the silliest manual cover of the year contest is quite different. It does not duplicate the information in help files. It's under half the nearly 700 pages of MS-DOS 5 and it has a more topic based approach.

CONFIG.SYS can have alternative configurations, and at long last CHOICE allows you to answer questions from inside a batch file, and we shall be examining later whether it really measures up to the task. Then there is DELTREE, a potentially lethal weapon which allows you to delete entire directories and their subdirectories.

There is a new much improved file back-up facility, anti-virus programs and other features, too, including DEFRAG, a disk defragmenter. The disk compression facility DoubleSpace has also been introduced, as have improved memory management facilities. Two new utilities for portable computers are on stream: Interlink allows you to link 2 PCs and access disk drives of one machine from the other, and POWER with portables using APM (Advanced Power Management) can save up to 25 per cent on batteries.

Version 6.2

Just as this book was going off to my long-suffering publisher, along came yet another upgrade to MS-DOS, Version 6.2. I must have blinked somewhere along the line and missed 6.1, although there was an upgrade with that name released which included increased power saving for portable machines.

The emphasis in this upgrade is on extending and expanding some of the more powerful facilities of Version 6, and there is a strong feeling that many of the features included are there to cope with some of the problems which have arisen with Version 6. For example, the improved scope of DEFRAG is obviously in response to people with huge hard disks and lots of files on them. In addition, the SMARTdrive add-on is probably an attempt to save some users from themselves.

Increased control is another feature – you can do a great deal more now with DoubleSpace and ScanDisk. All in all, then, this upgrade fills in a few minor gaps in Version 6 and adds some very useful features, which Microsoft itself indicates are aimed at increasing the safety of your system and its data, as well as enhancing ease of use.

Here is a brief run-down on what 6.2 has to offer. The first in line is the comprehensive, powerful and user-friendly replacement for CHKDSK, ScanDisk, which keeps you entertained with pretty pictures while it performs its excellent work.

ScanDisk examines disks and drives for errors, takes remedial action and offers a log of its activities. It can work on both uncompressed drives and drives which have been compressed using DoubleSpace. In addition, DoubleSpace now runs ScanDisk to ensure that a disk is in a fit state before setting about the work of compressing it.

If you try ScanDisk out on a 1.44Mb floppy disk, up comes a diagrammatical representation of the clusters on the disk (2847 in all), indicating which are fully used, which partly, which are not used, and which are faulty. You can see a running total of which clusters have been examined and which, if any, are bad.

If physical problems are found, data is moved to a safe area and the problem areas are marked as unusable. ScanDisk keeps a log of its efforts, and these can be saved to a file for reference purposes.

ScanDisk checks for media description, file allocation tables, directory structure, file system and it also offers a 'surface scan', CHKDSK still remains available, but you are advised to use ScanDisk instead, especially as a replacement for CHKDSK/F, the error fixing option for CHKDSK.

DoubleSpace now includes a feature called DoubleGuard. This checks memory for data corruption and closes down the system if it detects a fault in order to minimise damage. DoubleGuard can be turned off to save space – it is switched on by default.

DoubleSpace is now more flexible, in that a drive can be uncompressed, and now DoubleSpace itself can be uninstalled.

We turn next to HIMEM, which organises the use of extended memory in your machine. You should find it implemented in a DEVICE line in your CONFIG.SYS file. If it is not there, see the HELP information on HIMEM. In addition to its management role, HIMEM now tests for the integrity of extended memory at power-up time.

To switch HIMEM off, you need the switch /TESTMEM:OFF and to get more information on what it is up to, you need the switch /V (or /VERBOSE, if you want to be verbose!). It is also possible to inspect what HIMEM is up to by holding down the Alt key during its operation at boot-up time.

SMARTdrive, which speeds up operations as a cache (a fast halfway house between memory and drives), has been improved in two ways. First, it is now configured in such a way that it completes its operations before restoring the system prompt, so that it is much less likely that you switch the machine off while it is working.

SMARTdrive now also caches CD-ROM drives, but you must load MSCDEX before you include the SMARTdrive line in your AUTOEXEC.BAT file. On the subject of AUTOEXEC.BAT, it is now possible to step through it, as was the case with CONFIG.SYS, by holding down the F8 key.

The excellent DEFRAG now uses extended memory to allow it to deal with bigger hard disks with more files and directories on them. There's a cosmetic improvement, too, to DIR, MEM, CHKDSK (even though you are advised not to use it now) and FORMAT. Numbers greater than 999 are given commas – just when I was getting used to the old format, too. I have no information on whether the commas are replaced by full stops in German, and in other language conventions where appropriate.

DISKCOPY at last uses the hard disk as a halfway house, allowing copying between Drive A and Drive A to proceed at a good pace and without interminable disk-swapping. It not only tries to sort out bad sectors for you, it also – at long last – invites you to make another identical copy without your having to read the entire source disk again. MOVE, COPY and XCOPY now check with you if you are about to overwrite files, unless you use the /Y option, or put this command into your AUTOEXEC.BAT:

SET COPYCMD=/Y

All in all, a great deal has happened on the MS-DOS front since Version 4. In this book, I shall not be dealing with viruses, memory management, defragmentation, double space, or any of the features which you can read up from the manual or the screen-based help programs. We are going on a much more interesting voyage of discovery.

3

Going Ex-Directory

Let us get our explorations properly under way with the most frequently-used command in the entire canon: DIR. It has certainly been improved under MS-DOS 5/6 almost beyond recognition with new parameters and a sneaky way of customising it, but there are still a few more changes which could be made, some of which I shall be exploring.

Of all the MS-DOS commands, the internal command DIR is used far more than any other, providing as it does essential information about which files are where. Earlier versions of MS-DOS did not offer much in the way of options or switches: the only ones available were /P for a paused listing, in other words, the listing would halt after every screenful and invite you to continue, and /W for a "wide" listing, in other words, across the screen, but with only the filename and type given in each case.

It was also possible to go for both options – DIR /P/W – but that is the extent of the previous range of offerings for DIR. If you wanted to go beyond that level before MS-DOS 5, you would have to jump through a variety of hoops to obtain, for example, a sorted listing of a directory (by name, extension, size, date and so on), by using a hamfisted command like this one:

```
DIR | SORT/+10
```

That forgettable mouthful sorts in ascending alphabetical order by extension name by using the SORT filter. Note that the plus sign, for reasons best known to MS-DOS, is necessary. If you can work out (and remember) the appropriate column positions, you can sort under other criteria, too, and even include a pause option, by feeding the SORT output through the MORE filter. Equally, you can filter out lines containing or not containing specified strings by using FIND, so:

```
DIR | SORT | FIND /V "<DIR>" | MORE
```

– provides a listing which sorts the directory by filename, excludes subdirectories (lines containing the string "<DIR>") and pauses at the end of each page. It also takes its time to run, particularly if you are working from floppy disks. Just for the record, here are the column numbers for picking out each part of the directory listing:

1   – filename

10 – filetype

14 – file size

24 – day of the month

27 – month

30 – year

34 – time

Note that the contents beginning columns 24 and 27 will depend on which format of the date you have implemented. The information given here implies that you have set up the date in UK format.

Using filters is really only a practical proposition if you are running from a hard disk – as you will discover if you have floppies only, it takes a while to load the filters from disk and run them, and even that assumes you have the appropriate access to the files in the first place.

The possibilities under Version 5 are very greatly enhanced and far easier to use, and it is very well worth taking a closer look at them here, not least because hardened users of MS-DOS may not have considered the possibility that DIR has been touched up, and there are a few additional wrinkles which even the manual does not make very explicit. On top of that, there is a way of customising DIR which avoids the necessity for typing any additional options on every occasion you want a directory listing.

DIR consists of the command itself, a built-in command which is loaded as part of COMMAND.COM, and optional parameters and switches. The parameters are familiar enough, consisting as they do of the drive letter, the path, and the filename, so:

```
DIR D:\FRED *.BAK
```

– will list all BAK files in the FRED subdirectory of Drive D, provided both that the drive and path exist.

A new set of switches

The real interest focuses on the switches, which offer a wide range of options, far more than you are likely to need (rather than, as seemed to be the rule with options under earlier versions of MS-DOS, far less!). Before going down the list, there are two important points to bear in mind.

The first is that of the seven switches, which are all prefaced by the slash character ('/'), two can be followed by additional single letters which further specify the files you are after. These additional letters can optionally be preceded by a colon, so both the following make good sense to MS-DOS:

```
DIR /AH
DIR /A:H
```

The command means: List all files in the current directory with the hidden attribute set. As we shall see later, this attribute switch can be used to great effect (see Chapters 13 and 14).

The second point to note is that most of the switches and all of the single-letter specifiers can be preceded by a minus sign which negates the command. Here are just a couple of examples:

```
DIR /A:-D
DIR /-P
```

The first lists only the files in the current directory, not the names of subdirectories. The second lists the directory without pausing at the end of each screenful. What, you may be wondering, is the possible use of this command? Surely it is just the same as typing plain DIR. As you will see in the next Chapter, when we look at DIRCMD, there is a use for this variation on the /P switch, believe it or not.

Note, for the sake of completeness, that you can type DIR/A or DIR/-A, and DIR/O and DIR/-O.

Now for the switches in more detail.

The attribute switch

The /A switch, followed by a single letter, specifies files of a specified attribute only. One or more options can be used, but no spaces after the slash are allowed. As you may know, a file does not only have a name and type, a date stamp and a size, it also has one or more attributes, as follows:

A = 'archive'. What it means is that, every time you modify a file, the attribute byte is set. This allows the system to know which files to back up using XCOPY if you specify that only files with the attribute byte set are to be copied, like this:

```
XCOPY C: A:/A
```

– or the more useful:

XCOPY C: A:/M

– which switches the archive attribute off after each file has been copied, which, as we shall see, can be very useful indeed.

D = 'directory'. A filename and associated filetype can be used for three purposes: first, and most commonly, to name a file, so that you can access it for normal purposes, like reading, writing, copying or erasing it. Next, it can be used for the name of a subdirectory – for which purpose, it can have a filetype or extension just like an ordinary file. The filetype is not used very often in subdirectory names, but LocoScript on the PC, for example, creates two main directories: LS.PC, and LS.ETC.

Finally, the name of the drive itself, called the Volume label, in other words, the name of your hard drive or floppy disks, which can be up to eleven letters long (without a full stop in the middle).

If you ask for files which are not of directory status, you are, in effect, asking for a list of subdirectories in the current directory. Volume labels are not on offer.

H = 'hidden'. Your root directory should contain two hidden files, named IO.SYS and MSDOS.SYS or similar, which are loaded when the system is powered up.

R = 'read'. If this attribute is set (somewhat confusingly, to me at least), it means not that you can read it, but that you can't overwrite it. I would have thought that unsetting the read attribute would do that, but that is the way of the world. It is a useful security measure to prevent accidental erasure of important files.

S = 'system', for system files, which tend to be hidden files anyway.

A footnote on switches: one of the mega-grumbles about previous versions of MS-DOS was that ATTRIB could only be used to inspect and alter the A and R attributes. Not only has that omission been made good in Version 5, with A, H, R and S attributes able to be inspected and flip-flopped, but the addition of the /S switch allows this to be done to files in subdirectories of the current directory.

The basic switch

At least, I assume that /B stands for 'basic' or, possibly, 'bare', or 'bereft'. This option offers a vertical version of /W, but with the added omission, if that makes sense, of all the other detail normally associated with a directory listing: Volume label, directory identification, number of files, space used, and so on.

The lower case switch

If you opt for /L, the filenames and types – and subdirectory names – are listed in lower case. Apart from allegedly being more aesthetically pleasing than UPPER CASE, I have yet to think of a use for this particular switch.

There is one abstruse side effect of the /L switch, and that involves the use of unorthodox characters in filenames. If you have a filename containing an upper case e acute, it is not converted by /L, nor is a filename with a lower case e acute converted to upper case by /-L. Which all goes to prove something, but what that something is I have yet to discover.

The order switch

This switch, /O, is extremely useful, in that it allows you to determine the order in which the directory listing occurs, without the nightmare of having to tangle with SORT, which we described earlier. As in the case of /A, remember that the colon is optional, and that more than one option can be specified, just so long as there are no spaces after the slash.

Here is a list of options:

D = 'date'.   The directory listing is sorted by date and time, with the oldest filenames first. A minus before the D reverses the process. In the directory in which I have been developing programs for this book, my tinkerings around with information in the disk transfer area have led to a couple of files being created with these unorthodox and strictly illegal dates: 5/5/36 and 4/4/59. You will be pleased to know that this throws the D option into a state of some confusion.

E = 'extension'.   That is the alternative term for filetype, and sorts the directory listing in alphabetical order by extension. -E sorts by reverse alphabetical order, again by filetype.

G = 'group'.   That needs an additional word of explanation. The group referred to is the group of subdirectory names which tend to be scattered around the directory listing. If you ask for /O:G they are grouped at the beginning of the listing, and if you opt for /O:-G they appear at the end of the listing. By 'listing', I mean individual directory, as you may be asking for more than one directory to be listed overall, depending on the switches you have selected.

N = 'name'.   This performs exactly the same function for filenames as E above does for filetypes.

S = 'size'.   The option lists files, starting with the smallest, and -S asks for
                               the largest first.

Having run down the list of options and switches, here is an example of /A at work,
in conjunction with a few friends. See if you can work out what it does before I tell
you:

```
DIR /AD/S/P/B/L/OD
```

The answer is that it lists subdirectories names only in the current directory and all
subdirectories of the current directory in lower case and in alphabetically ascending
filename order, and it pauses at the end of every screenful.

The page switch

I include this at this point for the sake of completeness, and remind you that if it is
set, the directory listing pauses at the end of each screenful, and if it is not, the listing
whizzes past your very eyes until it is completed.

The subdirectory switch

Three cheers for the inclusion of this valuable tool. As we shall see later, this is one
of the new features of MS-DOS 5/6 which renders a familiar public domain program
redundant. It lists specified files in the current directory, and in all subdirectories of
the current directory.

The wide switch

This, with /P, is the other survivor from previous versions of MS-DOS, and lists files
across the screen. However, you will note that the names of subdirectories are now
usefully enclosed in square brackets, another helpful innovation.

Finally, don't forget DIR's partner in crime, TREE, which gives you a graphic picture
of the directory structure of your drive. Now we turn to another aspect of DIR.

4

DIR and the environment

It is particularly annoying to have to remember to type in /P each time, since most of the time you want to inspect the contents of a directory rather than just find out how much space is left over, and under previous versions you would have to create a batch file called something other than DIR, since MS-DOS looks first amongst the built-in commands for a match to a command typed in at the keyboard.

The problem arises from the fact that, unless you indulge in some fancy footwork, the command processor looks first for a match among built-in commands – like DIR, VER, CLS, COPY and so on), then for a match with the COM or EXE extension, and finally for a matching file with the BAT extension. This means that if you have a file called DIR.BAT, it will never get executed in the normal way of things. So customising DIR without either having a batch file with a different name presented something of a problem.

Even old-fashioned CP/M Plus, the ancestor of MS-DOS, contains a way round this particular bottle-neck. It includes a variant of a command called SET – not the same as the MS-DOS SET command, but related in that it modifies the operating environment – which enabled you to define which order the operating system would look for a match. For example:

`SETDEF M:,* [ORDER=(SUB,COM)]`

– would tell the operating system that, if you typed in the command LOGO, for example, it would look first for LOGO.SUB and only if LOGO.SUB did not exist would it look for LOGO.COM. The search would be carried out on Drive M and then on the currently logged-in drive.

This has the enormous advantage of enabling you to load LOGO.COM from the SUB file (the equivalent of an MS-DOS BAT file) after resetting certain keys on the keyboard to accommodate the editor. And when you exit from Logo itself, another command resets the keys to their default values before handing you back to the MS-DOS prompt.

Under MS-DOS, however, if there is a built-in command called DIR, you can have a file called DIR.BAT and another called DIR.COM and both would always be ignored, for reasons I explained a moment ago, unless you jumped through some fancy hoops, which are not worth describing here, since MS-DOS 5/6 avoids the problem. Just to say, though, that the batch file you would create would probably contain the one line:

`DIR/P`

There is a straightforward way of dealing with this matter now. If you type SET from the command prompt, you will see the environment variables currently in force. There are two kinds of such variables, those which you define, and those which have a special meaning to the operating system. In the latter category used to come just two: PROMPT and PATH.

The value of PROMPT

PROMPT tells the system what kind of command prompt you want, unless you have opted for the default prompt, which just gives the current drive. In any serious system, it should have the value:

`PROMPT=$p$g`

– which gives the drive and current directory. PATH tells MS-DOS where to look for commands and in what order.

Under MS-DOS 5/6 a new contender joins the fray. It has an unlovely name – DIRCMD – but it is extremely useful. To try it out, type:

`SET DIRCMD=/P`

Please note that SET is very fussy about spaces, so do not put any before or after the equals sign.

In case you are not too sure about SET and the environment, type SET at the MS-DOS prompt, and you will see the current settings of PROMPT, PATH and a couple of other system environment variables. It is possible for the user to extend the amount of environment space, if necessary, and also to create user-defined environment variables, which is particularly useful as an aid to the more efficient running of batch files.

DIRCMD is one of the new system variables and if it is present with the value /P, DIR acts as if you have typed DIR/P. Read on to see how this can be temporarily overruled in a batch file, after we have checked out DIRCMD to ensure that it functions properly.

Checking out DIRCMD

Now ensure you are in a directory with more than a screenful of files in it and type:

`DIR`

Lo and behold, this now has the same effect as if you had typed:

`DIR /P`

So DIR looks for the environment variable DIRCMD and, if it finds it, adds its contents as if they were a switch. Well, not quite, as we shall see in a moment, but this feature is so valuable that it is well worth incorporating that SET command in your AUTOEXEC.BAT file.

The obvious question that arises is: What if I want to override the /P option? The answer is that DIR doesn't just slavishly add whatever it finds in DIRCMD, it checks to see what you have put.

The rule goes like this. If you cancel out a switch – in our case, by putting /-P after your call of DIR – then you override it, but if you add a different switch, the current switch in DIRCMD remains in force.

In other words, if you have set DIRCMD as above:

`DIR /-P`

– produces a full directory listing with no pause between screenfuls (not a particularly useful exercise!), but:

`DIR /O:N`

– will produce a listing in alphabetical order by filename, pausing at the end of each screenful. Now that is what I call a sensible and useful improvement for DIR.

Unwanted pauses

There is one snag to setting the environment variable DIRCMD to /P which I came across by chance, and that was when I was experimenting with a command which would list all the subdirectories on the disk in alphabetical order, to ensure that I did not have two of the same or similar names lurking in different dark corners of my hard disk.

This is the command I came up with:

```
DIR /S/OG | FIND "<DI" | FIND /V "." | SORT
```

If you wanted to tip that lot into a file for further examination, add:

```
> TEMPFILE
```

to the end of the command, if you have enough breath left.

When I typed that in, the system responded briefly, with the hard drive light flickering on for a second, and then it hung. I pressed Enter, and on came the light again for a moment. I kept on pressing Enter – because by now it had occurred to me that the /P switch was in full swing, even though the information from the directory listing was not being sent to the screen!

So include the /-P switch in the command line. A better way of dealing with this kind of problem is to make use of the environment in a batch file which restores the default values of DIR for the duration of the batch file, like this:

```
SET OLDDIR=%DIRCMD%
SET DIRCMD=
SET
ECHO Now we run the batch file
SET DIRCMD=%OLDDIR%
SET OLDDIR=
SET
```

As I stated earlier, SET is enormously fussy about spaces, so ensure that no superfluous spaces creep into your version of this batch file. You should also distinguish carefully between:

```
SET JOE=FRED
```

– which sets JOE to the value FRED, and, assuming you had just executed that command, this line:

```
SET FRED=%JOE%
```

– sets FRED to the contents of JOE which, if you work it out, happens to be the string FRED! If that confuses you (and if it doesn't, why not?), try that out in a batch file. Then get rid of the two environment parameters like this:

```
SET FRED=
SET JOE=
```

– with no commas after the equals sign. So in our batch file, assuming that you have already typed (or included in your AUTOEXEC.BAT file):

```
SET DIRCMD=/P
```

– the effect of typing these commands:

```
SET OLDDIR=%DIRCMD%
SET DIRCMD=
```

is to put the current contents of DIRCMD into OLDDIR and to clear DIRCMD. Now the batch file can run safe in the knowledge that the default value of DIR is in charge of things, and at the end, you reverse the situation like this:

```
SET DIRCMD=%OLDDIR%
SET OLDDIR=
```

That sets DIRCMD to the contents of OLDDIR and erases OLDDIR from the environment. Try that out a line at a time from the MS-DOS prompt, typing SET after each line, to inspect the contents of the environment variables.

It is not necessary to do this in batch files with COPYCMD, as the /Y switch is turned on during the running of batch files.

Find that file

One of the much-used utilities of earlier versions of MS-DOS which helped to make up for its deficiencies was WHEREIS, a shareware program, I believe, which looked through all the directories for the file you asked for (wildcards are allowed).

If only, people have lamented often enough in the past, MS-DOS did the same. Now it does, using an option of DIR, but remember that it will only search from the current directory downwards:

```
DIR /S/P *.WP
```

– will look for all matching files in the current directory and subdirectories, and I've added the /P option for good measure to pause after every screenful, as this command can generate a fair amount of output, in fact, a great deal more information than WHEREIS was prepared to give away.

If you type from the root directory:

```
DIR/S
```

– you will list every file on the current drive in every directory, and I have just discovered I have 911 files on my 80Mb hard drive on my Notebook, which I only bought a couple of months back.

One useful application of this option is to see how many BAK files you have on a disk or drive which is filling up and which you wish to clear. That is a process which we are going to automate with a cunning little program in Chapter 15.

5

A better CHOICE?

Having written in *MS-DOS Revealed* quite a lot about batch files and their power and deficiencies, I turned with interest to see what MS-DOS 5/6 and its heirs and successors have done to alter and improve batch file handling. In particular, I was keen to know if some of the additional features which I and many others had suggested might have been incorporated.

Not a bit of it. As far as I can see, there have been no changes at all to batch files for Version 5. And that leaves quite a few niggling loose ends unresolved, one of the messiest of which concerns parameters and making sure that they work with you rather than against you. Then there is the vexed question of interacting with batch files.

In this respect, MS-DOS 6 has relented with a long-overdue command called CHOICE, which – although it doesn't go as far as I would like it to – is at least a vast improvement over PAUSE.

Let me explain the nature of the problem. In batch files, one of the things you are likely to want to do is to interact with them. One simple situation comes when a disk change is required, and the PAUSE command is ideal for this purpose:

```
ECHO Please insert a blank formatted disk in Drive A and press
Enter
PAUSE
```

The message Strike any key... comes up, and you duly insert your disk and away you go.

Incidentally, you can customise the PAUSE message like this:

```
ECHO Please now change disks and then press any key...
PAUSE > NUL
```

The message from PAUSE is redirected to the NUL device, in other words, it just disappears down the computing equivalent of a black hole, called in the jargon the "bit bucket".

Choosing from inside a batch file

The problem comes when you want to make a choice within a batch file. Very frequently, batch files are used to put up menus from which a selection has to be made, but up until Version 6 the only way round the problem has been to write a short assembler program to do the job for you.

The program is explained towards the end of Chapter 12, and in simple terms what it does is to flush the keyboard buffer – to avoid problems with any typing ahead you may inadvertently have done – and read one character from the keyboard.

Depending on requirements, this character can be converted to upper case or left as it is. The program returns to the batch file with a number corresponding to the ASCII code of the character pressed. This ASCII code, known as the exit code, can be inspected and acted on by a cumbersome mouthful called ERRORLEVEL (which I hope MS-DOS will in due course offer a human-friendly abbreviation for), which presents a few problems of its own. This is a technique which is used in MS-DOS to inform you of errors in commands like BACKUP and FORMAT.

We need to understand ERRORLEVEL if we are to use CHOICE in a moment or two, so let me offer an example to demonstrate how to handle it. Assume we have a menu in a batch file offering four options:

1 – Word processor

2 – Spreadsheet

3 – Database

4 – BASIC

We now insert the name of our custom-built program – let's call it READ – which waits for a keypress and then returns its ASCII value as an exit code. Now we need a number of commands to process this information, assuming that the exit codes we are after are the ASCII values 49-52, the decimal ASCII value of the characters generating the numbers 1-4.

At first sight, it may seem that you will get the result you are after if you type:

```
IF ERRORLEVEL 49 GOTO WP
IF ERRORLEVEL 50 GOTO SPREAD
```

– and so on, assuming that elsewhere in the batch file there are labels :WP, :SPREAD and so on followed by loading instructions. Not a bit of it. ERRORLEVEL returns the value true if the exit code is equal to or greater than the value it is testing for. In other words, IF ERRORLEVEL 49 will be true if the exit code is 49 or greater than 49, which means that if you wrote the batch file like that you would always get the word-processor loaded – unless you pressed a key which generated a value below 49, which we have not yet dealt with.

There are two solutions to the problem. The first is to produce a series of mouthfuls like this:

```
IF ERRORLEVEL 49 IF NOT ERRORLEVEL 50 GOTO WP
IF ERRORLEVEL 50 IF NOT ERRORLEVEL 51 GOTO SPREAD
```

– which tells the batch file to load the word-processor if the exit code is 49 and not equal to 50 or more, and so on. That is a nice tight way of proceeding, because it then allows you, after the four lines of IF commands, to put in the following:

```
ECHO Please press a key between 1 and 4
PAUSE
GOTO TRYAGAIN
```

The actual form of the command is a ghastly mouthful, though.

Descending exit codes

The second approach, and the one which you use by default with CHOICE, is to test for exit codes in descending order:

```
IF ERRORLEVEL 53 GOTO WRONGKEY
IF ERRORLEVEL 52 GOTO BASIC
IF ERRORLEVEL 51 GOTO DATAB
IF ERRORLEVEL 50 GOTO SPREAD
IF ERRORLEVEL 49 GOTO WP
:WRONGKEY
ECHO Please press a key between 1 and 4
PAUSE
GOTO TRYAGAIN
```

With the advent of CHOICE under Version 6, you are offered a tool which checks for keyboard input with an optional prompt and time delay. However, it still does not go that extra mile, to quote some politician or other, to take all the hassle out of batch programming. It still has to be processed using IF ERRORLEVEL, and there are a couple of messy switches to get on speaking terms with.

Here are some examples of CHOICE at work, with a fair range of options:

```
CHOICE
```

This is the default setting for CHOICE, which generates this output:

```
[Y,N]?
```

Note the question mark which is a nuisance if you are not asking a question but telling the user to make a choice, as the next example will show. The batch file will sit there waiting for you to press Y or N in upper or lower case. By default, CHOICE is not case sensitive. Now let's add a few embellishments, together with a warning:

```
CHOICE/C:abc "Choose between a b or c ---> "
IF ERRORLEVEL 3 ECHO c hit
IF ERRORLEVEL 2 ECHO b hit
IF ERRORLEVEL 1 ECHO a hit
```

The output on this occasion is:

```
Choose between a b or c ---> [A,B,C]?
```

There are quite a few points to note here. The first concerns the /C: option (the colon is itself optional), which is followed by the characters which you select as valid responses, in this case A, B or C in either upper or lower case. Note that the output converts the letters to upper case.

The next point concerns the double quotes. As you can see, they are stripped before the text appears. Their main function is to allow you to include a slash character. I have seen somewhere that you should not include piping or redirection operators even within quotes, but the chevron in the above example doesn't do any harm, maybe because it is the last character on the line. These are irritations we could again well do without.

The value of the quotes is that you can see the space at the end of the line – otherwise, the square bracketed options come immediately after the last character of the prompt string.

Now the important point: As in Miss World contests, the results have to be considered in reverse order, unless you use the IF ... IF NOT technique I described earlier. It is also essential, as you can see if you run this batch file without ECHO OFF, to follow the IF with GOTO, otherwise if you press A, each of the ECHO commands is obeyed.

Now for something slightly different:

```
CHOICE/C:123/T3,5
IF ERRORLEVEL 1 IF NOT ERRORLEVEL 2 ECHO 1 hit
IF ERRORLEVEL 2 IF NOT ERRORLEVEL 3 ECHO 2 hit
IF ERRORLEVEL 3 ECHO 1 hit
```

The prompt that comes up is:

`[1,2,3]?`

What about the /T option? This is a timer feature, which does two things. The character before the comma, which must be one of the options selected (or Y or N if none are chosen), is the option which CHOICE goes for if you do not press a key before the number of seconds after the comma has elapsed.

So the form of the option is:

`/Tcharacter pressed,time wait in seconds`

Case sensitivity

One further option concerns case sensitivity. The /S option tells CHOICE that the response should be case sensitive, so that with this command line:

`CHOICE/S/C:aBc`

– you get the following message:

`[a,B,c]?`

The batch file will only proceed if lower case a, upper case B, or lower case c is pressed.

A final option suppresses the square brackets, their contents, and – thankfully also – the question mark:

`CHOICE Yes or no?/N`

– simply waits for a response after printing:

`Yes or no?`

CHOICE can be used in the AUTOEXEC.BAT file, which allows you to select particular options and, in conjunction with the /T option, lets you power up the machine with you away from the keyboard. Here is a generalised example:

```
CHOICE Do you want feature X/Tn,5
IF ERRORLEVEL 2 GOTO NOTX
REM Line loading feature X
:NOTX
```

Add those lines to your AUTOEXEC.BAT file, and CHOICE waits for five seconds. If after that time Y has not been pressed, the feature concerned is not loaded, and execution of the batch file continues or concludes, as the case may be.

There are a couple of oddities about CHOICE, in particular the character selection option. The first is the pretty daft situation in which you can have the same character repeated in the /C option:

CHOICE/Cddd

– generates, not a bemused error message, but:

[D,D,D]?

I suspect that's the kind of choice which is put before the unfortunate victims in those Italian Mafia movies a few seconds before a bullet sprays their brains all over the expensive wallpaper. Another curiosity concerns non-keyboard characters. You can specify character 130, by pressing Alt+1+3+0 on the numeric keypad, but it comes out as [E]? in the prompt, not e acute as one might expect.

Other characters in the upper range are reproduced, but if you were thinking of using this feature in a batch file to cause your machine to 'hang' while you are away from the keyboard as a security measure, forget it. Pressing the Ctrl+C combination still generates the Terminate batch file(Y/N)? message, and that will soon get any unauthorised individual back at the MS-DOS prompt.

Unfortunately, there are some keys which CHOICE will not let you opt for, the space-bar being one of them. That is a commonly used key in menu situations, and again our customised program in Chapter 12 can be trained to deal with this for you.

So, all in all, CHOICE is a useful if rather fiddly tool, but you may well prefer the customised assembler program, or a number of variations on it.

A final word about CHOICE: although it doesn't make a great deal of sense to use it from the MS-DOS prompt, you can actually do so, and this will enable you to get used to CHOICE, go for a few dry runs with it, and see the pretty reasonable error messages that come when you make mistakes.

Do remember that if you are writing batch files for other users, you may have to assume that they have, say MS-DOS Version 3 and upwards, in which case you cannot assume access to CHOICE. Use VER to test for current version:

```
VER | FIND "blabla" > NUL
IF ERRORLEVEL 1 GOTO TIS6
```

Parameters for all

Now let me turn to the vexed question of parameters to batch files which I referred to at the beginning of this Chapter as a deficiency which MS-DOS has yet to make up for.

Let me begin with a brief survey of what parameters are and what they can and cannot do (until we have succeeding in bending them, that is). A batch file is a file with the extension or filetype BAT, which contains a sequence of MS-DOS commands that are carried out as if you were typing them in from the keyboard.

They are an important time-saving device, and your AUTOEXEC.BAT file is vital in automatically setting up your system in the way you want it, loading device drivers and setting up the appropriate path, for example, and possibly automatically loading a program like the MS-DOS shell.

One of the most useful and at the same time infuriating features of batch files is that of parameter substitution, which can best be explained by an example. Say that you have a batch file which you use to run a particular program in conjunction with one or more data files and depending on whether a parameter to the batch file was a particular day of the week. Nothing could be simpler:

PROCESS MYDATA TUESDAY

Or could it? The problem is that if you had typed in monday, tuesday etc, the only way to ensure that you coped with every possible combination of Monday mOnday, etc, would be a long list which the batch file command processor would laboriously have to struggle through, and if you are working from floppy disk, believe me, it would take an eternity. Not to put too fine a point on it, batch file parameters are infuriatingly case dependent.

One alternative would be to switch off the caps lock before the batch file is run, but that would be a high-risk strategy, as there is nothing to stop the user from switching it back on again. There must be some other way.

Solving the case problem

You will be relieved to know that there is, and the idea occurred to me purely by chance when I came across one feature of the operating system in which MS-DOS is particularly lenient. Most of the time, it's a pretty stern disciplinarian. Try jumping to a non-existent label in a batch file and you are unceremoniously dumped at the MS-DOS prompt with a flea in your ear and the curt message:

Label not found

But there are times when MS-DOS turns a blind eye, and that occurs in the case of non-existent environment variables. For those of you not too familiar with environment variables, here is a brief guide to them. If you are familiar with them, you can skip the next couple of paragraphs.

From the MS-DOS prompt, type:

SET

– and you will see the environment variables currently in operation, the first of which is almost invariably PATH, which tells the operating system where to look for programs to run regardless of what directory you happen to be in at the time. The environment space is limited, but it can be expanded by the user, and it is available for you to put your own variables in, although the rules are pretty strict.

You can examine the contents of user defined and other environment variables from within batch files. Now if you try and locate an environment variable that doesn't exist, you do not, to your great surprise, get an error message but a null string. This is how it operates.

Environment variables are in upper case only – and that is what gave me the idea. It takes a bit of explaining, so I'll try and make it as painless as possible. Maybe someone else has thought of this, or something similar elsewhere, but I have not come across it.

```
@ECHO OFF
CLS
IF "%TEST%"=="" GOTO SKIP
ECHO ON
:SKIP
IF "%1"=="" GOTO NOPARAM
SET %1=COMPARE
REM at this point you might like to add two lines:
REM SET
REM PAUSE
REM so you can see the list of environment parameters
IF NOT "%GAME1%"=="COMPARE" GOTO NOMATCH
ECHO MATCH FOUND
GOTO ENDBATCH
:NOMATCH
ECHO No match found
:ENDBATCH
SET %1=
GOTO FINISHBAT
:NOPARAM
ECHO No first parameter
:FINISHBAT
```

The first couple of lines demonstrate what I said a little while back about a non-existent environment variable. If there is no environment variable, MS-DOS treats it as a blank, which enables you to switch between having ECHO ON when developing a batch file to switching ECHO to OFF in production mode without having to modify the file in any way.

A dummy environment variable

What you do is to create an environment variable called TEST and put anything you like in it. Do remember, however, that SET is very critical when it comes to the string preceding the equals sign. If you leave a space, you have not created a variable 'TEST' but rather one called 'TEST '. So, from your prompt, type:

```
SET TEST=anything
```

If you now run the batch file I have just listed, ECHO will be switched on, as TEST is not an empty string. To ensure that ECHO stays OFF, simply wipe out the variable like this:

```
SET TEST=
```

– ensuring that there is no blank either before or after the equals sign. If you want to be a little cleverer, why not create a short batch file which acts as a flip flop, in other words, which switches between TEST existing and not existing?

Call the file SWITCH.BAT. It should contain the following:

```
@ECHO OFF
IF "%TEST%"=="" GOTO ON
SET TEST=
echo TEST is switched off
GOTO END
: ON
SET TEST=ANYTHING
ECHO TEST is switched on
: END
```

Try it with the first line omitted so that you can see how it functions. In case you were wondering why the second line does not simply test for the presence of the environment variable rather than its contents, the first answer is that they amount to the same thing, as one would not exist without the other.

The second is that it is a tall order to test for the absence of an environment variable by using IF. Consider these two lines:

```
IF TEST=="" GOTO LABEL
IF TEST== GOTO LABEL
```

In the first case, the answer will always be false (try it and see), and in the second you will get an error message, because you have in effect left out the comparator – there is nothing to compare TEST with.

Something else may have occurred to you as it did to me. The first five lines are a bit of a mouthful, with ECHO going OFF and ON like a yo-yo:

```
@ECHO OFF
CLS
IF "%TEST%"=="" GOTO SKIP
ECHO ON
: SKIP
```

So I thought I would be extra clever and replace them with just one line:

```
%TEST%ECHO OFF
```

– and switch between:

```
SET TEST=@
SET TEST=REM
```

– in the second case, REM is followed by a space before Enter.

The trouble is that it does not work. For some reason, the batch command processor rejects the substitution of @ for %TEST% to suppress ECHO on the current line, and that is why I have had to go round the houses in order to achieve the same effect.

Now to get down to the meat of the batch file:

```
IF "%1"=="" GOTO NOPARAM
SET %1=COMPARE
REM at this point you might like to add two lines:
REM SET
REM PAUSE
REM so you can see the list of environment parameters
IF NOT "%GAME1%"=="COMPARE" GOTO NOMATCH
```

The first line of this part of the file is essential. You have to ensure that there is a first parameter when the file was called, otherwise you will get an error message on the next line, and the whole process will fall apart.

The heart of the matter comes in the next line:

```
SET %1==COMPARE
```

Assume that the batch file has been called like this:

```
MENU game1
```

– or, for that matter:

```
MENU GaMe1
```

What happens is that an environment variable (in upper case, of course), called MATCH1 is created and its contents are set to the string "compare". It could be anything you fancy, but "compare" will do. So, if you type SET to examine your environment variables, the last line should read:

```
GAME1=compare
```

Now comes the crafty bit:

```
IF NOT "%GAME1%"= ="COMPARE" GOTO NOMATCH
```

What this line does is to see if there is an environment variable called GAME1 by inspecting its contents for the string 'compare'. If the parameter was not GAME1 but, say, GAME2, the answer comes out false, as you can see if you run this line with ECHO set to ON:

```
IF NOT ""= ="COMPARE" GOTO NOMATCH
```

So if it is not true that those two strings match (if you can work out the double negatives in the line and cancel them out), go to nomatch – and see if it matches GAME2 or whatever other comparators you are in pursuit of.

At the end of the batch file, it is vital to tidy up and remove any environment variables created during the running of the file, otherwise you will get the wrong result if the file is run again.

This points to the one hazard in using a technique like this – if you interrupt the batch file with Ctrl+C or Ctrl+Break, the result of running the batch file again will be uncertain, depending on the exact circumstances.

6

The Key to DOS

One of the odder aspects of MS-DOS, at least in Versions 1 to 4, is the fact that it is in some respects a step backwards from CP/M, the operating system which preceded it, and whose direct descendant it is.

Let me give you two examples: the first is PIP, CP/M's Peripheral Interchange Program, which is a powerful – if user hostile – tool for copying files and other data, usually from one disk drive to another, but also from the screen to the printer, from a file to an output port, and so on. It operated in two modes, single command mode and multiple line command mode, and it also enabled you with search and quit options to copy parts of files and perform other tricks like converting from lower to upper case. COPY is a pale shadow of PIP and its many options.

Example number two is the one we shall be examining in this chapter, CP/M's CCP (Command Control Processor) and its equivalent under MS-DOS. Here is an example taken from the best-known implementation of CP/M (CP/M Plus, actually), that on the Amstrad PCW range of word-processing computers.

If you type in a command on the PCW, you can edit that command simply and unfussily with the cursor control keys. If you mistype it, you can summon it up again by pressing the Copy key, and you will find the cursor sitting at the end of the line waiting for you to make any modifications you require.

Using MS-DOS, the equivalent, it seems, must have been put together by someone actually anxious for you not to make use of it. If you type in a command and make a mess of it, you need to remember how to deal with all the function keys and for the most part you are fumbling in the dark.

Surely there must be a better way. There is, under MS-DOS 5/6 at least, and it's called DOSKEY. Although it's a vast improvement on the old system and streets ahead of what is on offer under CP/M, there are still aspects of it which I am not too happy with. Anyway, let's give it a whirl and see what it can do for us.

DOSKEY is quite minute, taking up a mere 4K. In fact, with modern machines dripping with memory, it does seem odd that this and other features of MS-DOS are still referred to as if memory was gold dust. It ought to be installed by default. To do so, all you need to do is to add a line to your AUTOEXEC.BAT file. There is just one problem to note, which is that it may cause problems when you are running software which does not like any TSR to be present at all. It cannot be uninstalled once installed, unfortunately, but you could have it as an option in the AUTOEXEC.BAT file.

DOSKEY is worth it just for the fact that it offers a far more civilised and intuitive way of editing the command line than the standard MS-DOS method. The first point to note is that DOSKEY functions by default in overstrike mode. It seems to me – and this is not just because I spend quite a lot of my time with CP/M systems – that insert mode is preferable, so the line referring to DOSKEY in my AUTOEXEC.BAT file takes this form:

DOSKEY/INSERT

Do note, however, that if you are editing a command line and press Ins to go to overstrike mode, DOSKEY, blast it, does not 'remember' the switch and reverts to insert mode (or whatever you have determined was the start-up mode) as soon as you press Enter.

Memory is gold dust

But that isn't quite all there is to getting DOSKEY up and running. On the outdated memory is gold dust principle, a niggardly 512 bytes of memory are allocated by default, so it is preferable to increase that to somewhere around 1K, so:

DOSKEY/INSERT/BUFSIZE=1024

– or whatever you like, up to a theoretically unlimited maximum. There is a minimum of a quarter of a kilobyte.

I discovered quite by chance that if you have a full buffer you cannot assign a new macro, more of which later, and to do so you have to reinstall DOSKEY from the command prompt (using the /REINSTALL switch), which, as you might guess, wipes out the command line history. That is another negative aspect to DOSKEY.

An improvement I really would like to have seen is an increase in the niggardly size of the MS-DOS circular keyboard buffer. Maybe around MS-DOS 12 or so this will happen!

So now you have DOSKEY installed. You will find that you can edit the command line in a far simpler way than before – and do a great deal more besides. Instead of having to use the function keys to cut and paste bits of the command together, you simply go through the following procedure. Assume that you have typed this:

DOSKEY

– to get a demonstration up and running, then type a long command with the very first letter incorrect:

ZCOPY C:\THISSUB\THATSUB\TOTHER.SUB*.WP A:\BACK-UP

Press Enter to get an error message, and now let us consider what to do next. With the command line editor which comes with MS-DOS, you would first have to press the Delete key once, then add the X, then press F3 and hope that all is well. Did you remember that? Almost certainly not.

How is this for an improvement. Once you have got the error message, press the cursor up key once, and lo and behold the last command you typed (the ZCOPY ... line) reappears. Press Home and the cursor zips to the beginning of the line. If you are in overstrike mode, simply press X to overwrite the Z.

If you are in insert mode, press the Ins key and the cursor blob changes to let you know, and then press X. You can press Enter from anywhere in the command line and you can now execute your corrected command.

The key presses are pretty straightforward, but here is a quick run through them in case you are not familiar with them. The cursor up and down keys take you through the command line history, in other words, until its buffer fills up, DOSKEY "remembers" all the commands you typed in. More about that in a moment.

The cursor right and left keys move you one character position at a time along the line. Note that this does not erase or in any way alter the characters which you have typed, so that you can insert or alter characters at will.

For larger movements, Ctrl+ arrow key moves you back and forward a "word", which is defined as characters bounded by a space or spaces.

To go to the beginning of the line, type Home, and to the end type End. The Ins key toggles between insert and overstrike modes, and causes the cursor to change to remind you of what mode you are in.

Non-intuitive commands

One slightly less intuitive duo of commands is Ctrl+End and Ctrl+Home. These erase characters to the right and left of the cursor respectively, and where appropriate shunt text to the beginning of the line.

The sequence Home followed by Ctrl+End will, therefore, wipe out the contents of the current command line. So, I have just discovered, does F5.

The real power of DOSKEY begins to reveal itself with the even less intuitive F7 and F9 keys. The F7 key puts up the entire command history, as it is called, up on screen, a page at a time. But more than that, it numbers the commands in sequence for you, treating the first command typed in as number one, and so on up to the last command.

This allows you to review what you have typed from the keyboard, but more than that, the F9 key brings up the following invitation:

Line number:

Now type a number between 1 and the current highest number, and the command against that number will appear on screen. Note that it will not be executed, but will sit there waiting for you to take whatever action you wish – from editing it to pressing Enter to execute it unaltered.

If you press 0 or a number higher than the current total of the list, you do not, thank goodness, get an error message. DOSKEY just gives you the first or last in the list respectively. I sincerely hope that this is, at long last, the beginning of a trend away from the Calvinistic principles of computing which have held sway since the old mainframe days, where every miskey was an Error of some kind, usually accompanied by an inscrutable error code number or letter, which had to be chased up in one of the wallful of ring-bound manuals which appeared to be essential to the running of any computer in those days.

Instead of issuing error messages at the drop of a hat, operating systems ought either to provide the user with the nearest to what they asked for, in this case, or in other cases either to help out or prompt rather than simply wag a reproving electronic finger at them.

You know the sort of thing. You type COPY with no parameters and you are told that the required parameters are missing. Of course they are, anyone can see that. What ought to appear is a message on these lines:

Which file do you want to copy from?

And so on. I don't want to labour the point, but the emphasis ought in the 1990s at long last to be shifting away from informing us of the error of our ways, which we are more than likely all too aware of, to giving us a helping hand back on to the straight and narrow.

Anyway, let's get back to DOSKEY and its various abilities. You may have noticed that I referred to the F7 and F9 keys – but what about the one in the middle, F8?

If you can recall the first letter or letters of a previously typed command, type them followed by F8 and one of two things will happen. If DOSKEY can find a match in the command history, starting with the most recent and working its way backwards, then that command will be put up on screen.

Press F8 and the next most recent match, if any, will appear, and so on. If, on the other hand, DOSKEY cannot find a match, the cursor will just sit dumbly at the side of character or characters you have typed. At this point, the best course is to type Home, followed by Ctrl+End to clear the command line and then press F7 to see the list and remind yourself of what you were looking for.

Alternatively, F8 typed at the prompt will scan backwards throughout the command history. In this and other cases, the list is considered to be circular. Once you have reached item number 1, the next to be put up is whatever the most recent command was, and so on ad infinitum.

More possibilities of DOSKEY

This does not exhaust the possibilities of this aspect of DOSKEY. There are a couple more surprises to come. The first is that you can actually insert a command into the command history without carrying it out.

For example, if you wanted to copy a whole list of files from one drive to another, and you had just typed out a mouthful like this:

XCOPY C:\THISSUB\THATSUB\MYFILES*.WP B:\BACK-UP\MONDAY

– and then you realised that you could not remember whether you wanted to copy *.WP files or *.DAT files, you do not have to abandon all those painstakingly typed in characters and start again. Press F5, which inserts the command into the command history, then dig around to find out what kind of files you wanted to copy. Then the cursor up key brings the XCOPY line back for you to execute or edit and execute.

Two more points: the first is that it is possible to put more than one command on a line, by pressing Ctrl+T as a separator, which puts up the paragraph sign on screen. The second is that pressing Alt+F7 deletes the entire command history.

Advanced DOSKEY

The power of DOSKEY does not finish there. The next, underused but potentially powerful, feature to consider is that of the macro. A macro is a command which, when executed, causes another command or a whole predefined string of commands to be carried out. In the case of MS-DOS, macros are stored in memory rather than on disk, and that makes them quicker to execute.

Macros are one-liners, with a maximum of 127 characters allowed. You can put more than one command on the line, using the sequence '$t' as a separator.

One particularly odd aspect of DOSKEY is that, while Ctrl+T (producing, as indicated earlier, the paragraph sign) is used to separate two or more commands in a single line, acting as substitute carriage return characters, this will not work with macros. You have to use $t or $T to divide the lines up, which is an additional source of confusion, not just within DOSKEY, but also if you want to use DOSKEY to change a prompt. It appears not to be possible to create a macro creating a prompt displaying the time:

DOSKEY T=PROMPT $T

If you now type plain T, up comes the basic prompt giving just the current drive and the greater than sign. That is a piece of confusion I could well do without.

To stop a macro, press Ctrl+C for each command in the macro. Unlike batch files, in which GOTO allows you to hop back and forth within the file, the commands in a macro are strictly linear. They are carried out one after another in sequence. You can, however, run a batch file from within a macro.

Here is an example of how to create, edit and delete a macro. If you frequently wanted to make back-up copies (and so you should, too) of your data to, say, the back-up disks on drive A, you can do so with a couple of keystrokes. Create the macro like this:

DOSKEY BU=XCOPY C:\THISSUB\THATSUB\TOTHER.SUB*.DAT A:\DATFILES

Then to cause the whole command to be executed, just type:

BU

– and the BU expands into the command you typed. If you realised that the macro contains an error, simply recall the line which created it, using the cursor up key, and retype it. To erase the macro from memory, type:

DOSKEY BU=

To turn a line in the command history into a macro, just recall that line into the buffer and precede it with:

DOSKEY name=

– where 'name' is the macro name you decide to give it. Note that if you name a macro FRED then name another one FRED, you overwrite the first one with the second one.

It is apparently not possible for one macro to call another. In other words, if you create two macros:

```
DOSKEY A=DIR.COM
DOSKEY B=A
```

– you will find that the macro B just contains the letter A, but that it does not execute the macro called A.

A possible pitfall

On the subject of naming macros, I have not seen anyone point out a potential pitfall, which is that you can give the macro the name of an internal command, like DIR, and this name overrules the internal command.

So if you create a macro like this:

```
DOSKEY DIR=ECHO There are no files here
```

– it's the ECHO command which is executed when you type DIR. There is an interesting side effect of this, and that is that you could incorporate a measure of security in your system by renaming DIR as anything you like, and ensuring that DIR did nothing in particular, like clearing the screen, something along these lines:

```
DOSKEY CAT=DIR
DOSKEY DIR=CLS
```

That should keep a potential hacker guessing for a while at least! It would be even better if DIR was defined as a short assembler file which continuously rang the bell until you pressed a key combination known to you alone. For a sample program along these lines, see Chapters 12 and 27.

To make a macro more general, you can use the equivalent of %1 to %9, the replaceable parameters in batch files. In macros, the equivalents are $1 to $9.

First, a reminder of how replaceable parameters work. Here is a simple example. Consider a batch file which lists COM files. If we give it the name C.BAT and create it using EDIT, we need one line in the file:

```
DIR *.COM
```

Not very useful. But if we wanted a directory listing of files with a variety of different filetypes, here is a powerful way of achieving it, by using parameter substitution. Our file C.BAT should now contain these lines:

```
:AGAIN
MORE < DIR %1
SHIFT
```

```
IF NOT "%1"== "" GOTO AGAIN
```

This batch file could be called, for example, like this:

```
C *.COM *.BAK *.WP
```

– and it would produce paged listings of those three kinds of directory output. What happens is that the string '$1' is substituted for by the first parameter after the C, in this case '*.COM'. Then the SHIFT command moves all the parameters one to the left, leaving '*.BAK' as the $1 parameter, and so it goes on until the list is exhausted.

If the list is empty, the C.BAT file is the exact equivalent of plain DIR.

Dummy parameters

In macros, the %1, %2 ... %9 dummy parameters are replaced by $1, $2, ... $9. Incidentally, in case you are wondering about %0, the parameter which in batch files contains the name of the calling batch file itself, the equivalent $0 does not appear to work. In other words, you cannot use $0 as a parameter which is replaced by the name of the calling macro.

So you can create a macro which, to take our earlier example of copying WP or DAT files, can do all the work with one command:

```
DOSKEY XC=XCOPY C:\THISSUB\THATSUB\TOTHER.SUB\$1 A:\$B
```

The macro would be called as in these examples:

```
XC *.DAT DATFILES
```

```
XC *.WP WPFILES
```

The matter of macros is not over yet. There is one more dummy parameter, and that is $* which replaces everything after the macro, spaces and all, with what you type. For example:

```
DOSKEY D=DIR $*
```

Now type:

```
D *.BAK /OD
```

and you have the equivalent of a shorthand for DIR, in which $*=*.BAK /OD or whatever else you care to put after D. DOSKEY will not like it if you try and mix $* with any other dummy parameter in the range $1 – $9. I know – curiosity got the better of me, and I tried.

You can use redirection and piping with macros, but once again you have to unlearn and relearn the appropriate symbols. Here is a table of symbols, their meanings and when they are used:

Name	Normally	With Macros
input redirection	<	$L
output redirection	>	$G
output appending	>	GG
piping			$B

If it is any help, the letters after the dollar sign can be upper or lower case. Once more, the problem of confusion arises with PROMPT. Try this one on for size:

`DOSKEY P=PROMPT $P$G GREETINGS`

Instead of the result you might expect, a prompt ending in the word GREETINGS, what happens is that the prompt is redirected to a zero-length file called GREETING (note that, dangerously, MS-DOS still truncates overlong filenames in many circumstances without telling you!), and once again we end up with the basic 'C>' prompt again, if you are working with a hard disk, that is.

Additionally, it drew my attention to the fact that the $P is also ignored, which indicates that all characters following a dollar are ignored in macros, unless they are in the range 1-9, or consist of L, G or B. So that appears to put the proverbial kibosh on any attempt to create flexible prompts using macros.

However, the way round it is to double up. You will get the results you required by typing:

`DOSKEY P=PROMPT $$P$$G GREETINGS`

Which rather makes me wonder if it is worth all the effort in trying to remember which is which and whether the benefits outweigh the pain of getting it right.

Saving DOSKEY

Whenever you reboot or press Alt+F5, you lose the contents of the command history. The macros also go out of the window. Unless, of course, you do something about it. And, even with MS-DOS 6.2, what you have to do is a bit messy. Why is it that even now MS-DOS still makes us work so hard?

Let us consider the case of the command history first. It can be saved using:

`DOSKEY /HISTORY > HFILE`

– or whatever you want to call the file. /HISTORY can be abbreviated to /H. Do note that if you want to use this to create a batch file, you need to have the filetype BAT, and also you need to delete the last line of the file. Why? Because it contains the line:

```
DOSKEY /HISTORY > HFILE
```

– and if you run it as a batch file you get into an interesting on-going looping situation!

In order to see what macros are around, you need to type:

```
DOSKEY /MACROS
```

– which can be abbreviated to:

```
DOSKEY /M
```

To save them, you need to type:

```
DOSKEY /M > DMACROS
```

– or whatever you want to call the file. Do not forget a double chevron if you want to append the macros to existing macros. Now a snag arises, if you want to reinstate the macros when next you power up, because the file will contain the macro name, the equals sign and the macro definition, say:

```
D=DIR $1
P1=PROMPT $$P$$G
P2=PROMPT $$T $$P$$G
```

In order to insert them in the macro list, you need to have the text DOSKEY followed by a space in front of each of them. Also, you may well need some means of determining whether you actually want all of them saving or not. The program which performs this little exercise for you is on the disk which can be purchased with this book, and it is described in detail in Chapter 16.

7

Down to BASICs

When the reviews of MS-DOS 5 poured out in the computing press, they were universally favourable, even though there were quite a few snide comments suggesting – perish the thought – that Microsoft had only been stung into producing this class upgrade by competition from DR-DOS 5/6/7 with its extra features and user interface.

A great deal of fuss was made in the reviews about the new shell and the whole raft of upgraded commands, many of them recognised as long overdue, but hardly a mention of a new BASIC which comes with the package. One review does refer to its existence, and goes so far as to say 'it's wonderful', and it is 'the gem in the MS-DOS 5/6 collection', but for the most part you would never have guessed that it existed if you read most of the enthusiastic evaluations of Microsoft's new baby.

Up to Version 5, the standard BASIC available was GW-BASIC, a less than outstanding implementation of the language, and if you wanted a top quality compiler, you would have to go out and buy QuickBASIC and make something of a dent in your wallet. Now at last there is an interpreted version of the language, QBASIC, which offers a very high quality state of the art implementation of the language.

It isn't just another dialect of BASIC which offers a high degree of compatibility with GW-BASIC and BASIC-A, but far more importantly, is integrated with the MS-DOS operating system in that its editor is used in part for the EDIT and HELP facilities, and on top of that it encourages structured programming as never before. For convenience, I shall refer to the language as QBASIC from now on.

An excellent program

If you are a keen programmer, buy the compiled version – it really is worth it. I have written a couple of commercial packages using it and I have never come across a more powerful program development environment with outstanding trace facilities.

It has long been fashionable for computing professionals to turn their collective noses up at the very mention of the word BASIC – and if you add to that the dreaded keyword GOTO, you would instantly be regarded as a computing pariah. This BASIC, however, actually encourages structured program in a particularly striking way. If you type this line:

SUB fred

– something at first completely off-putting happens. You apparently lose sight of the program you are typing in or editing, the screen clears and up comes a more or less blank screen with these words on it:

SUB fred

END SUB

What QBASIC has done is to treat each subroutine as a separate program, if you like, and this encourages you to carve your program up into modules, each of which is distinct and separate from the rest. A press of the F2 key and you get an instant list of the current modules, including the main program module, and the ability to switch with equal speed between them.

It really is an astonishing programming tool, particularly if you build up a library of such routines for use across a variety of different programs.

Note at the same time that QBASIC bends over backwards to be helpful – as soon as you have typed SUB fred, not only does it open the new routine for you, it also provides you with an END SUB statement and, on top of that, it provides a DECLARE SUB statement for you in the main module. It almost makes you think favourably of the Nanny State.

Equally, when you are typing in a line of code, if you try to move to the next line with syntactical or other errors around, QBASIC warns you that you haven't got a valid statement.

BASIC with windows

The whole package is built round a series of windows to facilitate programming. The first thing you should do when powering up QBASIC is to opt for full menus (Alt+O for Options), and then you can use Alt+V to view split screens, in other words, you can edit different parts of the program simultaneously. Then there is the Help facility and two more windows, too.

The first of these is the Watch window, a special feature when you are debugging a program. The other is the immediate window, which enables you to type in direct commands and check the value of variables, and so on – and that, with a compiled BASIC, is some powerful feature.

You can also switch between windows, including the output window, program, immediate, and so forth, at the touch of a button.

There must be some negative aspects of QBASIC, but these are precious few. The one which I find most surprising is that there is no easy way of running MS-DOS commands from within the language. The FILES command, for example, is pretty feeble in contrast with DIR. However, these are minor grumbles, which can readily be overcome with a touch of ingenuity – particularly if you run EXE files within batch files – to make this the most pleasant and comfortable environment I have ever programmed in.

All right, I do have one real grouse, but that is one which I have with programming languages as a whole rather than with QBASIC. It refers to the notion of SHARED – or common – variables and arrays. I would like to be able to tell the program that everything, arrays included, are SHARED unless I tell it otherwise, but no, shared arrays – which have to be declared in the main module – and shared variables – which have to be declared as such within subroutines – have caused me much grief. I constantly fall into the trap of wondering why a variable has suddenly lost its value halfway through a program, and only discover after much struggling that I have failed to make it shared. Still, that is my problem.

With a powerful and flexible tool like this, it's no wonder that we are tempted to exploit it to expand the power of the operating system, and we shall be doing so, but only to a limited extent, since, as we shall see, DEBUG offers us complete access to the system and far more compact code, which at times can be counted in tens of bytes rather than tens of thousands.

We are going to look at three areas in which BASIC can come to your aid. The first is a simple program to extend the range of DIR, the second enables you to make flexible back-ups, and the third is a real brain-teaser, an attempt to automate drawing boxes on screen, a program which looks very easy at first sight, but which is in fact far from being so.

Finding the largest file

So let us begin with DIR. What if you wanted to know which the largest file in each subdirectory on your drive was? This is an invaluable guide to finding out if you have excessively large files floating around and cluttering up your disk space.

Quite often, the most sensible approach if you are needing to perform some fairly fancy tricks is to send the initial output from DIR to a file and then write a short program to extract the data in BASIC or assembler. One good reason for this is that it means you can clearly identify which subdirectory a particular file is sitting in.

The first step is to obtain a sorted listing and send it to a file:

```
DIR /S/L/O-S > DIRFILE
```

It really is a luxury to be able to invoke a powerful range of switches like this under DIR. That lists all files in the current directory and subdirectories of that directory in lower case (just for the fun of it) in reverse size order, in other words, with the largest file first and, using the redirection operator, sends the information to the file DIRFILE. The beginning of the file might look like this:

```
D:\>type dirfile

 Volume in drive C has no label
 Volume Serial Number is 3F56-17EA

Directory of C:\

command  com    47845 09-04-91    5:00a
wina20   386     9349 09-04-91    5:00a
list     com     8191 01-01-89   11:55p
demo     bas     7040 15-07-92    3:46p
whereis  com      403 28-08-85    1:04a
config   sys      357 13-07-92    9:22a
fred             342 22-09-92   10:20a
autoexec bat      148 13-07-92    9:10a
hotkey            69 05-07-92   11:36a
ls       bat       40 26-06-91    1:56a
```

At the end of each individual directory listing, there is a blank line, then the words:

```
Directory of C:\ ....
```

– followed by the appropriate subdirectory name. So it is a comparatively trivial matter to knock a QBASIC program together to extract the biggest file or files in each subdirectory and send them to a file or the screen, at the same time clearly identifying which subdirectory is involved. Here is the listing:

```
REM Program to extract the biggest file(s) from a listing

OPEN "dirfile" FOR INPUT AS #1
OPEN "bigfile" FOR OUTPUT AS #2
length = 99
CLS
PRINT #2, " Listing of largest file in each subdirectory "
PRINT #2,
PRINT #2, SPACE$(8); "Subdirectory Filename Size"; ""
```

```
PRINT #2,

REM This input skips over first line of file
LINE INPUT #1, fred$

WHILE NOT EOF(1)
  lastlength = length
  LINE INPUT #1, fred$
  length = LEN(fred$)
  WHILE lastlength = 0
      subname$ = MID$(fred$, 14, 99)
      check$ = fred$
      LINE INPUT #1, fred$
      LINE INPUT #1, fred$
      IF LEFT$(check$, 1) = "D" THEN
              subname$ = SPACE$(20) + subname$
              PRINT #2, RIGHT$(subname$, 20); "   "; fred$
      END IF
      lastlength = 99
  WEND
WEND
CLOSE 1
CLOSE 2
```

I hope you find that utility as useful as I have done. Of course, it is a relatively simple matter to pick up the three or four largest files in a subdirectory (if there are as many as that, of course), or indeed to highlight any file greater in size than 50K.

8

Flexible back-ups

One of the problems advanced users constantly seem to face with MS-DOS and other operating systems is that the facilities which are on offer are never quite what they are after, or if they are, they're couched in a non user-friendly format. The problem with a generalised utility, unless it is extremely comprehensive and unusual, is that we have to bend our requirements to fit it rather than the other way round.

It seems to be the case even if you bend the system using all the guile at your disposal. This is particularly true in the case of making back-up copies of files. Perhaps I perform this necessary chore in a way which nobody else does, but I suspect not.

I keep three back-up copies of work in progress. Every week I make back-ups which are kept in separate locations from the computer, and on a daily basis I make back-ups on to a disk which is kept by the machine.

This applies to three or four sets of disks at a time, each reflecting work done in different subdirectories. Sometimes a subdirectory isn't worked on for a few days at a time, and it becomes quite a chore to copy all the files created or modified since the last back-up. All the subdirectories are at the same level within the word-processor I use, which is LocoScript PC. In many circles, that is tantamount to admitting that one wears an anorak, rides a Lambretta and buys Max Bygraves records, but for strictly word-processing operations it takes a lot of beating for speed, features, price and ease of use. The more powerful LocoScript Professional is even better. I am a totally unrepentant and unreconstructed fan.

The options in making back-ups are to use the BACKUP facility provided by MS-DOS, which is a bit of a sledgehammer to crack the particular nut which I am interested in, or to type:

```
DIR A:/OD
```

This generates a directory listing in date order, the most recent files being listed last. Then using XCOPY a back-up is made of files modified on or after the last date, something like:

```
XCOPY C:*.WP A:/D:12-12-94
```

It would be nice to customise this into a couple of keystrokes which would let the computer do all the hard work and leave me to get on with something else.

My approach, which can readily be modified for your needs, depends on a batch file which runs a QBASIC EXE program, creates a couple of files and then deletes them. It's all very simple, and although it isn't completely idiot-proof, it is far quicker and more reliable than keying in those error-prone MS-DOS commands.

Here first is the batch file which drives the program:

```
@ECHO OFF
CLS
ECHO Batch file to copy files from subdirectory to A:\
ECHO created/modified on or after date of last files in A:\
ECHO Please wait a moment ...
DIR A:/OD > AFILES
ABACK
CALL DOCOPY
DEL AFILES > NUL
DEL DOCOPY.BAT > NUL
```

This batch file assumes that there is a formatted disk in Drive A, and sends a directory listing of the root directory of A via the redirection operator '>' to the file AFILES.

The reason why this operation is not done inside a program is that the FILES command of QBASIC is pretty feeble in comparison with DIR. You could, of course, go to the trouble of writing a routine of your own to winkle out the latest date, but if the facility is sitting there waiting for you in DIR, it seems pretty silly to do so. One anomaly of MS-DOS arises if the floppy disk is empty.

You can redirect anything sent to the current list device to a file, but the error message 'File not found' is sent to the screen. This means that when you are dealing with an empty disk, the file AFILES will contain something like this:

```
Volume in drive A has no label
Volume Serial Number is 092B-14D1
Directory of A:\
```

– but not the error message:

```
File not found.
```

We should not look for it in the file. It will pop up on screen during the running of the BAT file.

Note that I have written the batch file – and indeed the program – to suit specific requirements, which you can easily change. The drive letter can be readily altered, as can the subdirectory names and total in the program.

Exploring the program

In talking you through the program, I shall take it a chunk at a time and explain what is going on. The whole business is quite simple, as you can see. First, we have a couple of remarks to tell us what the program is about, and then come the DATA statements, the contents of which are read into the array subdirs$():

```
REM program to make copies of files with date on/after newest
    file on A
REM We assume a batch file has created a file AFILES using DIR/OD
DATA 12,apcwjan,apcwfeb,apcwmar,apcwapr,apcwmay,apcwjun,apcwjul
DATA apcwaug,apcwsep,apcwoct,apcwnov,apcwdec
READ total
DIM subdirs$(total)
FOR i = 1 TO total: READ subdirs$(i): NEXT
```

As far as the names of subdirectories are concerned and their total number, you will clearly have a different set to work with than I have. Change the 12 to the number of subdirectories, and then add the names of the subdirectories. They are assumed to be in the same path, as you will see later in the program, but again there is nothing to prevent you from adding in part or all of the path at this point if your subdirectory structure is more complicated.

Note that QBASIC allows dynamic array declaration. The REDIM command even allows you to change the bounds of arrays on the fly.

Next, the colours are set to yellow on blue. You can set them to what you like, unless you are content with a rather drab white on black.

```
COLOR 14, 1
PRINT
PRINT " *** Customised back-up program *** "
OPEN "afiles" FOR INPUT AS #1
REM look for line before line containing word "File"
thisline$ = ""
REM Skip initial lines
FOR i = 1 TO 4: LINE INPUT #1, discard$: NEXT
DO WHILE NOT EOF(1)
IF INSTR(thisline$, "File") <> 0 THEN EXIT DO
prevline$ = thisline$
LINE INPUT #1, thisline$
LOOP
CLOSE
```

The program first hops down the first four lines of AFILES, which contain the header information which comes with a DIR listing, and then it scans down the file AFILES looking for the string 'ile', in other words, the line containing the message telling you how many files there are, and the line previous to that is the one in which we are interested. That, as you can see, is kept on a rolling basis in the variable prevline$. It will contain information on the most recently created or modified file in the directory, together with its date, which is the bit we are really in search of.

These lines of code also cope with the situation in which the disk is empty, as we shall see in a moment. Note the flexibility of the DO ... LOOP iteration facility, which allows you to EXIT DO if a condition is satisfied, in this case the fact that the INSTR() command looking for a match for "File" finds one. Now we are ready to put together our customised XCOPY command and put it in a batch file:

```
OPEN "docopy.bat" FOR OUTPUT AS #1
from$ = "XCOPY C:\LS.PC\LS.ETC\"
to$ = "A:\"
mask$ = "*.PCW"
columns = 0
FOR i = 1 TO total
temp$ = LEFT$(subdirs$(i) + SPACE$(12), 12)
PRINT USING "##"; i; : PRINT ") "; temp$;
columns = columns + 1
IF columns = 4 THEN PRINT : columns = 0
NEXT
```

First, the batch file DOCOPY.BAT is opened. It requires the BAT filetype for the system to be able to recognise it as a batch file and act accordingly. Then we start to build up the command line with the XCOPY command and the first part of the path of the source directory for copying. As stated earlier, it will be different in your case, unless you are using LocoScript PC in a similar way to this. The to$ variable is the target drive and directory for the XCOPY command, and again this is up to you to vary if necessary.

The next item is the variable mask$. This limits the copying to word-processor format files, avoiding ASCII and BAK files, for example. Again, the format – or even the existence – of the mask is up to you.

Displaying subdirectories

Next duty is to put up on screen the subdirectories for the user to select the appropriate one for backing up. The PRINT USING command sets out the number for selection neatly against the close bracket, which is then followed by the name of the subdirectory.

Now the user has to select the appropriate number:

```
goof:
PRINT : INPUT "Type number of subdirectory + Enter --> ", subno
IF subno < 1 OR subno > total THEN GOTO goof
```

I make no apologies whatsoever for including a GOTO statement here. Structured programming is all very well and desirable, but the dogmatists can go too far. The most extreme example I have come across is the, in my view, incredible lengths to which the originators of BASIC in Dartmouth College in the early 1960s, John Kememy and Thomas Kurtz, have gone in their implementation of BASIC, True BASIC. They are so doctrinaire that they refer haughtily to GOTO and GOSUB as "older BASIC control structures", for which you actually have to use line numbers. Labels are nowhere to be found.

In their introduction, they seem to be overwrought by the tensions created by the concepts of structured programming on the one hand, and of what they call 'street BASIC' on the other. They are clearly upset by the creation of many a "horrible dialect of a beautiful language". Beautiful? BASIC may be many things, but this is the first time I have seen aesthetic qualities attributed to it.

A simple GOTO

Anyway, I take the view that a simple GOTO, appropriately used, is far easier to understand and recognise than a welter of WHILE ... WENDs, and I am happy to stand accused of using them in this and other programs.

Now we turn to back-up process itself. In case the disk is empty, we set up a default date of 1 January 1980, because that is the first legal date to which you can set the PC. Currently, the latest date is 2099. The test here for the length of thisline$ is to determine if the disk is empty. If it is not, the date is picked out of the line using the MID$() command:

```
lastdate$ = "1/1/80"
IF LEN(thisline$) <> 0 THEN lastdate$ = MID$(prevline$, 28, 8)
```

If at this point there is a valid date inside lastdate$, we come up against an odd little problem. The date is in the format day/month/year, with the slash as a separator. Unfortunately, the slash has a special significance for MS-DOS commands, introducing as it does a switch, as in:

```
DIR /W/P
```

– and so on. So the date needs to be in a different format, hence the use of INSTR() to detect and replace "/" with "-":

```
FOR i = 1 TO LEN(lastdate$)
IF INSTR(lastdate$, "/") <> 0 THEN MID$(lastdate$, INSTR(last-
date$, "/")) = "-"
NEXT
```

```
from$ = from$ + UCASE$(subdirs$(subno)) + "\" + mask$ + "/D:" +
lastdate$ + " " + to$
PRINT #1, from$

CLOSE
PRINT "I'm copying files to A from "; subdirs$(subno); " using
this formula:"
PRINT from$
END
```

Note that even with 6.2 XCOPY will not prompt for overwriting existing files because it is issued from within a batch file. Outside batch files, it is now necessary to put the /Y switch.

So much for the program in its basic form.

Locating the program

Where do you locate the program and batch file? Either in the root directory, or, if like most users, you prefer to keep that directory as uncluttered as possible, put it in the DOS directory, which should have a path open to it.

Also there is no security to ensure that you copy from the appropriate directory. But surely there is no way round that? Oh yes, there is.

There is a way of enhancing the operation of this back-up facility, which depends on the name which is given to the disk in Drive A. First, a word about the concept of labelling a disk.

Let's look at a typical floppy disk directory listing with a couple of files in it. The one I am using as temporary back-up for this chapter will do:

```
Volume in drive A is TEMPORARY
Volume Serial Number is 0C07-1BF5
Directory of A:\

XXX                        0 18/11/93   20:37
ABACK5    BAS          2,113 18/11/93   20:06
BUP       BAT            279 18/11/93   18:38
          3 file(s)          2,392 bytes
                          724,992 bytes free
```

First, for those of you who cannot quite believe their eyes – yes, those are commas separating off the thousands from the hundreds. This is an innovation of Version 6.2 designed to make these listings more human-friendly, but I must confess that I was put off by them when I first saw them, used as I was to a wedge of numbers indicating the byte size of the file.

The second point to note is that I was redirecting the directory listing to the file XXX, and you will see that it appears as a file of zero bytes in length, because the redirection operator causes the file first to be opened, then the directory listing is put into it, and after that the file is closed and acquires the appropriate number of bytes against its name.

However, back to the question of naming disks. This one is called TEMPORARY, and even though you cannot see it the line is padded out with spaces to make a total of eleven characters. The reason for the – literally – odd number of characters allowed is that the name of a disk or drive is a special case of a filename, which consists of up to eight characters plus up to three for the filetype. A subdirectory name is a similar special case of a filename, but the disk name is special in that you can include spaces in it.

You can include a wide range of other characters, including extended characters, but unless you are really desperate to do so, it's advisable to stick to the conventional range. The MS-DOS 5 manual (p. 134) gives a full list plus warnings about which code page to use if you insist on extended characters.

The title which MS-DOS gives to disk names is "Volume label", treating each disk as if it were the volume of a book which requires a label. This label can be either left blank or created by the user. There are two commands specifically designed to assist you with labels. The first is:

VOL

– which will tell you the contents, if any, of the Volume label. The second allows you to delete or create or alter the Volume label. Here are three variations on it:

LABEL
LABEL A:TEMPORARY
LABEL B:

In the first case, the label of the current drive is deleted. You have to be in the current drive if you want to delete its label. In the second, the disk in Drive A is relabelled as TEMPORARY. In the third case, MS-DOS does not delete the label to Drive B, but first tells you about the Volume label and invites you to change it:

Volume in drive B has no label
Volume label (11 characters, ENTER for none)?

If there is a label, that is of course given. If you type Enter to delete the current label, you are given a last chance to repent:

Delete current volume label (Y/N)?

The serial number is an innovation since Version 4, and is used by MS-DOS to identify the currently logged on disk.

Reading the Volume label

The modified version of the program relies on an addition to the BAT file, which
now goes like this:

```
@ECHO OFF
CLS
ECHO Batch file to copy files from subdirectory to A:\
ECHO created/modified on or after date of last files in A:\
ECHO Please wait a moment ...
DIR A:/OD > AFILES
VOL A: > AVOL
ABACK
CALL DOCOPY
DEL AVOL > NUL
DEL AFILES > NUL
DEL DOCOPY.BAT > NUL
```

The Volume name, if any, of the disk can now be winkled out from the file AVOL to
which output from VOL has been redirected.

The following listing is a modified version of the program. I have not reproduced the
whole thing, in order to save space, but I have started just before the modifications so
that you can see exactly where the new lines of code come:

```
OPEN "docopy.bat" FOR OUTPUT AS #1
dirline$ = ""
from$ = "XCOPY C:\LS.PC\LS.ETC\"
to$ = "A:\"
mask$ = "*.PCW"
columns = 0

REM Additional commands here to see if vol has the answer
OPEN "avol" FOR INPUT AS #2
INPUT #2, discard$
INPUT #2, volume$
subdir$ = MID$(volume$, 22, 99)
CLOSE 2
match = 0
FOR i = 1 TO total
IF subdir$ = UCASE$(subdirs$(i)) THEN match = 1
NEXT
IF match THEN GOTO labelfound
FOR i = 1 TO total
temp$ = LEFT$(subdirs$(i) + SPACE$(12), 12)
PRINT USING "##"; i; : PRINT ") "; temp$;
columns = columns + 1
IF columns = 4 THEN PRINT : columns = 0
NEXT

goof:
PRINT : INPUT "Type number of subdirectory + Enter --> ", subno
```

```
IF subno < 1 OR subno > total THEN GOTO goof
subdir$ = UCASE$(subdirs$(subno))

goof2:
yes$ = ""
PRINT : PRINT "Do you wish to (re)label your disk "; subdir$; "?
(Y/N)"
WHILE yes$ = ""
yes$ = UCASE$(INKEY$)
WEND
IF yes$ = "Y" OR yes$ = "N" GOTO labelfound ELSE GOTO goof2
labelfound:
lastdate$ = "1/1/80"
IF LEN(thisline$) <> 0 THEN lastdate$ = MID$(prevline$, 28, 8)

FOR i = 1 TO LEN(lastdate$)
IF INSTR(lastdate$, "/") <> 0 THEN MID$(lastdate$, INSTR(last-
date$, "/")) = "-"
NEXT

from$ = from$ + subdir$ + "\" + mask$ + "/D:" + lastdate$ + " " +
to$
PRINT #1, from$
IF yes$ = "Y" THEN PRINT #1, "LABEL A: "; subdir$
CLOSE
PRINT "I'm copying files to A from "; subdir$; " using this
formula:"
PRINT from$
END
```

The real problem with a routine like this is that, after a while, it begins to take on a life of its own, and it is tempting to keep on tinkering with it, adding a bell here, a whistle there, until the whole business gets entirely out of hand.

The question of a full target disk, for example, is one which is resolved more easily by ensuring that you never have more than a megabyte or so of material to back up from a single subdirectory and that you use 1.44 disks (or 1.2 if you have a 5.25 inch drive).

If there is a chance that back-ups have to run over more than one disk, a different approach is required, using the archive attribute or some other technique. But the best approach is to avoid over-complicating things in the first place.

9

Drawing boxes with EDIT – I

To those who suffered in the past from EDLIN, EDIT is a blissful relief.

EDLIN goes back to the old mainframe days when such on-line interaction as there was took place via Teletype machines, which rattled like machine guns and could be fed with punched tape as a means of input. The basis of the interaction was line by line. It would be something of a challenge to have a full screen editor on a sheet of continuous paper!

This meant that any editing of a file had to be done on a line by line basis, and EDLIN is in the long tradition of such editors. It is derived from the CP/M program ED, and shares most of its quirks and vices. One of the things I found most tiresome about it was the way in which it handled the two modes which editors require: command and edit mode.

In command mode, you issue commands to the editor, in edit mode, you are typing in text. Switching between the two in EDLIN and ensuring that you were not in edit mode when you thought you were in command mode, and vice versa, was always something of a nightmare. It was so easy to confuse the two and lose line of edit or mistakenly put editing commands into the file itself.

By the way, I keep speaking of EDLIN in the past, but it still hangs on like Marley's ghost in MS-DOS 5, in case you really feel the need to try it out.

The purpose of an editor in an operating system context is to enable you to design and modify batch files, not to perform word-processing, so you should not expect word wrap, spell checkers and all the paraphernalia of a fully-featured word-processor.

The new EDIT feature

EDIT is not designed to deliver such luxuries – and, in fact, it wasn't really designed as a replacement to EDLIN at all. The reason for this becomes apparent if you type:

```
DIR EDIT.COM
```

You'll probably find it in the DOS subdirectory. To your astonishment, you will see that it consists of 413 bytes, and it may well occur to you that it is something of a minor miracle to be able to write a screen editor in a couple of hundred assembler instructions.

Of course, this is not what happens, and the solution to the riddle is apparent when you see in the manual that in order to function, EDIT.COM needs to be able to find QBASIC.EXE. What happens in fact is that the program EDIT.COM uses the QBASIC editor, as neat a piece of smash and grab as you are likely to come across.

There are a couple of interesting side effects from this situation. One can be helpful if, like me, you can't be bothered to load up a word-processor to type short documents or letters. The trouble with EDIT – and similar programs – is that it doesn't allow a proper left-hand margin, so if you print out your document, it is flush with the left-hand side of the paper, and if you are using continuous stationery, like I tend to, that is a nuisance.

However, if you press the tab key at the beginning of the file, EDIT 'remembers' the tab at the beginning of all subsequent lines, creating an automatic hanging indent effect. That is a direct result of the indenting feature used when typing in programs in order to make loops and suchlike easier to pick out in the listing.

There is another side effect which I found less than pleasing, and that is that although EDIT supports the full IBM PC character set – the accented characters, mathematical symbols, and box-drawing lines which people the area above 7F – it is a real nightmare trying to draw boxes, because it was not possible to redefine keys on the keyboard to make it easier, since EDIT grabs them all.

A program to automate boxes

It was at this point that I thought I had a bright idea: why not provide you with a simple enhancement to EDIT which would enable you to type in boxes using, say, the open left square bracket character (or any other character that took your fancy), and letting a simple BASIC program convert them into boxes for you? All you would have to do is to put the open square bracket character wherever you wanted a box line to appear, and that's all there is to it. Or so I fondly believed.

I was thinking in terms of, say, a screenful of information which could be printed out as part of a batch file to make it more attractive on screen, or indeed for a rolling display with boxes to show, say, a flowchart or some similar effect. So I began with the concept of a file 80x25 characters in size, referred to as 0-79 and 0-24 respectively.

All the program would have to do is convert the open square bracket to the box character – but it rapidly became apparent that the crucial question was: Which box character? If you draw a box on graph paper, you will soon see the nature of the problem. There isn't just one character, there are the four corner characters, the horizontal line, the vertical line, the vertical line with a left branch, the vertical line with a right branch, and so it goes on.

A complex task

It was beginning to turn from a simple three-line program into something of a design nightmare. But at the same time, it was a challenge worth going for, since the outcome would be all the more worthwhile.

Several days later, and after the expenditure of huge quantities of blood, sweat and tears, I finally came up with a solution. Maybe my programming talents, such as they are, deserted me in droves, but I found this a really tricky challenge. You may come up with a different solution, but here is my attempt at cracking the problem. The program I have designed will produce single or double ruled boxes, but not a combination of the two.

The real challenge is to write a program which looks at each box-drawing character and makes the decision as to which of the eleven characters is required at a particular location. In case you think this is making a mountain out of the proverbial molehill, consider the following situation:

```
[[[[[
[   [
[   [
[[[[[
```

Starting at the top, the first character requires replacement by the top left-hand corner character, the second, third and fourth by horizontal lines, and the fifth by the top right-hand character.

None of these characters could be defined without reference to adjacent characters, and it soon became evident that, in order to find out what each stands for, we need a 3 x 3 matrix of some kind. It was at this point that the hairy complexities of the problem came to light.

Defining the box character

Imagine each character being at the centre of such a matrix. For a corner, there is no problem. In the following, the asterisk stands for any character other than an open square bracket:

```
***
*[[
*[*
```

That uniquely describes a top left-hand corner character. In other words, there is one character to the right and one below which makes up the pattern. So, I thought in my innocence, why not devise a model matrix consisting of, say:

```
1 2 3
4 5 6
7 8 9
```

– which could define the pattern in terms of the total of the squares containing square brackets. In other words, the top left-hand corner could be defined as 5+6+8 = 19. It would not take you long to work out the totals for the other corner characters (top right = 17, bottom left = 13, bottom right = 11).

The next question that arises is: Assuming that we have read the file into a two-dimensional array which we are scanning along, we shall of course need a dummy strip one character wide round the outside of the array, so that we don't fall off the edge when looking at characters on row 1, column 1, for example.

It is tempting to replace the open square bracket with the value of the corner character (201 in decimal) without further ado. Surely we have solved the problem. Not quite – because if you insert the box character in the two-dimensional array, you will be causing problems for the next character in line, because it, too, needs definition in terms of the surrounding characters, including the one which we have just defined as the top left-hand corner character. I warned you that this would be complicated.

Assume that we are now looking at the second character in the box, the first horizontal line. If you shift our matrix mask along one, you can begin to see that all is not as simple as it seems:

```
*  *  *
[  [  [
[  *  *
```

The first problem is that the bracket to the left of the one we are examining would now have been changed to character 201, so that we would be obliged to test for characters over 127 as well as for open square bracket. At this point, I opted for a three-dimensional array, in which the third dimension mirrors the page we are scanning, and contains empty strings except where we have found box characters are required.

This leaves the original text unaltered, and when the time comes later to insert the box-drawing characters, it is a simple matter of printing out two dimensions of the array, pausing when a bracket occurs and checking to see if there is a box-drawing character at the same location in the third dimension.

This also has the neat side effect of allowing isolated square bracket characters to remain as such, which means that any character you may choose for box-drawing isn't instantly taken out of commission for use on screen by itself, so long as it is not contiguous with another such character.

However, I suspect that you are beginning to see that something odd is happening to our matrix. The second character along is defined as $4 + 5 + 6 + 7 = 22$, if we use our original matrix of numbers, because on the bottom left-hand corner of the matrix, the beginning of the vertical line is still within the matrix.

I rapidly realised that there was not just one way of defining uniquely a horizontal or vertical line, depending on how close it is to other lines going off in different directions. If you discount some of the more exotic combinations, of which more later, there are nine different ways of describing a horizontal or vertical line.

Redefining the matrix

And – you guessed – this means that a matrix defined by the numbers 1 to 9 is not up to the task of offering a unique value for all the possible combinations of characters. Here is one example for you to try out where you will, in fact, end up with the same total:

```
* * *        [ * *
[ [ [        [ [ [
* [ *        [ * *
```

Both come out with the total 23, so that spoils Plan A. In fact, if I had looked closely at the numbers in the matrix, I would have seen that the way in which certain combinations come to the same value ($4+1 = 5$, $3 + 2 = 5$, and so on) made it almost inevitable that a clash would occur.

However, it simply had not dawned on me just how complicated the apparently simple conversion program was going to turn out. At this point I nearly abandoned the whole project.

However, I withdrew to lick a few wounds and eventually came up with a matrix mask which looked like this:

```
 1   4   9
16  25  36
49  64  81
```

I reckoned that succeeding squares should come up with a unique value for every possible combination. And so it nearly proved to be, if you include one restriction in the box-drawing, to which we shall come later.

However, now that I have the program in a more or less complete and working state, let me talk you through it. Again, if you are not inclined to type it in, there is an executable version of the program on disk, as well as the source code.

I have divided the program up into sections, each of which will be explained as we go along.

```
REM program to read file from edit and convert to boxes
CLS
LOCATE 8, 8
INPUT "Name of file please > ", filename$
OPEN filename$ FOR INPUT AS #1
DIM fileconts$(-1 TO 25, -1 TO 80, 1 TO 2)
DIM match(-1 TO 1, -1 TO 1)
DIM boxlines(300)
DATA 1,4,9,16,25,36,49,64,81
FOR x = -1 TO 1
FOR y = -1 TO 1
READ z
match(x, y) = z
NEXT y
NEXT x
```

The first part of the program grabs the file which we are going to convert and opens it. Then we define the array into which the file goes. As you can see, I have defined it as a text screen (80x24) with a border round the edge. You can make it any size that suits you. Remember that I am working on the basis of a file which will be put up on screen.

The array 'match' is the matrix we shall be using to create values based on the occurrence of square bracket characters. The reason for the odd bounds is quite simple, as you will see later. The array is filled up with the numbers in the DATA list.

When we have added up the appropriate figures in the matrix, we need to be able to map them on to the appropriate number corresponding to the required ASCII value. This has been painstakingly done for you in the next few lines. The DATA statements contain pairs of numbers. The first is the total which has been arrived at by adding the numbers in the matrix which correspond to locations containing square brackets, and the second number is the ASCII value of the box-drawing character.

For example, the first number is 125 (25+36+64), and the second is 201, the code for the top right-hand corner of a box.

As you will see, there are eleven different ways of defining each of the horizontal (205) and vertical (186) lines:

```
FOR i = 1 TO 300: boxlines(i) = 91: NEXT
DATA 125,201,65,200,105,187,45,188,129,204,109,185,81,202
DATA 141,203,145,206,41,205,61,205,77,205,78,205,126,205
DATA 127,205,158,205,86,205,167,205,87,205,207,205
DATA 29,186,89,186,93,186,94,186,142,186,102,186
DATA 103,186,174,186,223,186,143,186,183,186 ,186
FOR i = 1 TO 31: READ a: READ b: boxlines(a) = b: NEXT
```

Now that the preliminaries are over, let battle commence.

10

Drawing boxes with EDIT – II

First we read the text in a line at a time, padding out with spaces where necessary, and allowing in the EXIT FOR instruction for files of less than 25 lines:

```
FOR x = 0 TO 24
IF EOF(1) THEN EXIT FOR
LINE INPUT #1, tline$
tline$ = tline$ + STRING$(80, " ")
FOR y = 0 TO 79
fileconts$(x, y, 1) = MID$(tline$, y + 1, 1)
NEXT y
NEXT x
CLOSE 1
```

The x and y coordinates correspond to the conventional way in which columns and rows are referred to. The slice of fileconts$(x,y,1) is for the text, while fileconts$(x,y,2) is for the box-drawing characters. You may find it convenient to insert the following REM lines to remind you of the correspondence between numbers and characters:

```
REM now convert [[ to box double lines
REM top left = 201, horizontal = 205, top right = 187
REM bottom left = 200, vertical = 186, bottom right = 188
REM T = 203, inverted T = 202, I- = 204, -I = 185
REM cross = 206
```

The I- and -I characters are as near as I can get to lazy T's. Note that the box-drawing characters are for double lined boxes, so if you want, you can change them for single lines in the program, or have two different programs, one for each sort.

If by any chance you were thinking of the characters which link single and double boxes together, I will, if you don't mind, leave that problem for you to solve. I had enough trouble with just one kind of box.

Sorting out box characters

The next part of the program takes the file contents and tries to sort out the box-drawing characters:

```
CLS
FOR x = 0 TO 25
FOR y = 0 TO 79
    REM now we put in the box-drawing characters
    total = 0
    IF fileconts$(x, y, 1) = "[" THEN
      FOR xx = -1 TO 1
        FOR yy = -1 TO 1
            IF fileconts$(x + xx, y + yy, 1) = "[" THEN
            total = total + match(xx, yy)
            END IF
          NEXT yy
      NEXT xx
    END IF
    LOCATE 12, 12: PRINT "Searching line ..."; x
    IF total <> 0 THEN
    fileconts$(x, y, 2) = CHR$(boxlines(total))
    END IF
NEXT y
NEXT x
PRINT "Processing completed."
```

That is the engine of the program, which given the complexity of the whole business is very short and neat. We search the text row by row, a column at a time, for an occurrence of an open square bracket.

Matching characters

If one is found, then our array match() comes into play and you can now see why I have chosen the odd bounds -1 to 1. The actual lines which look for the pattern of square brackets are:

```
IF fileconts$(x + xx, y + yy, 1) = "[" THEN
        total = total + match(xx, yy)
        END IF
```

If an open square bracket is found on column 2, row 2 of the array, the first time round the value x+xx = 2 + -1 (= 1) and that of y+yy = 2 + -1 (=1), and so on, so that the matrix scans first the adjacent three characters on the line above, then with xx=0 on the same line, then with xx=1 on line three. Cunning and effective. If a match is found, total is updated accordingly from match(xx,yy).

A process of simplification

All programming, I have discovered over many years, is a process of simplification, and that I reckon is as simple a solution to a complex problem as you can get. The appropriate value is picked out from boxlines() and inserted into fileconts$(x,y,2). Now for the final stage of the program:

```
PRINT "Your input file was called " + filename$
INPUT "Output filename, please > ", ofname$
OPEN ofname$ FOR OUTPUT AS #1
FOR x = 0 TO 24
FOR y = 0 TO 79
  IF fileconts$(x, y, 1) = "[" THEN
    PRINT #1, fileconts$(x, y, 2);
    ELSE
    PRINT #1, fileconts$(x, y, 1);
  END IF
NEXT y
NEXT x
CLOSE 1
END
```

If an open square bracket is found, the contents of fileconts$(x,y,2) is printed. And that is the end of the story. Well, not quite.

Earlier I referred to a restriction on this program, and that is that all horizontal or vertical lines must be at least two characters long. Otherwise you can get into a situation like this:

```
* [ *
[ [ [
[ * *
```

– which adds up to 130 and defines the inverted 'T' character. Unfortunately, that is also the total for this combination:

```
[ [ *
* [ [
* [ *
```

– which defines the 'lazy T'. There is one other combination which clashes in very small squares, as a result of which the program needs a couple of extra lines, as well as twelve more DATA items. Still, the resultant output makes it all worth while.

11

Getting assembled

The time has now come to dig a little deeper into MS-DOS, to provide a suite of routines and utilities which even Versions 5 and 6 have not come up with, and in order to do this, we need to explore the world of assembler in some detail.

For those of you familiar with assembler, do feel free to skip the rest of this Chapter, and much of the next Chapter, although it does contain a couple of very useful little programs. Further supporting information on assembler and DEBUG will be found in the Appendices, which – for those who read *MS-DOS Revealed* – include expanded versions of the appendices in that book. For the rest of you, do not shrink back in awe from something which the experts keep telling you is difficult (they wouldn't be allowed to be experts if everyone found out how easy it was, would they?).

So here is a brief tour of assembler. At the heart of every computing system is a central processor which is driven by instructions written in machine code. This is what the machine code of a typical short assembler program looks like when represented in hexadecimal:

B40AB00731DBB91200CD10CD20

Now I'm fairly sure that those digits and letters make just about as much sense as the small print on the average insurance policy. The reason is quite simple: it's designed for the computer to understand, not humans. I'm not sure that the same applies to insurance policies, though.

In fact, if it was printed out in the actual number base used by the computer – binary – it would make no sense at all. The first instruction (B4) would look remarkably like this:

10110100

So human operators rapidly decided that binary was not for them, moved on to hexadecimal, which conveniently represents four binary digits (bits) at a time as a single hex value. As you can see from the above, B (11 in decimal) = 1011, and 4 = 0100. See the Appendix on binary and hex for further details.

However, a string of hex digits is also pretty obscure, so way back in the murky past some bright spark (to whom we should all be eternally grateful) came up with the notion of a mnemonic code. The term means a code with instructions which "remind" you of what they actually mean, so the first instruction in the program is:

MOV AH, 0A

The actual operand (the bit which tells you what the instruction does) is "MOV" – and it does not take a great deal of figuring out to determine that MOV stands for "move". The rest of the instruction tells the processor what to move and where to move it.

The reason why the fundamental language of the computer is called an assembler (rather than the compiler or interpreter we are familiar with from high-level languages) is that each line of instructions is "assembled" or converted into machine code a line at a time. With some exceptions, one line of instructions goes straight into machine code without any further ado.

What machine code?

Now let's turn to the question: What machine code? As you may well know, there are all kinds of different computers on the market, even though the IBM PC and its clones are the dominant force. The first personal computer which many people came across was the BBC Micro, which had a processor manufactured by Motorola, called the 6502. It uses a different approach to organising the internal workings of the machine from the chips developed by the competitor company Intel.

They started off with the 8080 chip (to cut a long story short), which was the basis of the CP/M operating system, and which is still alive and well and on Dixon's shelves now in the form of the PCW range of personal computers and their Z80 chip.

When the IBM PC came along, it took a newer version of the Intel chip, the 8088, as its basis. That became the 8086, and is now moving forward through a series of newer and faster chips, which is where you get the names 286 (based on the 80286 chip), 386, and now 486, with threats of a 586 to come. In broad terms, each chip is more powerful and faster than its predecessor and can address larger amounts of memory.

The instruction set for the 8086/8088 is what we shall be using here, as it is more than adequate for our purposes, and that covers all PCs. The fancier machines have additional instructions, but they all recognise the 8086/8088 set. There are also special instructions for the maths coprocessor, if fitted, but that is another story altogether.

Now for a quick guided tour of what from now on I'll call 8086 assembler, or just plain assembler, for short. The first point to remember is that all programming on the computer, whether it's a compiler or interpreter like QBASIC or QuickBASIC, an applications package like a word-processor or spreadsheet, a games program or whatever – is written, when it comes down to brass tacks, as they say, in assembler.

In other words, when you see in BASIC a line like:

PRINT "This is a demo"

– in order for that to run on the computer it has to be broken down into individual assembler instructions, which require far more detailed information than if you are programming in a high level language.

Let's take that line in order to show what I mean and to outline some of the fundamentals of assembler. First, though, comes the question of how to run assembler programs. Like BASIC, you can't just type them in from the MS-DOS prompt and press a button. IBM produce an assembler called MASM, which I find horribly bureaucratic. I much prefer a shareware package called A80 assembler, which is fast and very easy to use.

But for first steps in assembler – and for fairly fancy programming too – there is an external MS-DOS command which can do just about anything you require. Called DEBUG, it takes a bit of getting used to, designed as it was without undue reference to the term "user friendly", but it is great fun, and you will find it explained in detail in Appendix A.

What I will do here now is to give a quick introduction to its use, and from then on assume that you follow the same procedures in the other programs which we shall be exploring. The next bit is most productive if you are sitting at your machine and follow through the steps.

To ensure that as a beginner you inflict the minimum damage if – or should I say when – things go wrong, I suggest you format a blank disk in Drive A, copy DEBUG.COM (probably in the DOS subdirectory) to it, switch to Drive A and then type:

DEBUG MESSAGE.COM

Alternatively, set up a RAM disk as explained in Chapter 1 and copy everything to there.

Please note again that all the commands are in upper case (except when I am showing dumps of an actual session with DEBUG), but you can type in lower case. DEBUG converts commands to upper case – and when typing in commands and instructions, spaces are not necessary, only cosmetic.

When you have typed in the command as above, up comes a tart error message telling you "File not found", which is not surprising, as there isn't a file called MESSAGE.COM – yet. What you have done is to load DEBUG and tell it that you intend to make use of a file of that name later on.

DEBUG commands

The minus sign is DEBUG's prompt. DEBUG works with a number of commands which are single letters optionally followed by one or more numbers – and those numbers are exclusively in hexadecimal. To find out what is in DEBUG's repertoire, type ? and you will see a full list of the commands on offer. Don't get baffled by them, the most important ones will gradually make sense as we work our way through them.

Now type A (follow each command or line of text with Enter unless I tell you otherwise), and you will see a strange-looking number pop up on screen with the cursor sitting against it. Forget about the number for a moment. Type in these lines, and after the last line type Enter twice:

```
MOV AH,9
MOV DX,500
INT 21
INT 20
```

If you make a mistake, DEBUG will protest and invite you to type the line in again. One more thing to take on trust. Type the following from the minus prompt:

```
E 500 "This is a demo$"
```

Next, type this odd-looking command (explanations later):

```
R CX
```

– and you will see "CX 0000" followed by a line feed and a colon. At the colon prompt, type 600. Then type:

```
W
```

That will be met with a message telling you that you have written 600 (hex) bytes – to the file MESSAGE.COM. To run the program, type:

```
G
```

– and, all being well, you will be told that the program terminated normally. The only way to exit from DEBUG is to type:

Q

– for quit. Now, from the MS-DOS prompt, you can run your new command by typing:

MESSAGE

Here is a screen dump of how that DEBUG session should look (the numbers to the left of the colon will probably be different on your machine, but don't worry about that):

```
A:\>debug message.com
-a 100 107
1E10:0100 mov ah,9
1E10:0102 mov dx,500
1E10:0105 int 21
1E10:0107 int 20
-e 500 "This is a demo$"
-rcx
CX 0000
:600
-w
Writing 00600 bytes
-g
This is a demo
Program terminated normally
-q
```

That is a brief run-through of how to create and run a program under DEBUG. A lot of explanation is needed, and that will be provided in the pages that follow. In the meantime, why not go through that session again, this time putting a different message inside the double quotes – but do not forget the dollar sign, as 8086 looks for it as a terminator. For a reminder of how to use DEBUG in simple terms, see the beginning of Appendix A.

If things go wrong, try pressing Ctrl+Break. Failing that, you may have to reboot or reset your machine.

12

Ringing the changes

Now let us demonstrate DEBUG at work with a useful little program which offers a simple security measure to keep prying eyes away (there are more improved ideas in Chapter 27), locks out the computer, rings the bell, and waits for you to press the Escape key – or any other key of your choosing. As well as being a useful program in its own right, it's a neat way of learning more about DEBUG and assembler.

I shall be repeating some of the help I gave in the last Chapter with the MESSAGE.COM program to ensure that you follow what is going on. So now type:

DEBUG RING.COM

At this point you will again get the message "File not found", which does not matter, remember, since DEBUG has now got it into its head that it will be dealing with the file RING.COM, even if it doesn't yet exist.

This is as good a point as any to explain why the files we are creating have the COM filetype. Executable programs – files containing instructions carried out from the prompt – are either COM or EXE. If you examine the external MS-DOS commands you have, in the DOS subdirectory if you have a hard disk, you will see that they all have one or other of those filetypes, including DEBUG.

In this book, I am sticking exclusively to COM files. When you type the filename from the prompt, MS-DOS treats it like a program if it has the type COM or EXE – in the same way that it treats it as a batch file, but only if it has the filetype BAT.

Back to our program: at the minus prompt type A for Assemble (followed by Enter), and type these lines in carefully (at this stage, if you make a mistake you cannot escape from, type Q, press F3 to bring up the DEBUG command line again, and then start again from scratch):

```
MOV     AH,02
MOV     DL,07
INT     21
MOV     AH,0B
INT     21
CMP     AL,FF
JNZ     0100
MOV     AH,08
INT     21
CMP     AL,1B
JNZ     0100
INT     20
```

After the last line, press plain Enter, and you will be back at the prompt. A full explanation of what all this means will follow in a while. If you now type:

U 100

– you will see the listing with numbers against it. It should look something like this (again the numbers before the colon at the left will probably differ):

```
-u100
1E0F:0100 B402        MOV     AH,02
1E0F:0102 B207        MOV     DL,07
1E0F:0104 CD21        INT     21
1E0F:0106 B40B        MOV     AH,0B
1E0F:0108 CD21        INT     21
1E0F:010A 3CFF        CMP     AL,FF
1E0F:010C 75F2        JNZ     0100
1E0F:010E B408        MOV     AH,08
1E0F:0110 CD21        INT     21
1E0F:0112 3C1B        CMP     AL,1B
1E0F:0114 75EA        JNZ     0100
1E0F:0116 CD20        INT     20
1E0F:0118 48          DEC     AX
1E0F:0119 DA2B                FISUBR  DWORD PTR [BP+DI]
1E0F:011B D034        ???     BYTE PTR [SI],1
1E0F:011D 00E7        ADD     BH,AH
1E0F:011F 1E          PUSH    DS
-q
```

Note that U outputs 16 bytes worth of instructions at a time, falling off the end of the program in cases like this. The instructions at line 119 are DEBUG's brave attempt to make sense of the random data in the computer's memory at the time. Even so, sometimes it gives up the ghost, as the ??? in one attempted instruction indicates.

The program segment prefix

There are a number of other points to clear up now, before we go any further with explanation of the instructions. The first point to note is that all programs start at address 100 in hex. The area 0-FF is called the PSP, the Program Segment Prefix, an area set aside for housekeeping and other activities, and there are parts of the PSP which you can alter or use, with care.

Strictly speaking, we should not have typed A, but A100 (followed by Enter – last reminder). However, DEBUG starts off assuming you are operating from 100, and then it assumes you want to work from the address after the last one you used.

So now if we want to see what has been typed in, we need the Unassemble command (not D for disassemble, as D is used by DEBUG for Dump, as we shall see later) with the address number, which is what we did a moment or two ago.

The main difference in your output will be the number before the colon on the left. This is the number of the first free available segment (FFFF bytes, 65535 in decimal) in memory, which varies from one machine to another, depending what else you have loaded in memory at the time. So in future listings, I shall omit the segment number.

If you are happy that you have typed the instructions in correctly, go to the next stage. Otherwise, the best thing for the beginner to do is to type Q for quit (the only way of leaving DEBUG and returning to the prompt) and then press F3 to bring the command to load again, and type the instructions in again.

To save the instructions, you first have to tell the computer how many bytes you need to save. This is done by typing the following (explanations later):

R CX

A colon will appear. Type 50 (more than needed, but I always allow a generous margin). Then type:

W

You will see a message telling you that 50 (hex, remember) bytes are being written. You do not have to inform DEBUG of the name of the file. As you will recall, you told it when you first loaded it. For more details on naming, loading and writing files, and other DEBUG commands, see the Appendix, particularly the more detailed information on R CX.

Noting instruction addresses

Far more important than the segment number is the address at which each instruction begins. By pure coincidence, each of the instructions in our simple program takes up two bytes. The computer is bright enough to know how long each instruction is, which is rather a good thing, as data and instructions are all jumbled together, and if the machine tried to execute data instead of instructions the result would be chaos.

At the very least, the machine would hang and at worst, you might get random data scattered over your disks. Now let us examine the first line of the program so that we can see what is happening:

```
0100 B402          MOV      AH,02
```

First comes the address, in this case 100. Then comes a number in hex. This is the result of assembling the text and number(s) which take up the rest of the line into machine code, the raw bytes which make the PC tick.

In this case, MOV AH is converted to the code B4, and the 02 is the data which is manipulated by the instruction. More about what this and the other instructions mean in a moment.

If you look down the machine code, you will see some numbers repeated. CD is the machine code for INT, as you will see, and 3C is the machine code for CMP AL. Note that if the instruction is CMP AH or some other combination, the machine code is different. If you look at the listing, in fact, you will see that MOV AH has a different code from MOV DL.

Let me now take you through the program, explaining as much as possible as we go along the way:

```
MOV      AH,02
MOV      DL,07
INT      21
```

Each instruction falls into two parts (not all of which are necessarily present – only the first is always there). The first part is the opcode (operation code), the second the operand. In the first two lines, the opcodes are MOV AH and MOV DL. The operands are 02 and 07.

Before we explain exactly what these three lines do, we need to grapple with the concept of registers. If you type R at the DEBUG prompt, you will see this apparently bewildering array of information:

```
AX=0000 BX=0000 CX=0020 DX=0000 SP=FFFE BP=0000 SI=0000 DI=0000
DS=1F12 ES=1F12 SS=1F12 CS=1F12 IP=0100   NV UP EI PL NZ NA PO NC
1F12:0100 B402          MOV      AH,02
```

The registers are special locations in memory in which important operations are carried out. They consist of two bytes each, and some can be referred to a byte at a time. The AX register, the most important of all, can be accessed as AH and AL (in which the H and L stand for higher and lower bytes). The same applies to the CX and DX registers.

You will come across many of the other registers as we progress through this section of the book. The other points to note are that some of the registers in the second line are set to the current segment number (the first available space free in the computer for your program). The eight two-letter codes on the right indicate the state of the flags, which give us a variety of information about what is happening inside the machine. Again more of them later.

The third and final line of the listing gives the instruction about to be executed, the first of the program in this case. You can see almost immediately above the assembler instruction the IP register, the instruction pointer register, which currently points to the start of the program.

Now, although assembler is complex, DEBUG allows us to see exactly what is going on, and that is perhaps the best way to explain how the program functions. If you press P (for Proceed) three times, you should see something like the following on your screen:

```
-P
AX=0200 BX=0000 CX=0020 DX=0000 SP=FFFE BP=0000 SI=0000 DI=0000
DS=1F12 ES=1F12 SS=1F12 CS=1F12 IP=0102  NV UP EI PL NZ NA PO NC
1F12:0102 B207        MOV    DL,07

-P

AX=0200 BX=0000 CX=0020 DX=0007 SP=FFFE BP=0000 SI=0000 DI=0000
DS=1F12 ES=1F12 SS=1F12 CS=1F12 IP=0104  NV UP EI PL NZ NA PO NC
1F12:0104 CD21        INT    21
-P

AX=0207 BX=0000 CX=0020 DX=0007 SP=FFFE BP=0000 SI=0000 DI=0000
DS=1F12 ES=1F12 SS=1F12 CS=1F12 IP=0106  NV UP EI PL NZ NA PO NC
1F12:0106 B40B        MOV    AH,0B
```

This is called single-stepping through the program one instruction at a time – with a slight variation at the third instruction, as we shall see.

After the first instruction is executed, you can see that the high byte of the AX register has had 02 moved into it, so that is what MOV AH,02 means. A similar instruction comes next, and the DL register, the low byte of the DX register, now contains 07. Then comes INT 21.

Using interrupts

We access the BDOS (Basic Disk Operating System) and BIOS (Basic Input Output System), the heart of the computer's means of dealing with keyboard, screen, disks, and so forth, by what are known as software interrupts, which literally interrupt the program and execute a specially written subroutine which does all the dirty work for us.

Of all the interrupts, INT 21 (hex, of course) is the most frequently used. Each interrupt has a number of functions, as they are called, and INT 21 has the most of all. When an interrupt is called, the function number is loaded into the AH register, and, depending on the exact circumstances, information is loaded into other registers, and after the interrupt, information may be returned into registers for our use.

In the present case, then, we are summoning up function 2 of interrupt 21, which prints a character. The character has to be inserted into the DL register, and in this case it's character 07. As you might guess, this is not one of the printable ASCII characters, which range upwards from 20 hex. This is the character which rings the bell, so you will have heard the ping of the bell as you proceeded past the INT.

Do note two very important points. The first is that there is a T command, which Traces step by step, but if you try to type T at an INT, you will end up in the murky depths of the operating system BDOS. P carries out a single instruction or a complete subroutine, which is what INT is treated as. So at the point where interrupts occur, always use P.

The second point is that once you have started stepping or moving through a program, never – repeat, never – go back to the beginning and try to start it again. DEBUG will almost inevitably become hopelessly confused. Use Q to quit and then reload DEBUG.

Do note that using P to proceed through this particular program means that, because of the fact that you are typing from the keyboard, you never get the chance to press Esc, and the program keeps looping round and ringing the bell. To extract yourself from the loop, use an alternative form of P, that is, P followed by an address, in this case:

P 116

The bell will ring like fury, until you press Esc.

Now let me take you through the rest of the program. Having rung the bell, we summon up function 0B of INT 21:

```
MOV    AH,0B
INT    21
```

This function looks at the keyboard and tells us if a character has been pressed. If no character has been pressed, AL will return with zero. Otherwise, if a character has been pressed, it returns FF.

We now ask if AL contains FF, in other words, if a character is waiting to be processed:

```
CMP    AL,FF
JNZ    0100
```

If not, we jump to 100. JNZ states Jump Not Zero, in other words, if we compare the contents of AL with FF and the result is not zero, we jump to the location 100.

At this point, we can take our first look at the flags. JNZ examines the flags register to see if the zero flag is ZR or NZ – so watch out for the state of the flag.

Note that the machine code operand is not 0100, as you might expect. After all, we have asked the program to jump to address 100. Instead, the operand is a confusing F2. This means that the jump is a relative jump backwards. If you polish up your hexadecimal and count backwards F2, F3 ... FF and so on, you will find yourself back at location 100.

Identifying characters

Now we are at the point in the program at which a character has been detected. The way in which the program was written was for it to keep on pinging its blighted bell until Esc is pressed (the code generated is 1B). So when a character has been detected, we need to know what it is. Function 8 reads the current character, and the result is returned in the AL register. If it is not 1B, we go back to 100 and the bell rings again, and again... Otherwise, the program is halted:

```
MOV     AH,08
INT     21
CMP     AL,1B
JNZ     0100
INT     20
```

Interrupt 20 called without parameters halts the program. There is at least one other way of stopping a program and returning to the MS-DOS prompt, as we shall see later.

Now you have a program which will keep ringing the bell until you press Esc. If you want to change the key, alter the line CMP AL,1B. How do you do this?

Examine the address at the beginning of the instruction and then summon up A plus this address. In this case, you should type:

```
A112
```

– plus Enter, plus the replacement instruction.

That, then, is a whirlwind tour of assembler. But just to round things off, here is the program promised earlier which you can use in batch files as an alternative to CHOICE. Use the techniques described earlier to type these lines in, save them and run the program:

```
MOV AX,0C08
INT 21
AND AL,DF
MOV AH,4C
INT 21
```

This clears the keyboard buffer, or flushes it, to use the jargon, and waits for a key to be pressed. When that happens, the ASCII value of the keypress is placed in the AL half of the AX register. The AND instruction converts the keypress to upper case if necessary, and then the program is halted by a powerful technique, using function 4C of INT 21. What it does is to stop the program, leaving behind an exit code corresponding to the value in the AL register.

This means that if you call this program, say READUC.COM, then run it as part of a batch file, you can test for keypresses like this:

```
@ECHO OFF
READUC
IF ERRORLEVEL 41 IF NOT ERRORLEVEL 42 ECHO You pressed A
IF ERRORLEVEL 42 IF NOT ERRORLEVEL 43 ECHO You pressed B
```

– and so on.

If you press "A" or "a", the code returned in AL is 41 hex, and the mouthful of an ERRORLEVEL command looks to see if it is 41 and no higher than 41. The next line does the same for B, and so on. As you can see, the potential of this technique is enormous.

Now for some more applications of this powerful tool on your PC.

13

Switching directories – I

When MS-DOS 1 grew up and became Version 2, a hierarchical directory structure was one of the important features added. They were a vast improvement on the 16 user areas in CP/M, the operating system from which MS-DOS was directly descended. The more powerful subdirectories became, the more benefit users derived from them – and the more potentially confusing and tricky it became to handle them efficiently.

I often need to switch between subdirectories in different branches of the directory tree, and I have long been looking for a simple way of doing so. What we are going to explore in this Chapter is my favourite program in the book. It combines exploiting MS-DOS to the full with a touch of low cunning and deviousness. That is the best part of programming – being able to achieve something which at first sight seems quite impossible or hopelessly complicated.

Now with MS-DOS 5 and later Versions, a way has emerged of allowing us to do so with a single command, and I am going to let you into the secret of how to do so.

The challenge goes something like this. Assume that part of your hard disk contains in its directory structure two subdirectories called FRED and JOE which are, in turn, in directories which are a fair way off from the root directory, but in completely different branches of the tree. Here is the complete path to FRED and JOE:

```
C:\SUB1\SUB2\SUB3\SUB4\FRED
C:\THATSUB1\THATSUB2\THATSUB3\JOE
```

The question is: How do we switch from FRED to JOE without knowing where JOE is and without indulging in complex directory-hopping? The aim is to create a command like this:

```
SF JOE
```

– standing for Subdirectory Find to JOE, assuming that I am currently in FRED, or any other subdirectory for that matter. In this Chapter, we are going to concentrate on just moving about the C:\ drive, the name given to most hard disks. If your hard disk is different, or you want to inspect a different drive, just change what follows accordingly.

In fact, you can devise a version of SF which works on each of your drives. If, for example, you have two floppy disks A and B, and a hard drive C, you could devise variations and call them, say, SFA, SFB and SFC. The principles are exactly the same for each drive. All you have to remember is to have a path open to the subdirectory in which you put the appropriate files and, as usual, I am going to opt for the \DOS directory on drive C.

The way to tackle the problem is with a combination of a batch file and assembler program. Assume that the batch file is called SF.BAT and the assembler program SUBPROC.COM, and assume further that they are to be located, as I have just suggested, in the \DOS subdirectory. Do note one point, namely, that this will only work with MS-DOS Version 5 and above, because of the DIR switches.

How the program works

Before we look through the batch file and the program, here is a schematic description of what they are seeking to achieve, so that you can gain an overall view of the steps towards achieving the objective. First, if it does not exist, a file called SUBLIST is created in \DOS. It contains, amongst other information, the full path name of every subdirectory on the hard disk. This is achieved thanks to some of the new switches added to DIR in Version 5.

The FIND command is used to extract the line containing the appropriate path to the subdirectory we wish to switch to, and then the assembler program reorganises that information in such a way that it creates a temporary batch file containing a change directory command to switch us to the subdirectory we are after. In addition, there is a help facility and various messages which support this program, together with a facility for regenerating the SUBLIST file if you have added or deleted subdirectories since the program last ran.

Exploring the batch file

Now for the batch file in some detail. It contains a few interesting twists and turns, as you will see. The opening lines of the batch file first switch off ECHO (which you should leave on while writing or modifying the batch file), clear the screen, and the next two lines allow the user to summon help in one of two ways. If you call SF with a question mark as the first parameter, one of the conventional ways of asking for help, then the program lists details on how to run it.

If the user calls SF without any parameters, this ingenious line reruns the batch file as if it had been called with SF ?:

```
IF "%1"=="" %0 ?
```

This means that if the first parameter is empty, then execute the command %0 ?. The double quotes or something similar are necessary, otherwise %1 will generate a blank and an error message complaining that there is nothing between the IF and the double equals sign which IF for some reason insists on having.

The zero-th parameter of the batch file is the name of the file itself, so that command is equivalent to SF ?. Batch files have no qualms about calling themselves, and that is one way in which you can end up in infinitely looping batch files. Here are the first few lines, the first of which should be prefaced by a REM while you are developing and testing the file:

```
@ECHO OFF
CLS
ECHO *** This is a batch file for finding a subdirectory and
changing to it.
IF "%1"=="" %0 ?
IF "%1"=="?" GOTO HELP
```

The next part of the batch file deals with the SUBLIST file. If it does not exist at all – in other words, if you are running the program for the first time – SUBLIST is created, and if you have a second parameter in the SF call, SUBLIST is updated. The batch file says the second parameter should be UPDATE, but to be user friendly I have allowed it to be anything at all.

The heart of the matter is the DIR command, but here first are the batch file lines concerned:

```
IF NOT EXIST C:\DOS\SUBLIST GOTO UPDATE
IF "%2"=="" GOTO NOUPDATE
:UPDATE
ECHO *** Please wait - I'm creating a file of subdirectories for
you...
DIR C:\/AD/S > C:\DOS\SUBLIST
:NOUPDATE
```

Now for the DIR command, which basically is in this form:

```
DIR /A:D/S
```

The first switch is the attribute switch, and one of the file attributes is 'Directory', in other words, a subdirectory name, which is a special case of a filename. The /S switch tells DIR to look not just in the current directory, but in all subdirectories as well. As in the case of other DIR switches, the colon after the A is optional.

Listing the directory

The output from this directory listing is redirected to the file SUBLIST. The relevant information we are after is in the lines beginning "Directory". Here are a few lines from a typical SUBLIST, with some of the Windows subdirectories:

```
Directory of C:\WINDOWS

.              <DIR>          31/07/91   11:58
..             <DIR>          31/07/91   11:58
SYSTEM         <DIR>          31/07/91   11:59
MSAPPS         <DIR>          07/03/92   22:13
        4 file(s)                 0 bytes

Directory of C:\WINDOWS\MSAPPS

.              <DIR>          07/03/92   22:13
..             <DIR>          07/03/92   22:13
WORDART        <DIR>          07/03/92   22:13
MSGRAPH        <DIR>          07/03/92   22:17
MSDRAW         <DIR>          07/03/92   22:18
EQUATION       <DIR>          07/03/92   22:20
GRPHFLT        <DIR>          07/03/92   22:33
        7 file(s)                 0 bytes

Directory of C:\WINDOWS\MSAPPS\EQUATION

.              <DIR>          07/03/92   22:20
..             <DIR>          07/03/92   22:20
        2 file(s)                 0 bytes

Directory of C:\WINDOWS\MSAPPS\GRPHFLT

.              <DIR>          07/03/92   22:33
..             <DIR>          07/03/92   22:33
        2 file(s)                 0 bytes
```

As you can see, each of the lines beginning "Directory" contains in turn the full path of each and every subdirectory on the disk. All we have to do now is to winkle out the one we want, and the first stage in doing that is to use FIND with the /I option, which makes it case insensitive, to extract the appropriate line.

Say, for example, we looked for EQUATION. The FIND string is prefaced by the backslash to ensure that the Directory line is found, the one containing the full path name of the subdirectory concerned, not the earlier line listing EQUATION as a subdirectory of \WINDOWS\MSAPPS. Note that if you have more than one subdirectory with the same name, you need to add more information – for example, its superior directory name plus a backslash first – to ensure that you light on the one you are after.

Redirecting the output

The output from FIND is redirected to the file SUBNAME.BAT (which, like SUBLIST, is kept in \DOS) and takes this form:

```
---------- SUBLIST
Directory of C:\WINDOWS\MSAPPS\EQUATION
```

FIND always prefaces its information with that unlovely line of dashes plus the name of the file it has been looking through, and that is just another piece of garbage to have to sweep out of the way when it comes to subsequent processing by the assembler file. Our objective is that it will change the file contents to:

```
CD C:\WINDOWS\MSAPPS\EQUATION
```

After the FIND command in the batch file, you will see that I have made use of the fact that, under Version 6, FIND returns an exit code of 1 if nothing has been found. Under Version 5, the batch file will just crash with an error message. You could make a minor modification to the assembler program to cause it to return with an exit code indicating that the file did not contain what it should – I leave that refinement to you.

We then invoke SUBPROC and then the rest of the file tidies up any odd files lying around and closes, hopping over the help information:

```
FIND/I "\%1" C:\DOS\SUBLIST > C:\DOS\SUBNAME.BAT
IF ERRORLEVEL 1 GOTO NOFILE
SUBPROC
CALL C:\DOS\SUBNAME
DEL C:\DOS\SUBNAME.BAT
GOTO END
:HELP
ECHO ***
ECHO *** To change to a subdirectory, name it as the first
parameter, e.g.:
ECHO ***
ECHO ***          SUBFIND SUBNAME
ECHO ***
ECHO *** Do not precede the subdirectory name with a backslash -
it's been
ECHO *** done for you by a kind programmer.
ECHO *** If you have added or deleted one or more subdirectories
since you
ECHO *** last ran this program, or you are running this for the
first time,
ECHO *** please type:
ECHO ***
ECHO ***          SUBFIND SUBNAME UPDATE
ECHO ***
```

```
ECHO *** In fact, you can put anything as the second parameter
and it will
ECHO *** perform an update, which just takes a few seconds.
ECHO *** Please note that the program finds the first match for
/SUBNAME
ECHO *** only, so it is advisable to ensure that your search
request is
ECHO *** unique. You can also type:
ECHO ***
ECHO ***            SUBFIND first_part_of_subname
ECHO ***            SUBFIND SUBNAME\ANOTHER_SUBNAME\....
ECHO ***
ECHO *** - just so long as you know what you are after.
GOTO END
:NOFILE
ECHO *** I'm sorry, I can't find the subdirectory %1
:END
```

So much for the batch file aspect of the project. I turn now to the assembler part of the exercise.

14

Switching directories – II

Now for the assembler program, which will take the information generated by FIND and process it. The program is created using:

DEBUG SUBPROC.COM

– and saving, say, 600 (hex) bytes to memory. In addition to the program listing, which is one continuous piece of spaghetti programming, you also need to insert data into memory like this:

E 500 "C:\DOS\SUBNAME.BAT",0

That is the ASCII string terminated by zero to identify the file SUBNAME.BAT, which is first opened for reading from, and then for writing the CD command line for it to be executed by the batch file.

The assembler program begins by opening the file SUBNAME.BAT and it returns with an exit code of FF if the file is not found (causing carry to be set). This is strictly superfluous, but I have added it in case you want to modify the batch file and need this feature:

```
0100 B8003D      MOV     AX,3D00
0103 BA0005      MOV     DX,0500
0106 CD21        INT     21
0108 7305        JNB     010F
010A B8FF4C      MOV     AX,4CFF
010D CD21        INT     21
```

Now that the file is opened, the file handle is copied to the BX register, where function 3F needs to find it. The handle is a number ranging upwards from 5 which will be used to identify the file.

Function 3F also needs to know how many bytes to read, so I have put an excessive value into the CX register. BDOS will either read that number of bytes or as many bytes as there are in the file, whichever is the lesser.

In addition, 3F needs to know the first address of the buffer to read to, and that is in DX. Just out of curiosity, you might like to single step through this part of the program using P, and after INT 21 has been called you will find in AX the actual number of bytes which have been transferred. This is invaluable information in many circumstances.

Closing files

When the file has been read, it needs to be closed. Always close a file you open, even though it appears not to be necessary. You may come along later and modify the program by writing to a file open for reading and wonder why you get inscrutable error messages. Here are the appropriate lines of code:

```
010F 89C3        MOV    BX,AX
0111 B43F        MOV    AH,3F
0113 B90005      MOV    CX,0500
0116 BA0010      MOV    DX,1000
0119 CD21        INT    21
011B B43E        MOV    AH,3E
011D CD21        INT    21
```

At this point, the contents of SUBNAME.BAT are in the buffer beginning at address 1000 and if you examine it, it looks like this:

```
-d1000
1F13:1000  0D 0A 2D 2D 2D 2D 2D 2D-2D 2D 2D 2D 20 53 55 42   ..---------- SUB
1F13:1010  4C 49 53 54 0D 0A 44 69-72 65 63 74 6F 72 79 20   LIST..Directory
1F13:1020  6F 66 20 43 3A 5C 57 49-4E 44 4F 57 53 5C 4D 53   of C:\WINDOWS\MS
1F13:1030  41 50 50 53 5C 45 51 55-41 54 49 4F 4E 0D 0A E2   APPS\EQUATION...
```

What we have to do now is to juggle the data so that it consists of CD plus a space, plus the full path, followed by a carriage return line feed. Then we open the file SUBNAME.BAT for writing just that number of bytes to it.

So we first need to orientate ourselves in the data, and the way I have chosen to do this is to look for the occurrence of a lower case i – which will skip past however much stuff precedes it and land on the second letter of "Directory". Do not look for upper case I – you would end up most of the way down the first record, and that is not where you want to be.

So this simple loop scans along and stops when it gets to the point we are looking for. Note that SI is now actually pointing to the byte after the lower case i, because the increment occurs before the comparison. There is no particular reason for this – it's just the way I have written the program:

```
011F BE0010          MOV     SI,1000
0122 8A04            MOV     AL,[SI]
0124 46              INC     SI
0125 3C69            CMP     AL,69
0127 75F9            JNZ     0122
```

Now we do a bit of rough and ready arithmetic, and find that adding 8 to SI will land us in the case of our example at address 1020, pointing at the first letter of the word "of", which is nice and convenient, as we can now add the letters "C" and "D" and a space (not strictly necessary, as there is one already there, but I am a born pessimist when it comes to assembler programming), which have the hex codes 44, 45 and 20 respectively:

```
0129 83C608          ADD     SI,+08
012C B043            MOV     AL,43
012E 8804            MOV     [SI],AL
0130 46              INC     SI
0131 B044            MOV     AL,44
0133 8804            MOV     [SI],AL
0135 46              INC     SI
0136 B020            MOV     AL,20
0138 8804            MOV     [SI],AL
```

Moving the data

Now we are going to move this data to the beginning of the buffer area. You could handle it in situ, but I am just demonstrating how easy it is to move stuff around, and anyway it's less confusing to have a buffer always starting at the same point in memory. So we now subtract 2 from SI, which leaves us pointing at the C of CD.

The reason for using SI now becomes clear, as we are about to use the REPNZ MOVSB instruction, which moves data a single byte at a time from the address pointed to by SI to the address pointed to by DI (1000, the beginning of the buffer). Then SI and DI are incremented, the contents of CX are decremented (again I have set them at a value greater than anyone is ever likely to need) until CX is zero:

```
013A 83EE02          SUB     SI,+02
013D BF0010          MOV     DI,1000
0140 B90002          MOV     CX,0200
0143 F2              REPNZ
0144 A4              MOVSB
```

If you are single-stepping round this point to see how the powerful pair REPNZ MOVSB works, do note that if you get to 143 and type P, DEBUG assumes you want to proceed until the loop count is exhausted, so when you get to 143, type T to watch the count proceed one step at a time.

A pause for breath, and we continue by calling function 3C of INT 21. Note that it is important not to call function 3D, which opens a file for reading. The function 3C either creates a non-existent file or it opens an existing file (if the state of the attributes allow this, which they do by default) for writing. Again the handle ends up in AX and needs to be moved to BX for the writing process:

```
0145 B8003C          MOV       AX,3C00
0148 BA0005          MOV       DX,0500
014B CD21            INT       21
014D 89C3            MOV       BX,AX
```

Before we can actually write, though, we need to find out where the data we want ends, so we look for the 0A which is the carriage return at the end of the first line:

```
014F BE0010          MOV       SI,1000
0152 8A04            MOV       AL,[SI]
0154 46              INC       SI
0155 3C0A            CMP       AL,0A
0157 75F9            JNZ       0152
```

Now for the writing process. We copy SI to CX, where function 40 – write file – expects to find the byte count for writing. Then we AND it with FF, to ensure only that the lower byte of the count is included (removing the 1000 part – if you are not sure what is going on, single step through this bit to see what happens). BX already contains the file handle, so away we go, finally closing the file before returning to the calling program, which in our case will be the batch file:

```
0159 89F1            MOV       CX,SI
015B BA0010          MOV       DX,1000
015E 81E1FF00        AND       CX,00FF
0162 B440            MOV       AH,40
0164 CD21            INT       21
0166 B43E            MOV       AH,3E
0168 CD21            INT       21
016A CD20            INT       20
```

There is something very satisfying in writing a routine which makes life easier for the programmer, and even more so if it appears a pretty impossible task at the time. I use it just about every day – I hope you will, too.

Just one footnote: to examine areas of memory for data, use D for Dump, followed by either the start of the area you are interested in, for example:

```
D 1000
```

– which puts several lines of information up on screen, or, if you want to limit the amount, say to 16 bytes:

```
D 1000 100F
```

– and so on. Use this command as you single step through the part of the program in this Chapter which moves data around, so that you can see exactly what is happening.

15

Deleting lots of files

There are a number of reasons for this Chapter, which in many ways is a follow-on from the last Chapter, in which we explored how to switch from one subdirectory to another. The programming in the example we are about to look at is broadly similar, but I shall be explaining it in full for you.

The first main reason is to air my own personal prejudice about data compression as a means of cramming more files into less space. I regard it – even given the extra security built into MS-DOS 6.2 – as a potentially hazardous business, if only for the reason that it introduces another level of complexity into the business of managing a computer system, and the more complex anything becomes, the more error-prone it gets. As I was proofing this Chapter, I noticed in today's Independent newspaper an article in their weekly computing section by a reporter whose compressed disk crashed and was only repaired with some difficulty and loss of data. True, he was running 6.0, but I would rather adopt strategies to save space than run the risk of spending hours, if not days, of valuable time trying to recover from an avoidable situation.

My view is that memory is cheap, so cheap that it is tempting to squander it rather than discipline ourselves to use it properly. I refer not just to disk storage, but to RAM. I am old enough to remember the days when the (paper tape in, paper tape out) first mainframe I dealt with had a massive 5K of memory, so every byte counted when devising a program, but now memory is so lavishly available that it makes program design far easier now than it ever has been.

Instead of having to worry about every last byte in a situation when old-fashioned core storage was limited, or its successor, the first chips, offered a meagre amount of program space (remember the BBC micro's massive 32K being eaten away by the memory-hungry screen modes?), we can now program away, almost regardless of the amount of memory we squander.

I remember being taught that programming was a trade-off between size and speed – the bigger the program, the faster it ran, but the greater the danger of running out of memory. Now things are radically different, and no more so than in back-up storage.

A hundred megabytes of hard disk and more are nothing unusual nowadays, and if the disk is getting perilously close to filling up, what better approach than to use the data compression facilities that MS-DOS now offers? Well, personally, I would only use them as a last resort, and check first that I do not have two kinds of data unnecessarily cluttering up the disk before I went down that road.

The first kind of clutter concerns subdirectories which have been created containing vast numbers of files which I do not need to have on the disk, and may well never need again. It only takes – to take just one example – a few of the cover-mounted disks from the monthly computing comics to sprawl over several tens of megabytes.

You pick at the offerings in a desultory fashion, then turn your back on them and never need them again. But they still remain, cluttering the disk up until you remove them. The other kind of clutter is back-up files. If you think I am joking, try this command from the root directory of your hard disk:

```
DIR *.BAK/S
```

Much of my work is word-processing and program development, but even I was astonished to find that on a hard disk of 110Mb or so, nearly 1.5Mb were taken up by back-up files, despite my regular clean-up campaigns.

Not all of these files were superfluous – in most directories, they were, but I wanted to keep a few, and the only way out of the situation seemed to be a tedious piece of housekeeping.

Automating the process

So that is why I wrote this batch file and assembler program to automate the process. It may need doing only every month or so, but it does free up a large amount of space, and running that plus DEFRAG (see MS-DOS HELP for further details) can certainly improve your disk's capacity and performance.

Before showing you the batch file and program, though, it may be useful to talk through the design of a method to solve a problem like this, in order to help you write your own programs in particular with the maximum of efficiency and the minimum of grief.

One of the real difficulties with using DEBUG is that it can be something of a pain inserting program lines and displacing existing lines of code. They have to be physically moved to another part of memory and then moved back again, but not without potentially disastrous results.

The vital thing is to experiment with non-crucial data in order to ensure that things do not go wrong in such a way that you create bugs which are impenetrably difficult to resolve. Here are some key examples culled from bitter experience.

Let us take a few lines of code from the program we shall be examining in Chapters 22 and 23, and show you what can happen to CALL, which at first sight looks pretty mystifying. I have removed the segment number in each case, to avoid confusing clutter.

First, I have listed the instructions from address 14D to 15A, just an arbitrary chunk of code, but one which contains a CALL to a subroutine at 400:

```
-u14d 15a
014D B8003D        MOV      AX,3D00
0150 BA1E12        MOV      DX,121E
0153 CD21          INT      21
0155 E8A802        CALL     0400
0158 B43E          MOV      AH,3E
015A CDB4          INT      B4
```

Next, I move the rest of the subroutine from address 14D onwards to 800, in order to be able to insert an instruction at that point. The instruction in question is a harmless NOP (which does nothing) in this case – or is it so harmless? Let's see:

```
-m14d 160 800
-a14d
014D nop
014E
```

Now to move the rest of the routine from 800 (I'm using arbitrarily large numbers to ensure that all the code gets copied to and fro – never mind the garbage tagged on the end), and to inspect what has happened now I have stitched a one-byte command in place:

```
-m 800 850 14e
-u14d 15c
014D 90            NOP
014E B8003D        MOV      AX,3D00
0151 BA1E12        MOV      DX,121E
0154 CD21          INT      21
0156 E8A802        CALL     0401
0159 B43E          MOV      AH,3E
015B CDB4          INT      B4
```

The result is apparently quite astonishing. Even though the hex code for the CALL remains exactly the same, the CALL is now to location 401, and if you went to that address, you would in all likelihood end up in the middle of an instruction, with entirely unpredictable but almost certainly catastrophic results!

Mysterious moving bytes

What is going on? It took me a little while to figure it out, I must confess. I wouldn't admit this to everyone, but at first I thought that in some way DEBUG was trying to be helpful, as it appears to be in some cases with JMP, more of which in a moment, but got itself confused. It was only when I got my scientific calculator out and did some sums that I realised what was happening.

If you look back at the first chunk of code, the hex for the CALL 400 instruction is E8 (the code for CALL), followed by 2A8 – remembering that addresses are stored backwards way on, as ever. That is supposedly the address of the CALL, but it bears no resemblance to the 400 which I typed in. If, however, you look at the address to which the program returns after the call, in other words the address of the instruction immediately after the CALL, we end up with 158+2A8 = 400. Mystery solved. The CALL is a computed call of a subroutine, and that is why it mysteriously adds a byte for each byte we interpose.

If you have to move instructions around in order to insert pieces of code, do as a matter of routine check for all CALL instructions. With jumps the story is a little different.

Here is another part of the same program, before and after adding a NOP using the same technique:

```
-u44d 456
044D 7503          JNZ     0452
044F E8AE00        CALL    0500
0452 46            INC     SI
0453 F2            REPNZ
0454 E2E8          LOOP    043E
0456 C3            RET
-m 44d 470 800
-a44d
044D nop
044E
-m 800 850 44e
-u44d 458
044D 90            NOP
044E 7503          JNZ     0453
0450 E8AE00        CALL    0501
0453 46            INC     SI
0454 F2            REPNZ
0455 E2E8          LOOP    043F
0457 C3            RET
0458 6D            DB      6D
```

This requires a different kind of mathematical dexterity. LOOP and JMP instructions (and all the variations on JMP) are relative jumps. There is only a single byte describing the target address, allowing you to move within the range that FF back and forward allows.

That relative jump back is pulled one forward for every byte you insert, so again keep your eyes skinned for that kind of problem whenever you add lines of code.

Modular program design

I split programs into the following broad sections:

1. The start-up process – initial message, opening files, and so on.

2. The main operations of the program, which are usually expressed in a series of subroutines.

3. The shut-down process – final message, output of data, closing files, and so on.

This may sound rather obvious, but it is far from common practice among all too many programmers.

Let me apply this top-down technique to the program before us. What I intend to do is to insert the program inside a batch file which first issues this command:

```
DIR *.BAK/S > DFILES
```

This puts the output of all the directories containing batch files into the file DFILES.

The program will first read the contents of DFILES into a buffer, then list each subdirectory in turn, asking the user if the BAK files in that subdirectory can be erased.

An output file called DFILES.BAT is opened, and the command:

```
DEL *.BAK
```

– plus the complete path name for the subdirectory is put into the file for every time the user answers in the affirmative to the question about erasing files.

At the end of the program, DFILES.BAT is closed.

The start-up part of the program opens the file DFILE and reads it into memory. A decision has to be made at this point as to how the program will recognise the end of the file when it has finished scanning through the subdirectories.

One way is to store the contents of the CX register, which records the number of bytes read, in a particular location, but that means fishing it out and comparing it with the current location rather a lot of times, so I opted to fill the two bytes after the end of the file with FFFF. This is particularly convenient, because the two bytes which end the file contain 0D0A.

Program output

Typical output which we are aiming for is:

```
DEL C:\ALDUS\USENGLSH\SET-UP *.BAK
DEL C:\LS.PC\LS.ETC *.BAK
DEL C:\LS.PC\LS.ETC\APCWFEB *.BAK
```

A short batch file

The batch file which runs the whole proceedings is very short:

```
@ECHO OFF
ECHO Please wait - I'm reading files for you ...
DIR C:\*.BAK/S > DFILES
ECHO Directory >> DFILES
DPROG
DFILES
DEL DFILES.*
```

The reason for the odd-looking ECHO on line 4 is explained in the detailed comments on the subroutine beginning at line 200.

It is, of course, up to you to specify which drive you are searching for the back-up files on. You can specify any kind of filetype instead of BAK, so long as the search pattern in the batch file matches the filetype read into memory at address 1050 and following.

The following data needs to be entered into memory:

```
E 1000  "DFILES",0
E 1010  1B,"[2J$"
E 1020  0D,0A,"Delete these files? (Y/N) $"
E 1040  "DFILES.BAT",0
E 1050  "\*.BAK",0D,0A,FF
E 1060  "DEL",20
```

In the strings beginning at addresses 1000 and 1040, the last character is a zero. The two-digit numbers are all hex.

To save the program, ensure the BX register is empty. Then put 1500 – more than enough, as usual – into CX and write the file to disk in the usual way.

This is the program listing, which I have annotated in full in case you want to be taken all the way through it. If not, ignore those parts of the text which you are familiar with and type in the program. The detailed text also includes information on modifications you could make to the program.

The main program module

The main module begins as usual at address 100. An analysis of the instructions follows the listing:

```
0100 B8003D      MOV     AX,3D00
0103 BA0010      MOV     DX,1000
0106 CD21        INT     21
0108 7304        JNB     010E
010A B44C        MOV     AH,4C
010C CD21        INT     21
010E 89C3        MOV     BX,AX
0110 B43F        MOV     AH,3F
0112 B9AAAA      MOV     CX,AAAA
0115 BA0012      MOV     DX,1200
0118 CD21        INT     21
011A 50          PUSH    AX
011B B43E        MOV     AH,3E
011D CD21        INT     21
011F 58          POP     AX
0120 89C3        MOV     BX,AX
0122 81C30012    ADD     BX,1200
0126 B8FFFF      MOV     AX,FFFF
0129 8907        MOV     [BX],AX
012B B43C        MOV     AH,3C
012D 31C9        XOR     CX,CX
012F BA4010      MOV     DX,1040
0132 CD21        INT     21
0134 A34E10      MOV     [104E],AX
0137 BF3012      MOV     DI,1230
013A E8C300      CALL    0200
013D B409        MOV     AH,09
013F BA1010      MOV     DX,1010
0142 CD21        INT     21
0144 E8B900      CALL    0200
0147 80FAFF      CMP     DL,FF
014A 7408        JZ      0154
014C E8B101      CALL    0300
014F E8AE02      CALL    0400
0152 EBE9        JMP     013D
0154 B43E        MOV     AH,3E
0156 CD21        INT     21
0158 CD20        INT     20
```

The program begins by opening the file DFILES, returning an exit code if there is an error, a response to which you can build into the batch file if you wish. The most likely error would be a full disk, if you are operating from Drive A or B.

At address 10E, the handle is copied to BX for reading the file contents. CX is set to a ridiculously high figure as usual, and the buffer begins at address 1200. The file is closed to tidy things up and release the handle, after AX – which contains the byte count from the file – is pushed into safety, popped back again and added to 1200 to find the address of the byte immediately following the last byte in the file.

Testing for end of file

That address and its neighbour, just for good measure, is set to FF. The reason for this is that I find testing for FF as a means of finding out where the end of the file is presents far fewer problems than storing the location somewhere, digging it up every time you move along the file and checking to see if it matches the current location.

If I do that, I invariably fail to check at one point or another, usually the crucial one, and the program goes sailing on through memory and out into oblivion, making me reboot the machine, nine times out of ten just after I have made a crucial alteration to the program which I promptly forget about in the panic. One way round the problem is to routinely use the F for Fill instruction to fill the entire segment with the INT 20 instruction.

Next, at address 12B, we set about opening the file DFILES.BAT for writing, using the create file function of INT 21. At address 134, I save the file handle to a spare location in memory. I always recommend doing this in preference to pushing it on to the stack, because that is an open invitation to disaster, especially if you then try and pop it back in the middle of the subroutine, at which point you will find that you are grappling with the return address of the subroutine rather than the file handle.

If you are not too sure as to what happens on the stack when you enter and leave subroutines, write a short program to do so and watch the values, as well as reading them off using D – and remember that, as ever, 8086 saves two-byte values (words) backwards way on, so to speak, the least significant byte first, as you will find if you inspect address 104E when you have saved the contents of AX there.

Now we load 1230 into DI. The reason for this becomes apparent if you type D 1200 to inspect the beginning of the buffer in which the file contents of DFILES are stored. Each subdirectory listing of BAK files takes the form:

```
Directory of C:\LS.PC\LS.ETC\GLOSSARY

PP38-9    BAK        14,960 09/10/93    10:06
GLOSS1    BAK         2,560 28/05/93    21:28
GLOSSJ-Z  BAK        12,880 11/10/93    10:46
GLOSSPCW  BAK         3,888 28/05/93    21:31
GLOSS     BAK        24,640 28/05/93    21:32
P40-1     BAK        13,136 09/10/93    10:07
GLOSSDEC  BAK        18,480 11/10/93    10:54
          7 file(s)          90,544 bytes
```

The whole lot is preceded by the Volume label of the file and its serial number, so I have started a fair way into that information and proceeded to search for a unique letter which indicates that I have found the first line of a Directory listing (or FF to tell me I have got to the end of the file altogether). The first unique letter is the lower case "c" of "Directory". The first call of the subroutine at 200 hops over the opening information and ends up, with a little adjustment, pointing at the "D" of "Directory".

Neat on the screen

Using the subroutine at 200 saves typing out extra code just to get things going. Now we print the string starting at address 1010 which clears the screen. That is always neater than simply scrolling untidily up from the prompt, ensuring as it does that no superfluous information is cluttering up the screen.

Now we are ready to call 200 for the first time proper, which as you will see later returns the location of the first and last bytes of the listing of the first directory or subdirectory containing *.BAK files.

If DL = FF, in other words, if the file has come to an end, the program jumps to 154, closes the file and stops. Otherwise we call 300, which prints the next directory on screen, then we call 400, which asks if those files are to be deleted and does the necessary fiddly bits, and then we loop back again to 13D.

The first subroutine is at address 200:

```
0200 89FE          MOV     SI,DI
0202 83C706        ADD     DI,+06
0205 8A14          MOV     DL,[SI]
0207 80FAFF        CMP     DL,FF
020A 7501          JNZ     020D
020C C3            RET
020D 8A15          MOV     DL,[DI]
020F 47            INC     DI
0210 80FA63        CMP     DL,63
0213 75F2          JNZ     0207
0215 83EF05        SUB     DI,+05
0218 C3            RET
```

The contents of DI, which points to the line beginning with the word "Directory" (except for the first time round, when it searches for the first occurrence of the word), are copied to SI, where it sits pointing at the beginning of this part of the listing ready for being printed out in the subroutine beginning at 300. Now we add 6 to DI, for the simple reason that if we start scanning down the buffer from the current address looking for the next lower case "c", we would find one soon enough – the same one we have just found!

So DI is pointing to the letter after the "c", and the search goes on for the next occurrence at the beginning of the next subdirectory listing. At the end of the file, I appended – in the batch file – a dummy occurrence of "Directory", as a sneaky way of ensuring that the last subdirectory gets listed without having to make special allowances for the last item in the list. We simply look for the "c" as normal and backtrack, and the next time round FF is found and the subroutine returns for the instruction at address 147 to pick it up and finish off the program.

At instructions 20D and following, we loop round looking for 63 (lower case "c"), and when it is found, 5 is subtracted from the value of DI so that it points to the beginning of the line.

The next subroutine is at address 300:

```
0300 89F9        MOV      CX,DI
0302 29F1        SUB      CX,SI
0304 56          PUSH     SI
0305 B402        MOV      AH,02
0307 8A14        MOV      DL,[SI]
0309 CD21        INT      21
030B 46          INC      SI
030C E0F9        LOOPNZ   0307
030E 5E          POP      SI
030F B409        MOV      AH,09
0311 BA2010      MOV      DX,1020
0314 CD21        INT      21
0316 B401        MOV      AH,01
0318 CD21        INT      21
031A 24DF        AND      AL,DF
031C 3C4E        CMP      AL,4E
031E 7501        JNZ      0321
0320 C3          RET
0321 3C59        CMP      AL,59
0323 75EA        JNZ      030F
0325 C3          RET
```

In this routine, the contents of the subdirectory are printed out. First, the word pointing to the beginning of the list (in DI) is copied to CX, for reasons which will become clear in a moment. Then SI – which points to the last byte of the subdirectory list – is subtracted from CX, which means that CX now contains a value corresponding to the number of bytes in this part of the list. Now we push SI, which copies the contents of the SI register to the top of the stack.

A powerful looping instruction

At this point we are ready to make use of a very valuable instruction, which is like REPNZ: LOOPNZ, which is sitting at address 30C. What LOOPNZ does is to jump to an instruction, in this case at address 207, and at the same time decrement CX. It loops round until CX is zero and the zero flag is set.

So, with the aid of function 2 (character output) and the contents of SI, this loop prints out the contents of the current subdirectory on screen. When that is completed, SI is popped to restore the word pointing to the address of the beginning of the list, and the message starting at 1020 is printed. The message asks if you want these files deleted, and the rest of the subroutine ensures that a Y or N is returned.

The final subroutine is at address 400:

```
0400 3C59          CMP    AL,59
0402 7401          JZ     0405
0404 C3            RET
0405 83C60D        ADD    SI,+0D
0408 BB6410        MOV    BX,1064
040B 8A04          MOV    AL,[SI]
040D 3C0D          CMP    AL,0D
040F 7406          JZ     0417
0411 8807          MOV    [BX],AL
0413 43            INC    BX
0414 46            INC    SI
0415 EBF4          JMP    040B
0417 BE5010        MOV    SI,1050
041A 8A04          MOV    AL,[SI]
041C 3CFF          CMP    AL,FF
041E 7406          JZ     0426
0420 8807          MOV    [BX],AL
0422 46            INC    SI
0423 43            INC    BX
0424 EBF4          JMP    041A
0426 89D9          MOV    CX,BX
0428 81E96010      SUB    CX,1060
042C 8B1E4E10      MOV    BX,[104E]
0430 B440          MOV    AH,40
0432 BA6010        MOV    DX,1060
0435 CD21          INT    21
0437 C3            RET
```

The subroutine first interrogates AL to see if 59 (capital "N") is there, and if so, the rest of the subroutine is ignored. Otherwise, we prepare to output to the file DFILES.BAT the delete files instruction for BAK files in this subdirectory, which requires a little bit of nifty footwork.

Let us take the example quoted above:

Directory of C:\LS.PC\LS.ETC\GLOSSARY

If you recall, the last part of our data area was filled as follows:

```
E 1050 "\*.BAK",0D,0A,FF
E 1060 "DEL",20
```

The object of the exercise is to take the path from the Directory line – the bit that goes "C:\LS.PC\LS.ETC\GLOSSARY" – and place it after the DEL followed by a space, and then copy immediately after that the "*.BAK" plus carriage return and line feed from the area beginning at 1050. Then that piece of patch and mend will look like this:

DEL C:\LS.PC\LS.ETC\GLOSSARY*.BAK

– and it is ready to add to the file DFILES.BAT. How is this achieved?

First, we take SI (pointing to the "D" of Directory, remember) and add 0D to it, which leaves it pointing now to the first letter of the path (in this case, "C"). We put the address 1064 into BX, which points to the byte after the space following "DEL", and copy the path across, stopping just before the carriage return and line feed which follow that.

Now we can copy the filetype, the address of the beginning of which is copied into SI (in the instruction at address 41A). The FF at the end of the buffer area is used to determine when the copying is complete. Of course, you can replace *.BAK with anything you like. It doesn't have to be a three-character filetype, either – that's why I test for FF rather than blindly copying across a fixed number of bytes, so that you can have flexibility in your own implementation of the program.

If this all sounds a bit complicated, single-step through this part of the program and all will make good sense.

Finally, we output the DEL command plus carriage return line feed to DFILES.BAT, starting at address 426. The byte count is arrived at by moving BX into CX and subtracting the start address – 1060 – from it. Then the file handle is retrieved from 104E and 104F and placed into BX. DX is given the start address for the write function 40. That completes the program, which I run every week or so just to keep my back-up files in order.

16

Saving those macros

As I said earlier in the book in the Chapter on DOSKEY, one of the benefits of this new MS-DOS tool was the ability to save macros, but it was strange indeed that they could neither be saved selectively, nor in a form in which they could immediately be reloaded.

Let me explain. Assume we have used the /M (or /MACROS) switch to save three macros in a file called DOSFILES. I have simply called the macros A, B and C – there is no reason why they should not be given more sensible names. They are saved using the command:

```
DOSKEY/M > DOSFILES
```

– which redirects the listing of macros to the file DOSFILES. The form in which they are saved is as follows:

```
A=DIR *.COM
B=DIR *.WP
C=XCOPY C:\LS.PC\LS.ETC\MDSDOS2 A:
```

In order to load them as macros, they need to be in this format:

```
DOSKEY A=DIR *.COM
DOSKEY B=DIR *.WP
DOSKEY C=XCOPY C:\LS.PC\LS.ETC\MSDOS2 A:
```

In addition to prefixing each line with "DOSKEY ", it would also be nice to be able to select which of the macros is worth saving.

Both objectives can be achieved with the help of this assembler program, which is best run as part of a batch file which begins by saving the files. Note that I have called the file DOSFILES – you can call it what you like, except that there should be

no filetype, as the program adds the suffix ".NEW" to the file containing the
unprocessed files.

You should ensure in your batch file that if by chance a file called DOSFILES.NEW
– or whatever – exists, it is first deleted. That saves the program the fiddle of
checking.

You make your own arrangements if you have more than one file of macros. That can
be done at the end of the batch file like this:

COPY ALLMACS.NEW+ALLMACS.BAT ALLMACS.BAT

– where %1 contains the name you have given the file containing the unprocessed
macros. Ensure that ALLMACS.BAT exists – even as an empty file first time round.
If you are not going to add to an existing file, you need to rename ALLMACS.NEW
as ALLMACS.BAT so that it can be run the next time you want those macros to be
used with DOSKEY.

A modular program

The program is neatly divided up into modules. The main module, beginning at 100,
calls three subroutines at 200, 300 and 400, closes the .NEW file, and then halts.

In addition to the program instructions, you need to type:

```
E 1000  "File name please > $"
E 1019  ".NEW",0
E 1040  "Save this macro (Y/N) ?$"
E 1050  "DOSKEY "
```

Note in the second line that the last character is a zero, not a capital O, and in the last
line the word DOSKEY is followed by a space before the closing quotes.

When using R CX and W to save the program, allocate around 1500 (hex) bytes.
Remember, if you are saving or altering this program during running, that BX must
be cleared (using R BX and then filling it with zero) when saving, otherwise you may
well find yourself filling huge amounts of space inadvertently – or even running out
of space.

The program begins by asking you what the name of the file containing the macros is,
using the familiar print string function, which expects to find the value 24 as a
terminator:

```
0100 B409          MOV     AH,09
0102 BA0010        MOV     DX,1000
0105 CD21          INT     21
```

Now the answer to the question needs to be read into a buffer. Using function 0A (buffered keyboard input), which takes care of line editing as it's being typed in, we need first to allocate a buffer. This is done starting at address 1020.

The rules for buffered keyboard input are simple, but you have to be precise about using them. The first byte of the buffer, in this case at address 1020, contains the maximum number of characters you can type in, which, as you can see, I have set to 8, the maximum number of characters in a filename plus one.

Why plus one? The answer is that when you reach the maximum minus one and try to type another character, the system bleeps at you and won't let you. The last character space – if you use up the complete allocation – is set aside for the 0D (carriage return) terminator. The absolute maximum allowed is FF-1 characters.

The second byte of the buffer will return the actual number of characters keyed in, not counting the carriage return, which is supplied immediately after the last character you type. That palaver is dealt with in the following instructions:

```
0107 BB2010       MOV     BX,1020
010A B009         MOV     AL,09
010C 8807         MOV     [BX],AL
010E BA2010       MOV     DX,1020
0111 B40A         MOV     AH,0A
0113 CD21         INT     21
```

Now the string has been read in, we need to convert it to a form in which we can try opening the file. We need, of course, to know if it exists before reading from it. So we extract from the second byte of the buffer (1021) the number of characters typed in, clear AX – using the exclusive OR instruction, or by MOV AX,0 if you like – and move the number of bytes into AL.

Moving pairs of bytes

Do note that if you MOV AX,[BX] you are moving a pair of bytes (a "word" in the jargon) into the complete register. That's why I emptied the high byte first and ensured that only the contents of 1021 get into the low byte. As it is sitting around doing nothing, that information is moved into the SI register:

```
0115 BB2110       MOV     BX,1021
0118 31C0         XOR     AX,AX
011A 8A07         MOV     AL,[BX]
011C 89C6         MOV     SI,AX
```

Now I add the start address of the buffer to the SI register, which means that if the file name was four characters long, BX would contain 1022 and SI would contain 4.

So if I move the contents of AH – zero, remember – to the address pointed to by BX+SI I am effectively terminating the file name with a zero, which is precisely what the file handling functions of the BDOS need in order to look for the file and open it:

```
011E BB2210        MOV     BX,1022
0121 8820          MOV     [BX+SI],AH
```

Now the moment has come to open the file. First, I clear AX and load 3D, the function to open file, into AH. AL now contains the normal access mode, zero. DX contains 1022, the start address of the ASCII string terminated by zero:

```
0123 31C0          XOR     AX,AX
0125 B43D          MOV     AH,3D
0127 BA2210        MOV     DX,1022
012A CD21          INT     21
```

When this function returns, AL contains either the file handle, the number by which the file is referred to in subsequent operations, which will normally be 5, or an error message.

Remember 0-4 are reserved by the operating system for the devices keyboard, screen and so on. I suppose another way of checking to see if all is well is to see if carry is set (if it is, something is wrong). In any event, if we do not find the file number we expect, the program is terminated using 4C, which allows the return code in AL to be examined by the batch file using IF ERRORLEVEL so that you can add into the batch file appropriate comments, usually to the effect that you have gone for a non-existent file:

```
012C 3C05          CMP     AL,05
012E 7D04          JGE     0134
0130 B44C          MOV     AH,4C
0132 CD21          INT     21
```

Now we have successfully opened the file. The file handle is in AL, which I shunt off to DI for safe keeping. It is probably not necessary, but it is always wise to save the handle somewhere where you cannot accidentally tread on it and cause the program to crash. For the purposes of what we are doing here, DI is safe enough. Then the data is loaded and saved into the .NEW file according to the programmer's instructions in the subroutines at 200, 300 and 400.

Then, finally, the .NEW file is closed using function 3E of INT 21 (BX at this point contains the file handle for closing):

```
0134 89C7          MOV     DI,AX
0136 E8C700        CALL    0200
0139 E8C401        CALL    0300
013C E8C102        CALL    0400
013F B43E          MOV     AH,3E
0141 CD21          INT     21
0143 CD20          INT     20
```

Exploring the subroutines

Now we examine the subroutines, beginning with the one starting at address 200. The function 3F reads from the opened file with the file handle in BX and the buffer to read to, starting at the address pointed to by DX. CX contains the number of bytes to read, which I have set at a ridiculously high figure.

If you manage to create more macros than that space allows for, I leave it to you to do the necessary twiddling. Remember that the function returns the number of bytes actually read in the AX register, if you need that information:

```
0200 B43F          MOV     AH,3F
0202 BA0020        MOV     DX,2000
0205 89FB          MOV     BX,DI
0207 B9AAAA        MOV     CX,AAAA
020A CD21          INT     21
```

At this point, we save the number of records read in 1FFE and 1FFF, which happen to be free just before the buffer into which the file contents have been loaded. Finally, the file is closed and we return back to the main calling module:

```
020C BBFE1F        MOV     BX,1FFE
020F 8907          MOV     [BX],AX
0211 B43E          MOV     AH,3E
0213 89FB          MOV     BX,DI
0215 CD21          INT     21
0217 C3            RET
```

Up comes the subroutine starting at address 300. Now for the fiddly bits. First, we find out the address of the byte after the last byte of the filename (the one we earlier zeroised), and move into it ".NEW" followed by zero to form the name of the output file. The REPZ MOVSB instruction, which DEBUG spreads over two lines, does quite a lot of hard work for you.

First, you set up the start address for the data move in the SI (source index) register, and then you put the start address for the target area in DI. Then the CX register is set to the number of characters to move. The move single byte instruction moves a byte from the address pointed to by SI to that pointed to by DI, and then the REPZ adds one to SI and DI, decrements CX, and round and round we go until CX is zero:

```
0300 31DB          XOR     BX,BX
0302 8A1E2110      MOV     BL,[1021]
0306 81C32210      ADD     BX,1022
030A 89DF          MOV     DI,BX
030C BE1910        MOV     SI,1019
030F B90500        MOV     CX,0005
0312 F3            REPZ
0313 A4            MOVSB
```

Now we create the .NEW file, clearing AX first, just for tidiness, so that AH can take the function number while leaving AL as zero. Note that this either creates the file or, if it exists (and the read attribute is not set), truncates it to zero length ready for writing.

The start address of the filename is in DX, and CX contains the file attribute (zero):

```
0314 31C0        XOR      AX,AX
0316 B43C        MOV      AH,3C
0318 BA2210      MOV      DX,1022
031B 31C9        XOR      CX,CX
031D CD21        INT      21
031F A31E10      MOV      [101E],AX
0322 C3          RET
```

The file handle is saved at 101E.

Saving the macro definitions

In the final subroutine, the one starting at 400, we do the hard work of prefacing each line with "DOSKEY = " and asking if the user wants to save the macro definition.

Now I insert FF at the end of the data read into the buffer starting at address 2000. The byte count is first extracted from 1FFE and 1FFF into SI, and then 2000 is added to it:

```
0400 8B36FE1F    MOV      SI,[1FFE]
0404 B0FF        MOV      AL,FF
0406 81C60020    ADD      SI,2000
040A 8804        MOV      [SI],AL
040C BE0020      MOV      SI,2000
```

Now we take one line at a time from the buffer, copying it to bytes 1507 and following. If you remember, bytes 1500 to 1506 contain the string "DOSKEY" plus a space. The check for FF – which we have inserted after the last byte of the buffer – is of course superfluous the first time round, but it is most conveniently located here.

The reading from the file buffer concludes with 0A, the line feed character, and 24 is added to the target buffer as a terminator for function 9. The line preface by DOSKEY is now printed on screen, together with a line asking if you wish to save this particular macro:

```
040F BF0715      MOV      DI,1507
0412 8A04        MOV      AL,[SI]
0414 8805        MOV      [DI],AL
0416 46          INC      SI
0417 47          INC      DI
0418 3CFF        CMP      AL,FF
041A 7501        JNZ      041D
041C C3          RET
041D 3C0A        CMP      AL,0A
041F 75F1        JNZ      0412
0421 B024        MOV      AL,24
0423 8805        MOV      [DI],AL
0425 B409        MOV      AH,09
```

```
0427 BA0015          MOV     DX,1500
042A CD21            INT     21
042C B409            MOV     AH,09
042E BA4010          MOV     DX,1040
0431 CD21            INT     21
```

Now we wait for a response. The instruction starting at address 437 converts input to upper case. If Y is found (ASCII value 59), we jump to location 443, if N is found (ASCII 4E), we go to location 45B to add a carriage return line feed to avoid overwriting the screen before going back to load the next line, and if neither is found, we go back to location 433 to ask the question again:

```
0433 B401            MOV     AH,01
0435 CD21            INT     21
0437 24DF            AND     AL,DF
0439 3C59            CMP     AL,59
043B 7406            JZ      0443
043D 3C4E            CMP     AL,4E
043F 75F2            JNZ     0433
0441 EB18            JMP     045B
```

The modified line containing the macro definition is now written to the file. I do it the lazy way, one character at a time – hence the 1 in CX – stopping at character 24, the dollar sign terminating the string printed on screen:

```
0443 BA0015          MOV     DX,1500
0446 B440            MOV     AH,40
0448 BB1E10          MOV     BX,101E
044B 8B1F            MOV     BX,[BX]
044D B90100          MOV     CX,0001
0450 CD21            INT     21
0452 42              INC     DX
0453 89D7            MOV     DI,DX
0455 8A05            MOV     AL,[DI]
0457 3C24            CMP     AL,24
0459 75EB            JNZ     0446
```

We come to 45B whether or not the line has been saved, as it is necessary to print 0D followed by 0D to prevent the current line on screen from being overwritten.

Then we go round again for the next line:

```
045B B402            MOV     AH,02
045D B20D            MOV     DL,0D
045F CD21            INT     21
0461 B402            MOV     AH,02
0463 B20A            MOV     DL,0A
0465 CD21            INT     21
0467 EBA6            JMP     040F
```

That finishes off a valuable addition to MS-DOS. Pity it wasn't provided off the shelf, though.

17

Can I have some MORE? – I

I often feel that MS-DOS is a bit like the Meccano set of fond memory. You are provided with all the bits and pieces, if only you knew where to look for them, and all the instructions, if only you could make sense of them, and given a Ph.D. in logistics and civil engineering you could probably – just – create some kind of useful artefact, like a left-handed windmill or a scale replica of the Titanic, complete with iceberg. There are still times, though, when you get the distinct impression that your chosen project needs set Number 5 and all you have is set Number 4.

Take the requirement for outputting text files on screen, hardly an exotic and little-used utility. Old-fashioned CP/M Plus on the PCW has an inbuilt TYPE command which obligingly pauses at the end of each screenful of information, and waits politely for you to ask for the next page, or abort the operation.

In order to override the pause at the end of each screen, you actually have to use the transient utility TYPE.COM in this format:

TYPE filename [NOPAGE]

With MS-DOS, on the other hand, the information scoots up the screen like a frightened rabbit, requiring you to press the Pause or some other panic button to halt it in its tracks. I can never get the hang of Pause, which requires a key other than Pause to be pressed for the listing to continue, then Pause again, and so on. I get the distinct impression that features like these were designed for an ancient PC with an 8088 processor, and that no allowance has been made for the additional clock speed of a 286, let alone a 486 with clock doubler.

If you want a page at a time, you have to resort to a different piece of the Meccano set, MORE.COM, and use the redirection operator "<":

MORE < filename

That takes the file to the right of the operator as input to the MORE command, using the redirection operator "<", and lists information a screenful at a time.

Twenty lines at a time

Never easily satisfied, I had a requirement to create a variation on MORE which would list a file 20 lines at a time – or, to be more accurate, two files 20 lines at a time, one file on my main PC, the other on the portable sitting next to it, so that I could ensure that the contents of two sets of pages matched up.

It's a bit of a long story, but I was editing a text for a forthcoming Viewbook based on their already successful Shakespearian series. The Viewbook is a software package produced by Information Education of Stoke-on-Trent which enables you to create computerised books on screen.

The concept involves – amongst a lot of other things – being able to switch instantaneously from a screenful of text to a screenful of glossary, giving explanations and meanings of words and phrases at the touch of a button.

I was working (believe it or not) on the first of a series of French 17th century texts – the famous comedy by Molière called *L'Avare,* The Miser – and I wanted to ensure that my glossary "pages" matched the pages with text on them, and that the line numbers also married correctly.

The simplest way of doing this was to have two computers side by side – and by this time the files were plain ASCII files – with each page set at 20 lines, so it occurred to my devious brain that it might be rather a nice idea to bend the MORE.COM program to produce 20 lines at a go, or any other number the user might require.

This would enable you, for example, to check a list of names and addresses one at a time, or any other set of data which was divided up into a fixed number of lines.

However, as we shall see, it wasn't exactly plain sailing. Consistency isn't one of the stronger points of MS-DOS, and in MORE.COM this characteristic is carried over into a lack of internal consistency.

Let me explain how I got to the point of being nearly successful. First of all, I copied MORE.COM to MYMORE.COM, just in case I made a mess of it, and then had a go at examining its contents by typing:

```
DEBUG MYMORE.COM
U
```

The Unassemble command, remember, converts the program instructions (or whatever DEBUG finds at the specified locations) into assembler commands a chunk at a time. If you do not specify a number after U first time round, DEBUG assumes 100.

I found the instructions which altered the line count, and it worked fine in MS-DOS 3.3 I think it was at the time, but it was no use as a flexible general purpose MORE command, with the additional problem that the first screenful was one less than subsequent screenfuls! So I rolled up the programming sleeves and came up with this general-purpose utility.

MS-DOS, by the way, will not let you use a version of an external command which was not designed for a particular version of the operating system. It uses function 30 of INT 21, which returns the Version number in AL and AH. For Version 6.2, AL returns the 6, and AH 14, presumably the Microsoft code corresponding to the ".2" – Version 3.1 returns 0A in AH, for example.

A better version of MORE

The requirement is for a program which will list text files, a number of lines (in the range 1-24) at a time, with the screen being cleared between displays and the number being able to be changed at any point during the listing. Let us first decide which keys do what.

Here is a useful tip about which buttons to get the user to press and at the same time how to make life as easy as possible for yourself as a programmer. In so doing, we take advantage of the feature known as extended ASCII codes.

The function keys, the Home, End, PgUp, PgDn, arrow and other keys (plus their Shift+, Ctrl+ and Alt+ combinations) do not generate a single ASCII character – all the individual ones between 0-255 are fully occupied. For this reason, extended ASCII codes were invented, which generate two values, of which – and this is where we can save a lot of checking in the program – the first is always a zero. At the same time, we have to be a little careful, as the function which we are going to use (function 8 of INT 21) reads one character only at a time. We will look at this in detail when we examine the subroutine starting at address 300.

First, here are the memory insertions you need to perform. Be particularly careful with the byte count of the one starting at 1030, because the program assumes that the tens and digit of "24" are at addresses 108D and 108E respectively. Note that the "25;0" is 25 plus a semi-colon plus a zero, and that the last three memory areas have zeros throughout:

```
E 1000 "File name please > $"
E1030 1B,"[2J",1B,"[34;47m",1B,"[25;0fCursor left/right adjusts
length, PgUp/Dn for screen, Esc to quit",1B,"[33;44m 24$"
E 1090 18,00
E 10A0 1B,"[0;0f$"
E 10B0 1B,"[K",0D,0A,"$"
```

The ANSI sequence ending in lower case "m" alters the screen colours. You can either leave it out or change it to suit your requirements. I normally run the screen with yellow on blue (33;44), which I find the most restful combination for working for long periods of time. The highlight bar is set to blue on white, resetting the values to yellow on blue at the end.

Note also that the bar ends with the number "24", which is the default number of lines printed on screen at a time. We shall see how that number gets changed when we come to look at the routine at 500.

The main program module

Here comes the main module. It begins with a message on screen – the one at address 1000 and following – to ask for the filename you want to read from. The buffer to read from begins at 1020, and that first address needs to be filled with the maximum permitted number of characters (minus one), hence the 0C being loaded in the instructions at addresses 10A to 10C.

Now, in order to get a filename which MS-DOS can deal with, we replace the trailing 0D with a zero, then try opening the file with function 3D. In the event of an error, the program terminates with exit code set to the error message number.

This you can handle, if you wish, in a batch file which drives the program. That takes us to the point at which we get down to business proper in a succession of subroutines, after which the program is brought to a close with INT 20:

```
0100 B409        MOV      AH,09
0102 BA0010      MOV      DX,1000
0105 CD21        INT      21
0107 BB2010      MOV      BX,1020
010A B00C        MOV      AL,0C
010C 8807        MOV      [BX],AL
010E BA2010      MOV      DX,1020
0111 B40A        MOV      AH,0A
0113 CD21        INT      21
0115 BB2110      MOV      BX,1021
0118 31C0        XOR      AX,AX
011A 8A07        MOV      AL,[BX]
011C 89C6        MOV      SI,AX
011E BB2210      MOV      BX,1022
0121 8820        MOV      [BX+SI],AH
0123 31C0        XOR      AX,AX
0125 B43D        MOV      AH,3D
0127 BA2210      MOV      DX,1022
012A CD21        INT      21
012C 3C05        CMP      AL,05
012E 7D04        JGE      0134
0130 B44C        MOV      AH,4C
0132 CD21        INT      21
0134 E8C900      CALL     0200
0137 E8C601      CALL     0300
013A CD20        INT      20
```

Incidentally, there is nothing magical about where these routines are located in memory. I have just got into the habit of putting the main module – fairly obviously – at the beginning of memory, at 100 and onwards, and subroutines at 200, 300, 400 and so on, with data starting at 1000, which leaves plenty of space for all but the longest pieces of spaghetti programming. But there is nothing sacred about these locations, as you can see in this case, where I decided at the last moment that an additional routine at 450 would serve to modularise things even better.

Loading the file into memory

The first of these subroutines starts at address 200. It reads the file into memory, starting at address 1500, and allows for just over 60K of file:

```
0200 89C3       MOV    BX,AX
0202 B43F       MOV    AH,3F
0204 B9EEEE     MOV    CX,EEEE
0207 BA0015     MOV    DX,1500
020A CD21       INT    21
020C BE0015     MOV    SI,1500
```

Then the byte count, returned in AX, is added to the start address, so that we can find the address of the end of the file when we scan through it by setting it to FF (I've set two bytes to FF – one will do), and then we go on to the subroutine at 400:

```
020F 01C6       ADD    SI,AX
0211 B8FFFF     MOV    AX,FFFF
0214 8904       MOV    [SI],AX
0216 B409       MOV    AH,09
0218 BA3010     MOV    DX,1030
021B CD21       INT    21
021D BE0015     MOV    SI,1500
0220 BF0015     MOV    DI,1500
0223 E8DA01     CALL   0400
0226 C3         RET
```

So far, so good. We next have to turn to the actual printing out of the required number of lines on screen, and that we shall do in the next Chapter.

18

Can I have some MORE? – II

Now we get to the routine at 400. After a bit of fiddling around, including setting up SI and DI (SI is the address of the current top of page in memory, and DI is the address of the last top of page – both set initially, of course, to 1500), we clear the screen with the routine at 450 – details follow this routine – and read into CX the contents of 1090 (and 1091, which is set to zero – it's easier than fiddling around with single bytes, but it's 1090 that matters).

In 1090 we have the default number of lines per screen, 18 in hex or 24 in decimal. The rest of the routine prints out eighteen lines, by decrementing CX each time a carriage return is encountered and stopping at zero. If that value is altered, then less than 24 lines will be printed. The instruction at 41D tests for the end of the file. After each byte is printed, SI is incremented – at address 427 before we loop round for the next byte:

```
0400 8B0E9010        MOV     CX,[1090]
0404 01C3            ADD     BX,AX
0406 89F7            MOV     DI,SI
0408 E84500          CALL    0450
040B 8B0E9010        MOV     CX,[1090]
040F 8A14            MOV     DL,[SI]
0411 80FA0D          CMP     DL,0D
0414 7501            JNZ     0417
0416 49              DEC     CX
0417 83F900          CMP     CX,+00
041A 7501            JNZ     041D
041C C3              RET
041D 80FAFF          CMP     DL,FF
0420 7501            JNZ     0423
0422 C3              RET
0423 B402            MOV     AH,02
0425 CD21            INT     21
0427 46              INC     SI
0428 EBE5            JMP     040F
```

Tidying up the screen

The mini-routine at 450 performs some necessary housework to tidy up the screen. First it outputs the string at address 10A0, an ANSI sequence which moves the cursor to the "home" position at the top left-hand corner of the screen. Then the string at address 10B0 and following, which clears the current line, hops down to the next line and performs that operation 18 hex times, to clear the screen except for the information bar across the bottom. Finally the cursor is deposited again at the home position in readiness for the text to be displayed:

```
0450 B409          MOV      AH,09
0452 BAA010        MOV      DX,10A0
0455 CD21          INT      21
0457 B91800        MOV      CX,0018
045A B409          MOV      AH,09
045C BAB010        MOV      DX,10B0
045F CD21          INT      21
0461 E0F7          LOOPNZ   045A
0463 B409          MOV      AH,09
0465 BAA010        MOV      DX,10A0
0468 CD21          INT      21
046A C3            RET
```

Once everything is set up, with the first page on screen, we are ready for the user to decide what to do next. At this point we come back to the question of extended ASCII codes. If we had decided on F for forwards and B for back, L for less and M for more lines per page, the checking to see if a valid key has been pressed would be messy, to say the least.

As you can see from the message which starts at address 1030 (given above in the data needed to be inserted into memory), I have chosen Esc to quit, PgUp to go to the beginning of the file, PgDn to go to the next page, cursor left to decrease and cursor right to increase the number of lines shown at a time.

This means, as you can see from the next few instructions below, that all I need to do is to check for 1B (Escape), then for an incoming zero, failing which we simply loop around for another incoming character. If a zero is detected, then we perform function 8 again to pick up the second character in the extended ASCII duet, and if we do not find a 4B, 4D, 49, or 51 (for left and right arrow, PgUp and PgDn respectively), then we scoot back to 300 for another keypress:

```
0300 B408          MOV      AH,08
0302 CD21          INT      21
0304 3C1B          CMP      AL,1B
0306 7501          JNZ      0309
0308 C3            RET
0309 3C00          CMP      AL,00
030B 7402          JZ       030F
030D EBF1          JMP      0300
```

```
030F B408          MOV     AH,08
0311 CD21          INT     21
```

I have interrupted the listing at this juncture to make an important point. If you are single-stepping through the program to see what makes it tick, do note that if you use G or P to get you to address 304 and you press any key which generates extended ASCII, a zero will appear in the AL register, but the second character will be lost and appear at the minus prompt as the ASCII equivalent. So it's best to use G to go to 313, where both characters will have been processed.

Looking for keypresses

Here we are looking for the legal keypresses apart from 1B. If 51 is pressed (PgDn) we call 400, which puts the next page up on screen:

```
0313 3C51          CMP     AL,51
0315 7505          JNZ     031C
0317 E8E600        CALL    0400
031A EBE4          JMP     0300
```

If 49 (PgUp) is pressed, we reset the top of page values to 1500 in SI and DI and reprint the first page to the value currently in 1090:

```
031C 3C49          CMP     AL,49
031E 750B          JNZ     032B
0320 BE0015        MOV     SI,1500
0323 BF0015        MOV     DI,1500
0326 E8D700        CALL    0400
0329 EBD5          JMP     0300
```

If 4B (cursor left) is pressed, we call the subroutine at 500, and if 4D (cursor right) is pressed, we go for 600:

```
032B 3C4B          CMP     AL,4B
032D 7505          JNZ     0334
032F E8CE01        CALL    0500
0332 EBCC          JMP     0300
0334 3C4D          CMP     AL,4D
0336 75C8          JNZ     0300
0338 E8C502        CALL    0600
033B EBC3          JMP     0300
```

Here is the first of the cursor subroutines. The two have some features in common, so let me explain in general terms what is going on to avoid getting repetitive.

Altering the line count

First we use the BP register – because it happens to be lying around doing nothing –

to load the current contents of 1090, and 1091, and then we check for the current value. If cursor left has been pressed and the current value is 1, then it doesn't make sense to print less than one line, so we jump out of the routine. At the other end, if the value is 24 in decimal then it can't be added to, so we again return.

Now that we have agreed that a valid request for decreasing or increasing the line count has been made, we increment or decrement BP and store the result back in our data area:

```
0500 8B2E9010      MOV      BP,[1090]
0504 83FD02        CMP      BP,+02
0507 7D01          JGE      050A
0509 C3            RET
050A 4D            DEC      BP
050B 892E9010      MOV      [1090],BP
```

The next part is a bit messy, so let's follow it through in the first routine in some detail. If the value in 1090/1091 has been changed, we need to change also the number which appears at the end of our information bar at the bottom of the screen. Let me talk you through how to do this when decrementing (the routine at 600 does exactly the same, but the other way round, so to speak).

First, we look at the digit, which is of course an ASCII value, by copying it to Al from 108D. If it's "4", say, then we just decrement it and return it, but if it is "0", then we need to take further action, in other words, if the value is "20", we need to set the digit to "9" and decrement the "2" in 108D:

```
050F A08E10        MOV      AL,[108E]
0512 3C30          CMP      AL,30
0514 7F0F          JG       0525
0516 B039          MOV      AL,39
0518 A28E10        MOV      [108E],AL
051B A08D10        MOV      AL,[108D]
051E FEC8          DEC      AL
0520 A28D10        MOV      [108D],AL
0523 EB05          JMP      052A
0525 FEC8          DEC      AL
0527 A28E10        MOV      [108E],AL
```

Finally, the current screen is printed out with the new number of lines:

```
052A 89FE          MOV      SI,DI
052C B409          MOV      AH,09
052E BA3010        MOV      DX,1030
0531 CD21          INT      21
0533 E8CAFE        CALL     0400
0536 C3            RET
```

Now for the routine at 600, which deals with incrementing the line count up to the permitted maximum of 18 hex and increasing the number in human-readable form at the end of the highlighted bar at the bottom of the screen. The programming is more or less the same as in the routine at 500:

```
0600 8B2E9010    MOV    BP,[1090]
0604 83FD18      CMP    BP,+18
0607 7C01        JL     060A
0609 C3          RET
060A 45          INC    BP
060B 892E9010    MOV    [1090],BP
060F A08E10      MOV    AL,[108E]
0612 3C39        CMP    AL,39
0614 7D07        JGE    061D
0616 FEC0        INC    AL
0618 A28E10      MOV    [108E],AL
061B EB0D        JMP    062A
061D B030        MOV    AL,30
061F A28E10      MOV    [108E],AL
0622 A08D10      MOV    AL,[108D]
0625 FEC0        INC    AL
0627 A28D10      MOV    [108D],AL
062A 89FE        MOV    SI,DI
062C B409        MOV    AH,09
062E BA3010      MOV    DX,1030
0631 CD21        INT    21
0633 E8CAFD      CALL   0400
0636 C3          RET
```

And that's just about it.

Switching the cursor off

I left the cursor switched on, but if you want to kill it during the running of the program, just write two short routines, both using functions of INT 10, the first of which switches the cursor off:

```
0100 B401        MOV    AH,01
0102 B520        MOV    CH,20
0104 CD10        INT    10
0106 CD20        INT    20
```

– and the second restores the default MS-DOS cursor:

```
0100 B401        MOV    AH,01
0102 B90403      MOV    CX,0304
0104 CD10        INT    10
0106 CD20        INT    20
```

If you feel adventurous, try changing the values in CX. It can be especially interesting if you set the top line higher than the second. If you set CH to 20 in hex, the cursor disappears altogether.

19

Down in the dumps – I

One of the technical problems in putting a book like this together concerns the question of grabbing source listings from DEBUG and inserting them in the text. As you might gather, it's a matter of life and death for every single character to be accurate, otherwise disaster will result and the phone lines to the publisher will be humming with angry calls as to why this or that doesn't do what the author claims it should.

The problem is that program files created with DEBUG are in COM format, which means that they cannot be listed using the TYPE command – they can only be accessed from within DEBUG itself. True, you can print them out using Print Screen, but that depends on the quality of the printer you have, and hard copy is both an inflexible medium and one which modern publishers would rather avoid.

And if you are thinking that the best way is to print out and then read in via a scanner and a piece of OCR software, forget it: it just needs one fault in the paper, one blemish in the inking, and 'O' comes out as 'C' and disaster results. No, we need a foolproof method which doesn't involve too much programming.

So how do we go about grabbing what appears on screen and saving it to a file – a text file, that is, not some graphics format which would be just as inscrutable for the purposes of reading into a word-processor? The answer lies in an area which is full of fascination for the inveterate tinkerer like myself: the video RAM or buffer of the PC.

Exploring the video buffer

This is an area of memory where a copy of what appears on screen is stored. Strictly speaking, as we shall see later, there are several video buffers, but we shall be looking at the default page in text mode which you will find located at B800:0000 (or A000:000, depending on your machine – the latter address is for CGA screens). Try B800:0 first and see what happens.

In order to see what this area of memory looks like, put some text up on screen, then load DEBUG and type:

D B800:0000

If that doesn't come up trumps, try the alternative address. The result is something of a surprise. Here is a sample piece of output from a VGA screen with yellow text on a blue ground. It begins with a directory listing, using DIR/W/ON, then DEBUG is loaded and the top half of the screen examined:

PW1.COM	PW4.COM	READUC.COM	RING.COM	S.COM
SDUMP.COM	SDUMP1.COM	SDUMP2.COM	SDUMP3.COM	SEARCH.COM
SET-UP.COM	SF.BAT	SPACE2.COM	SPACE3.COM	SUBFIND.BAT
SUBLIST	SUBNAME.BAT	SUBPROC.COM	SUBX.BAT	TEMP.COM
TENS.COM	TFIND10.COM	TFIND12.COM	VRAM.COM	WCOUNT
WIPE.BAT	WIPEIT	WIPEOUT.BAT	WPAGE.COM	X.BAT
XC1.COM	XXX	YEAR.COM		

```
        73 file(s)         235,522 bytes

                    449,536 bytes free


A:\>debug
-db800:800
B800:0800  53 1E 2E 1E 43 1E 4F 1E-4D 1E 20 1E 20 1E 20 1E   S...C.O.M. . . .
B800:0810  4F 1E 4D 1E 20 1E 20 1E-20 1E 20 1E 20 1E 20 1E   O.M. . . . . . .
B800:0820  53 1E 55 1E 42 1E 4C 1E-49 1E 53 1E 54 1E 20 1E   S.U.B.L.I.S.T. .
B800:0830  20 1E 20 1E 20 1E 20 1E-20 1E 20 1E 20 1E 20 1E   . . . . . . . .
B800:0840  57 1E 49 1E 50 1E 45 1E-49 1E 54 1E 20 1E 20 1E   W.I.P.E.I.T. . .
B800:0850  20 1E 20 1E 20 1E 20 1E-20 1E 20 1E 20 1E 20 1E   . . . . . . . .
B800:0860  20 1E 62 1E 79 1E 74 1E-65 1E 73 1E 20 1E 20 1E   .b.y.t.e.s. . .
B800:0870  72 1E 65 1E 65 1E 20 1E-20 1E 20 1E 20 1E 20 1E   r.e.e. . . . . .
-
```

The reason why I asked for addresses from 800 bytes into the segment is because if you request B800:0 the text you are watching scrolls right off the top of the screen.

The output looks rather odd. The first point to strike us is that the actual characters or text printed on screen only occupy alternate locations – there appears to be a consistent byte after each character.

This is known as the attribute byte, the byte which tells the video display what the text character should look like: if it is to be yellow on blue, black on white, underlined or whatever. So, to cut a long story short, the video buffer, which holds the text which is on screen, is twice the length of the number of characters you can fit on to the screen, as each character is accompanied by a byte telling us what colour it is, what intensity, and whether it blinks.

As you might guess, it is even more complicated than that, because the attribute byte also has to tell us what the background colour is to be as well as the foreground

colour. How is this all done? The best way to explain it is to give an example which
will allow you to explore the whole business for yourself. Here is a crafty little
program which does just that. As it is a bit fiddly, I'll talk you through it and explain
the attribute byte at the appropriate time. First, enter these values into memory:

```
E 500 1,2,4,8,10,20,40,80
E 520 1B,"[A",0D,0A,"Esc to quit any key to go on $"
E 550 0A,"0-3 fore, 4-6 back, 7 blink, Enter to see $"
```

All will be made clear in a moment or two. Note that all values separated by commas
and not in double quotes are hexadecimal numbers.

Writing the colour change program

Call the program ATT.COM and, when writing it to memory, allow 600 bytes. First,
ensure that the screen is full of data – a directory listing will do, then run the
program. The first thing that will pop up will be the message starting at address 550:

```
0100 B409        MOV      AH,09
0102 BA5005      MOV      DX,0550
0105 CD21        INT      21
```

The 0A at the beginning of the message ensures that it starts flush with the left of the
screen. Now down to business. Try and work out what is happening in these lines of
code:

```
0107 31DB        XOR      BX,BX
0109 B408        MOV      AH,08
010B CD21        INT      21
010D 3C1B        CMP      AL,1B
010F 7502        JNZ      0113
0111 CD20        INT      20
0113 3C0D        CMP      AL,0D
0115 7415        JZ       012C
0117 3C30        CMP      AL,30
0119 7CEE        JL       0109
011B 3C37        CMP      AL,37
011D 7FEA        JG       0109
011F BE0005      MOV      SI,0500
0122 240F        AND      AL,0F
0124 30E4        XOR      AH,AH
0126 01C6        ADD      SI,AX
0128 021C        ADD      BL,[SI]
012A EBDD        JMP      0109
```

First, BX is set to zero. Then function 8 waits for a keyboard input without echoing
it, and if it is in the range 0-7 or it is Enter, the input is acted on, otherwise we loop
back to 109. We shall see in a moment or two what the effect of Enter is, but now to
discover what is going on, let us assume that the key 3 has been depressed.

As it is in the range 0-7, the instruction at address 11F is executed. SI is set to 500 and AL (in which the value of the keypress is returned) is ANDed with F. In hex, the AL register contained 33, and the result of performing a logical AND is to retain in AL all the bits which match the F, in other words:

```
33   110011 AND
0F   001111 =
     _____
     000011
```

In other words, the value 3 is returned, and if we extend that operation in the range 30-37 hex, the values 0-7 are returned respectively. Now what happens is that the ANDed value is added to the contents of SI, and if we look at the values we entered into memory at addresses 500-507, we will see that opting for 3 yields the value 4 (all in hex remember), opting for 6 produces 40, and so on. Every time we press a key in the range 0-7, one of these values is added into the BL register at address 128. What is going on?

The answer becomes clearer if we ask ourselves what the values in addresses 550 to 557 look like in binary:

1 = 1

2 = 10

4 = 100

8 = 1000

10 = 1000

20 = 10000

40 = 100000

80 = 1000000

In other words, what we are doing is building up a bit pattern in BL which will in the next part of the program become the attribute byte for the current screenful of text. And the way I have set the program up, the keys correspond to the bits which are set to create particular effects, from 0 – the least significant bit, to 7.

Building up the text colours

Here are the colours you get (remembering that you can mix red, green and blue together in various combinations):

0 = foreground blue

1 = foreground green

2 = foreground red

3 = intense foreground colour

4 = background blue

5 = background green

6 = background red

7 = blink foreground

So if you have pressed 1, 3 and 6, you will get a migraine-inducing bright green on a red background, and for a real blinder you could add in 7, which causes the green to blink. Now we have to put the attribute into memory so that we can see the effect on screen:

```
012C BA00B8       MOV     DX,B800
012F 8EDA         MOV     DS,DX
0131 B90008       MOV     CX,0800
0134 BE0100       MOV     SI,0001
0137 881C         MOV     [SI],BL
0139 46           INC     SI
013A 46           INC     SI
013B E0FA         LOOPNZ  0137
```

At this point, we have to be particularly careful. The address we are after is not B800:0, but B800:1 and every second byte thereafter. But how do we ensure that the byte gets into the B800 segment?

The answer lies in an assumption which we make quite happily most of the time, namely that when we refer to an address in an assembler program, we take it for granted that it will go into the current segment, which it does if the DS (data segment) register is not changed. In other words, if you opt for the address pointed to by SI, for example, you are telling the computer that you want the address DS:SI. So we have to change DS to B800, but – and it's a big but – we must change it back if we want to print out a message, which we shall do soon, otherwise the results will be unpredictable, to put it mildly.

So the instructions at 12C and 12F move B800 into DS – it is not possible to load DS directly, hence we have to go via the scenic route, so to speak. Then SI is set to 1, in other words the first address to be filled with the attribute byte is B800:0001, it is duly filled – the assumption, remember, being DS:SI – double incremented, and then we go round the loop until CX (which contains a value which just about fills the screen) is exhausted.

There is no need to save the previous value of DS, as it is sitting by default in the extra segment register, so we use that to copy it back (again in two stages) before printing out an invitation to continue or halt the program:

```
013D 8CC2        MOV      DX,ES
013F 8EDA        MOV      DS,DX
0141 B409        MOV      AH,09
0143 BA2005      MOV      DX,0520
0146 CD21        INT      21
0148 B408        MOV      AH,08
014A CD21        INT      21
014C 3C1B        CMP      AL,1B
014E 75B0        JNZ      0100
0150 CD20        INT      20
```

Now we have explored this aspect of the video buffer, we turn to the main objective of this chapter, namely to peel off from the screen DEBUG program listings and save them to a file.

We have already learned that we need to grab alternate characters – the even numbers – but now it is necessary to look at the program requirements in more detail.

Reading a text screen

Let's first determine what our actual objective is. If we load DEBUG and type U (for unassemble) to put the mnemonic codes up on screen, we should be able to gain access to them by reading them out of the video buffer and saving them to a file. Repeat that process a couple of times, concatenate the files together, and we should have a rough and ready ASCII file to read into our word-processor and trim as necessary – a perfect copy of the listing on screen straight from the electronic horse's mouth, so to speak.

There is a little snag or two to overcome along the way, so let us start with a program which takes whatever text is on screen and save it to a file. Snag number one is that you have to exit from DEBUG, by typing Q, and then the name of your program.

In that process, the screen scrolls up, and that means you will lose the top line of the screen, and the last couple of lines won't be of much interest, but that is just something to remember. You have to leave a couple of lines at the top of the screen to allow this scrolling up to occur. This is not a perfect art form, strictly a practical tool.

Snag number two is: What are you going to call the file to which you save the screen? DUMP, perhaps – but what if you already have a file called DUMP? Do you overwrite it, or do you call it something else? The sensible answer is that you will probably want to create a sequence of files, called, say, DUMPA, DUMPB and so on, so let us add a touch of sophistication to our program which will achieve that objective by automatically finding out if DUMPA exists and, if so, calling the file DUMPB, and so on.

We begin by loading DEBUG as usual:

```
DEBUG SDUMP.COM
```

– and studiously ignoring it as usual when it tells you it cannot find the file SDUMP.COM.

Our program won't be very long, so let us put the filename we want to access starting at address 500:

```
E 500 "DUMPA",0
```

As we shall be writing the program to disk and loading it back again during the development process, I have included a couple of lines at the beginning which are not strictly necessary when the program has completed its development, but they are there to ensure that if and when you want to add to the program, you always start back at DUMPA, and not at the filename you ended up with the last time you saved the memory to disk:

```
0100 B041          MOV     AL,41
0102 A20405        MOV     [0504],AL
```

This simply loads upper case A (remember all numbers are in hex) into AL, and saves it into address 0504. The square brackets, remember, mean 'the address of the number in the brackets'.

Address 500 contains 'D', 501 'U', and so on, so we are resetting the last letter of the filename to ensure that we start off with 'DUMPA' each time the program runs. You could remove those two lines if you were sure that you were never going to develop the program further, but why bother – computers are blindingly fast nowadays, and we have long since past the era where speed is a serious problem for the programmer, and equally, we are not bothered about wasting a few bytes on redundant commands.

Now we have to find a means of determining whether DUMPA or any other filename in that sequence already exists. By the way, I have not included a test to see if we fall off the end of the alphabet. I have assumed that you do not want more than 26 files available at any one time.

It would not be too difficult to add a couple of lines to test to see if you have fallen off the end of the alphabet and, if so, to stop the program. Or, if you are really clever, to add another letter, so that you could, if you really must, have files DUMPAA, DUMPAB, and so on until you fill up your hard disk with them.

The best way of going about this is to try function 5B of INT 21, the create file function:

```
0105 B45B         MOV      AH,5B
0107 31C9         XOR      CX,CX
0109 BA0005       MOV      DX,0500
010C CD21         INT      21
```

This function requires AH to be loaded with the value 5B. The CX register contains the file attribute, which is usually the normal attribute, in other words, it is open for reading and writing. The normal attribute is zero and performing an exclusive OR operation on a register with itself causes all the bits to be turned off, in other words, it's a showing off way of zeroising the register.

The other attributes are read only (not particularly useful when creating a file!), hidden and system.

Next, you have to tell the operating system the address at which the filename starts, and I am assuming that you want the file in the same directory, otherwise you modify the name accordingly. That address is loaded into the DX register. Then we fire away by calling the interrupt.

Creating an output file

At this point, life gets interesting. The system tries to create a file with the given name. Now this means that if it is to be successful, there must be no file in that directory with the same name, otherwise the function fails. There are other ways in which the function can fail, but this is the one that interests us. If a file called DUMPA already exists, the carry flag is set, and the AX register contains the appropriate error code.

If, on the other hand, there is no file called DUMPA, carry is left clear and the AX register contains the next available file handle number. This needs a word of explanation. The handle numbers 0-4 are reserved by the system for the standard devices (keyboard, screen and so on) and the numbers 5 and upwards are allocated to the user's open files.

The important point to bear in mind is that, when you are referring to the file from now on, whether you are writing to it, reading from it, closing it, erasing it, or whatever, you refer to it by number rather than name, which, if you think about it, is far more convenient, just so long as you remember to save the handle number somewhere if need be.

The next piece of code checks to see if carry is set (JNB is the same as JNC or JAE), and if so the 'A' of DUMPA is incremented, and we loop back to location 105, try creating a file (DUMP second time around), until we come across one which is vacant:

```
010E 730A          JNB      011A
0110 A00405        MOV      AL,[0504]
0113 FEC0          INC      AL
0115 A20405        MOV      [0504],AL
0118 EBEB          JMP      0105
```

Now we have opened the file, we can start peeling information out of the video buffer, remembering that we are interested in alternate even locations only – that is, the text characters, not the attribute bytes. At this point another problem arises.

The memory of the PC is divided into segments, and the segment number in which you are currently programming is the next one which happens to be free inside your machine. This will vary according to a number of factors, but whatever the segment is, it certainly won't be the video buffer! Now, if you refer to an address inside the program, the assumption, as I said earlier, is DS:DX, in the same way that a reference to an address SI or DI assumes DS:SI and SD:DI respectively.

When DEBUG is loaded, you will find that the data segment, code segment, stack segment and extra segments are all set by default to the same value. You are free to change them at will, but this is only likely to be necessary with large programs or where, as here, we need to inspect or alter other parts of memory.

It's up to the programmer to change these as and when necessary, as we saw earlier in our colour changing program. So if we ask for the contents of address 0, the assumption is XXXX:0000, where XXXX is the current data segment. This means we have to change that value if we are to get at B800:0000 (or A000:0000). To do that, we need to alter the contents of DS, and as you recall, this has to be done in two stages:

```
011A BA00B8        MOV      DX,B800
011D 8EDA          MOV      DS,DX
```

So now, when we refer to address 0000, we are referring to B800:0000. At this point we are ready to read the information from the video buffer into DUMPA (or DUMPB, and so on, as the case may be). That is the topic we turn to next.

20

Down in the dumps – II

Now we start extracting information from the video buffer and saving it to our file DUMPA (or DUMPB or whatever). The first instruction moves the file handle to the BX register. As I have pointed out before, for some reason best known to those far wiser than ourselves, the handle is returned at file opening or creation time to the AX register, but for the other file operations the BX register is required. Once again, ours is not to reason why:

```
011F 89C3      MOV     BX,AX
0121 31D2      XOR     DX,DX
0123 B440      MOV     AH,40
0125 B90100    MOV     CX,0001
0128 CD21      INT     21
```

The DX register is first of all zeroised, AH is loaded with 40, the write file function, CX is set to 1, the number of bytes to be transferred, and the interrupt set going.

Now we double increment DX to skip over the attribute byte and get to the next character. We check to see if DX is 0E60 – in other words, if the whole buffer has been read – and if it is not, we jump back to address 123, and out goes the next character to the file:

```
012A 42        INC     DX
012B 42        INC     DX
012C 81FA600E  CMP     DX,0E60
0130 7CF1      JL      0123
```

If we have peeled off what we can, we close the file, and end the program in the normal way:

```
0132 B43E      MOV     AH,3E
0134 CD21      INT     21
0136 CD20      INT     20
```

At this point, we have saved a file to disk from screen and our troubles appear to be over, until, that is, you try importing it into a word-processor. As you will rapidly discover, two unpleasant things have happened: the first is that the screen is padded out with blanks where no character has been written, and the second is that there are no carriage returns!

If you print it to the screen, using TYPE, fine, because it is simply going back where it came from – but we need to get it into a word-processor, which means killing off the trailing blanks and inserting carriage return line feeds. Undaunted, we march on to program number two.

It's always the tidying up routines which seem to take up more time and effort than the original program, and this time it takes 68 instructions to sort out the trailing blanks and missing carriage return line feeds.

Naming the conversion file

We start by asking what file needs to be converted, so perhaps it is best to concatenate the existing files first, by using a variation on the COPY program:

```
COPY DUMPA+DUMPB+DUMPC DFILE
```

The asking is done by putting a message at location 500:

```
E 500 "Filename please > "
```

We need one other insertion in memory, this time of a hex byte:

```
E 520 0F
```

Then we call it with function 9 of INT 21:

```
0100 B409          MOV     AH,09
0102 BA0005        MOV     DX,0500
0105 CD21          INT     21
```

We now need to read in a string corresponding to the filename and to this end, we need function 0A, which is very useful, but a bit fiddly. Say we locate the input string at address 520.

Address 520 should be loaded by us, using the E command of DEBUG, with the maximum number of characters allowed to be typed in, which for our purposes would be 0A. When the function is completed, the address 521 contains the number of characters actually typed in.

This means that addresses 521 and onward contain the name of the file we are after. However, there is a slight snag, and that is that the string is terminated with the carriage return character, 0D, and we require an ASCIIZ string, a string of ASCII characters followed by zero, to hand over to the system for the purpose of opening the file. That's where the contents of 521 come in handy – they let us drop a zero on to the end of the string, by adding the value in 521 to 522:

```
0107 B40A          MOV     AH,0A
0109 BA2005        MOV     DX,0520
010C CD21          INT     21
010E A02105        MOV     AL,[0521]
0111 30E4          XOR     AH,AH
0113 BB2205        MOV     BX,0522
0116 01C3          ADD     BX,AX
```

Opening for reading

At this point, we open the file for reading:

```
0118 8827          MOV     [BX],AH
011A B8003D        MOV     AX,3D00
011D BA2205        MOV     DX,0522
0120 CD21          INT     21
0122 7305          JNB     0129
0124 B8014C        MOV     AX,4C01
0127 CD21          INT     21
```

We terminate with exit code 1 if things go wrong, otherwise we continue now that the file is opened by saving AX – the file handle – at address 900 (or anywhere else that's free and takes your fancy). Then the input file has a full stop, a "Z" and a zero added so that an output file is created, which will eventually contain the output stripped of trailing spaces and with a carriage return and line feed at the end of each line. You can add whatever filetype you like, of course.

Note that, as always, assembler stores values backwards way on, and that is why at address 12C 5A2E is stored ("Z" plus full stop) and not the other way on. Single step through this if you are not clear as to what is happening. BX is double incremented to ensure it is pointing at the byte after the "Z":

```
0129 A30009        MOV     [0900],AX
012C B82E5A        MOV     AX,5A2E
012F 8907          MOV     [BX],AX
0131 43            INC     BX
0132 43            INC     BX
0133 B000          MOV     AL,00
0135 8807          MOV     [BX],AL
```

Now we use the Create file function to open DUMPA.Z, or whatever it is called, for writing, or to truncate an existing file DUMPA.Z. It is up to you to ensure that if the output file already exists, it is surplus to requirements. The address 522 is the start address of the filename (plus type plus zero):

```
0137 B43C          MOV    AH,3C
0139 31C9          XOR    CX,CX
013B BA2205        MOV    DX,0522
013E CD21          INT    21
0140 7305          JNB    0147
0142 B8024C        MOV    AX,4C02
0145 CD21          INT    21
```

The new file handle is saved at address 902, because we need both files open at the same time:

```
0147 A30209        MOV    [0902],AX
014A 8B1E0009      MOV    BX,[0900]
014E B43F          MOV    AH,3F
```

The next part of the program needs a bit of careful planning.

Stripping trailing spaces

The screen saved by our first program saves complete rows of text, that's 80 characters in decimal, so the best way to examine each row and add a carriage return line feed before the trailing spaces is to read one row at a time, so:

```
0150 B95000        MOV    CX,0050
0153 BA5005        MOV    DX,0550
0156 CD21          INT    21
0158 3C00          CMP    AL,00
015A 7502          JNZ    015E
015C CD20          INT    20
```

The buffer starts at address 550. If A=0 the entire file has been read, and the program is stopped. As you can see, I have omitted to close the two files just to prove that MS-DOS does it for you with INT 20, but if you want to be super-cautious, like I usually am, there is nothing to stop you getting the handles at 900 and 902 and closing each file in turn.

I put FF in the byte immediately preceding the buffer, in case we have a completely blank line (these two lines could have come before address 150, but it is only a couple of instructions and assembler is so fast that you need not worry about little programming peccadillos like this). Next, we move the address of the last byte of the buffer into DI (or SI or any other suitable spare register pair):

```
015E B0FF          MOV    AL,FF
0160 A24F05        MOV    [054F],AL
0163 BF9F05        MOV    DI,059F
```

Modifying the buffer

To demonstrate what we are about to do, here is a "before and after" picture of the buffer with a typical screen row read into it from a DEBUG session. If you examine them carefully, you will see that the second dump shows a carriage return and line feed at 575 and 576, effectively stripping the trailing spaces in the buffer:

```
0550  31 46 31 33 3A 30 31 30-30 20 42 34 30 39 20 20   1F13:0100 B409
0560  20 20 20 20 20 20 20 20-4D 4F 56 20 20 20 20 20           MOV
0570  41 48 2C 30 39 00 00 20-20 20 20 20 20 20 20 20   AH,09..
0580  20 20 20 20 20 20 20 20-20 20 20 20 20 20 20 20
0590  20 20 20 20 20 20 20 20-20 20 20 20 20 20 20 20

0550  31 46 31 33 3A 30 31 30-30 20 42 34 30 39 20 20   1F13:0100 B409
0560  20 20 20 20 20 20 20 20-4D 4F 56 20 20 20 20 20           MOV
0570  41 48 2C 30 39 0D 0A 20-20 20 20 20 20 20 20 20   AH,09..
0580  20 20 20 20 20 20 20 20-20 20 20 20 20 20 20 20
0590  20 20 20 20 20 20 20 20-20 20 20 20 20 20 20 20
```

This is achieved by inspecting the last address in the buffer and then decrementing DI until we come across a non-space character which, if the line is empty, will of course be the FF we have inserted earlier at 54E, and if the last byte in the buffer is non-space, at addresses 5A0 and 5A1:

```
0166  8A05        MOV     AL,[DI]
0168  3C20        CMP     AL,20
016A  7503        JNZ     016F
016C  4F          DEC     DI
016D  EBF7        JMP     0166
016F  47          INC     DI
0170  B80D0A      MOV     AX,0A0D
0173  8905        MOV     [DI],AX
```

Now that we have located the carriage return line feed, we need to set things up for the output of the correct number of bytes. This is done by first retrieving the file handle from 902 and 903 into BX. Next, the subtraction at address 179 gives the number of bytes before the trailing spaces start, and that value is copied to CX, where the byte count is expected.

Two is added to CI to ensure that the 0D and 0A are output as well, and the line is output. Then we jump back to 14A until the entire file has been read, which might consist of several screenfuls:

```
0175  8B1E0209    MOV     BX,[0902]
0179  29D7        SUB     DI,DX
017B  89F9        MOV     CX,DI
017D  83C102      ADD     CX,+02
0180  B440        MOV     AH,40
0182  BA5005      MOV     DX,0550
0185  CD21        INT     21
0187  EBC1        JMP     014A
```

The procedure requires a little effort on your part, first dividing up the program into manageable chunks for output, and then merging them together for the trailing spaces program, then tidying up the output for use in your word-processor or as input to an assembler package proper.

A final note: When running these two programs – let's call them SDUMP.COM and STRIP.COM – ensure that you have first typed DOSKEY, because otherwise you will be typing:

```
DEBUG SDUMP.COM
STRIP
```

– in succession until you have built up a complete listing of your program. With DOSKEY, all you need to do is to press the up arrow key to get back to these two lines and press Enter. It's a valuable labour-saving device. Those two programs have saved me endless hours of meticulous copy typing and painstaking checking to ensure that the program listings reach you exactly as they leave me.

21

Tick, tock

It is often useful, if not vital, to know the time and the day and the month on your computer. No problem, you say: just key in DATE or TIME and press Enter twice, and there it is before your very eyes.

You can alter the time and date, both to reset them and to change between, say 24-hour clock and am/pm formats, and also to switch the date to US or Scientific International format, which puts the year first, then the month, then the day. That might be just right for scientists, but it presents the information in exactly the reverse order of priority to what most humans require.

The only trouble is that all this information is not in the form you need it to act upon it in, say, a batch file or even an AUTOEXEC.BAT file. If you wanted to automate a back-up every Friday, for example, or to perform a particular task on the first day of the month, how do you get at the information?

There are a variety of ways of tackling the problem. The simplest and most direct is to put together a couple of assembler programs which return exit codes which you are free to act on as you will.

Which day of the week?

Let us take each of them in turn, starting with the day first. Please note that throughout this Chapter I have given the batch files in their basic form – once you have them up and running, they can be incorporated into other files or provided with @ECHO OFF commands as appropriate.

MS-DOS function 2A of INT 21 gets the date from the system and deposits it neatly in various registers. The one which we are in pursuit of for the day of the week is the

AL register, which from Version 1.1 of MS-DOS onwards returns with the day of the week in the form 0-6, where 0 is Sunday, 1 is Monday, and so on.

The program is simplicity itself, as you can see:

```
0100 B42A          MOV     AH,2A
0102 CD21          INT     21
0104 B44C          MOV     AH,4C
0106 CD21          INT     21
```

The program consists of two calls of INT 21, the first to pick up the date, and the second to terminate the program with an exit code, which can be picked up by ERRORLEVEL, and which, conveniently, should be located in the AL register. It could hardly be neater!

So, if you call the program WHATDAY.COM (and allocate a massive eight bytes for it), you can simply put it in a batch file, find out what day of the week it is, and take whatever action you wish. The information can be put in an environment variable with a command like:

```
IF ERRORLEVEL 0 IF NOT ERRORLEVEL 1 SET TODAY=SUNDAY
IF ERRORLEVEL 1 IF NOT ERRORLEVEL 2 SET TODAY=MONDAY
```

And so on, until you arrive at the end of the week. If you think that wins few prizes in the programming concours d'elegance, I agree, so here is an interesting technique which depends on the peculiar characteristic of IF ERRORLEVEL that it returns the value true if the return code is equal to or greater than the value tested for.

In other words, if the exit code is 4, IF ERRORLEVEL 4 is true if the value is 4 or 5 or anything up to and including the maximum value of 255.

The exercise of winkling out the day and returning it as an environment variable requires two batch files and just a handful of lines of commands. The outer file – let's name it WHATDAY.BAT – contains a call to an inner file, which we'll name GETDAY.BAT. This is what you put into the WHATDAY batch file:

```
GETDAY Sunday Monday Tuesday Wednesday Thursday Friday Saturday
```

The inner file consists of the follow piece of low cunning:

```
DAY
FOR %%A IN (1 2 3 4 5 6) DO IF ERRORLEVEL %%A SHIFT
SET TODAY=%1
```

Note that the FOR command requires a double per cent sign before the variable. In case you are not quite sure what is happening, here is a run-down of the way in which the batch file works. First, the COM file DAY is executed, and it returns with an error code in the range 0-6. Then the clumsy FOR command is executed.

What it does is to repeat what comes after the DO six times, one for each of the variables in the brackets, and each time it takes on the value of the next variable in turn, so the first time round, %%A has the value 1, the second time 2, and so on until the list is exhausted.

What comes after the DO is the command SHIFT, which moves all the parameters from GETDAY one to the left, so that the first time round, Monday is shifted to become the first variable, and so on. If the exit code is zero, no shifting takes place, so the day is returned as Sunday. Alternatively, you can return the day as a digit in the range 1-7 by changing the parameters in the GETDAY.BAT file.

The mistake I made when designing this technique was to start the list inside the brackets with a zero, which caused the days to end up one out, because if you work through it, DAY delivers an exit code of zero if the day is Sunday, which means that you do not want to shift at all.

So, if the day is Wednesday, the exit code is 3, and this means that the FOR command is executed three times, remembering that IF ERRORLEVEL returns the value true if the code is equal to or greater than the matched value.

Try running this with ECHO set to ON, and you will soon see how it works. Now you are in a position to interrogate the environment variable to see if it is Friday:

```
IF %TODAY%= =Friday ...
```

Remember that in a batch file %TODAY% means "the contents of the environment variable TODAY". Or, alternatively, you can enter information into a log file to name the day of the week:

```
ECHO Batch file accessed on %TODAY% >> LOGFILE
```

Do note that the information in TODAY and tests for its contents are case sensitive, so ensure you check for Friday and not FRIDAY, for example.

You will also by now have gathered that I have started with the easiest part of the date, so now comes the time to turn to the more demanding challenges of the rest of the date information. The day of the month and the month are not too bad, but the year is quite a challenge.

The day of the month

To find out the day of the month is only a little more tricky. It requires first a program which is only slightly longer called, I suggest, DDATE.COM. You cannot call it DATE.COM, because DATE is an MS-DOS internal command and every time you type DATE, you will get the date, not any program or batch file you give the same name, because of the MS-DOS precedence rules:

```
0100 B42A          MOV      AH,2A
0102 CD21          INT      21
0104 88D0          MOV      AL,DL
0106 B44C          MOV      AH,4C
0108 CD21          INT      21
```

As the day of the month is returned in DL, it is necessary to swap it across to AL to make it an exit code. Very conveniently, the day is returned as a number in the range 1-31. Next, you need just one batch file this time called WHATDATE.BAT, containing:

```
FOR %%A IN (1 2 3 4 5 6 7 8 9) DO IF ERRORLEVEL %%A SET DATE=%%A
FOR %%A IN (10 11 12 13 14 15 16 17 18 19) DO IF ERRORLEVEL %%A
     SET DATE=%%A
FOR %%A IN (20 21 22 23 24 25 26 27 28 29 30 31) DO IF ERRORLEVEL
     %%A SET DATE=%%a
ECHO Date is %DATE%
```

I have split the FOR into 3, simply for legibility and convenience. What it does is to give the variable %%A the value 1, 2, 3 and so on until it matches the exit code, at which point the environment variable DATE is set to that value. The outcome is a number in DATE which corresponds to the day of the month, which you can act on in your own batch file.

The month of the year

This variable can be extracted by a similar process to that used for the day of the week. This time the value we are after in our COM file is in the DH register, so the program should look like this:

```
0100 B42A          MOV      AH,2A
0102 CD21          INT      21
0104 88F0          MOV      AL,DH
0106 B44C          MOV      AH,4C
0108 CD21          INT      21
```

Next we require the outer batch file, called WHATMONT.BAT (we have to trim off the "H" as only 8 letters are allowed in the filename):

```
FINDMONT 1 2 3 4 5 6 7 8 9 10 11 12
```

The inner batch file is called FINDMONT:

```
MONTH
FOR %%A IN (1 2 3 4 5 6 7 8 9 10 11 12) DO IF ERRORLEVEL %%A
     SHIFT
SET MONTH=%1
```

I leave it to you to decide whether you want the parameters to FINDMONT as 1, 2, 3

... or January, February, ... or their abbreviated forms, but do note that the batch file at the end of this Chapter requires the information in number format.

What year is it?

The most interesting challenge is the year, which is stored in the CX register. A simple program and batch file can cope with the year up to 1999. Here is the program (which I have called YEAR.COM:

```
0100 B42A          MOV     AH,2A
0102 CD21          INT     21
0104 81E9C607      SUB     CX,07C6
0108 88C8          MOV     AL,CL
010A B44C          MOV     AH,4C
010C CD21          INT     21
```

All becomes clear when you recognise that 7C6 is hex for 1990, and that the year as a value in the range 0-9 (for 1990 to 1999) is transferred via the CL half of the CX register to AL for use as an exit code with this batch file:

```
YEAR
FOR %%A IN (0 1 2 3 4 5 6 7 8 9) DO IF ERRORLEVEL %%A SET
    YEAR=199%%A
```

This returns the year by adding "199" to the value of %%A.

But I suspect that no one is really satisfied with that. We need something a little more future-proof. This requires two slightly more complicated COM files and a batch file.

What we are going to do is to get a date in the range 1990-2099, the current upper limit for the date under MS-DOS (although the registers can actually go further than that). The program DIGITS.COM is designed to return a value in the range 0-9 if the year is 1990-1999, and in the range 10-19 if it is 2000 or more.

If the year is 2000 or more, we invoke another program (only slightly different from DIGITS.COM) which picks up the tens of the year as a number in the range 0-9, thus coping with the whole range between 1990-2099. These two programs are processed by a short batch file.

First, the COM file called DIGITS.COM:

```
0100 B42A          MOV     AH,2A
0102 CD21          INT     21
0104 81E9C607      SUB     CX,07C6
0108 88C8          MOV     AL,CL
010A 3C0A          CMP     AL,0A
010C 7D04          JGE     0112
010E B44C          MOV     AH,4C
```

```
0110 CD21          INT     21
0112 30E4          XOR     AH,AH
0114 B30A          MOV     BL,0A
0116 F6F3          DIV     BL
0118 80C40A        ADD     AH,0A
011B 88E0          MOV     AL,AH
011D B44C          MOV     AH,4C
011F CD21          INT     21
```

The program works like this: The year is returned, as we saw a little earlier, in the CX register. If we subtract 7C6 from the year, we end up with a value which starts at zero for 1990, 1 for 1991, and so on, and most importantly, as 0A (10 in decimal) or more for 2000 and onwards.

That is why, once CL is moved to AL – partly in readiness to serve as an exit code, and partly in case a division is required – there is a test at address 10A to see if the value of the year is greater than 0A.

If it is, we need to do some division. The instruction DIV operates either on a byte or a word (two bytes). In the present case, we are dealing with a single byte, so DIV divides AX (hence I clear AH at address 112) by the byte concerned, in our case BL, containing 0A. The result ends up in AL, and any remainder, if we are interested in it, in AH.

Just for the record, the other version of DX divides AX:DX by the byte pair specified and the result ends up in AX, with the remainder, if any, in DX.

If you find this confusing, single step through the program, changing the year – using DATE from the prompt – each time. Do note that MS-DOS is fussy: although there is no ambiguity or overlap, after 1999 you have to type the full four digits of the year. The tens and units are not enough. For the terminally lazy or forgetful, there is a routine to save and restore the current date at the end of this Chapter.

Dealing with the tens

Now that we have got the digit of the year sorted out, we need to look at the tens with a program called TENS.COM, which you can save a lot of time with by first typing:

COPY DIGITS.COM TENS.COM

Then load it with DEBUG and type:

A118

At this point, replace the existing instructions with those that follow below for addresses 118 and following. For the sake of clarity and completeness, I am listing the whole of TENS.COM for you now:

```
0100 B42A        MOV     AH,2A
0102 CD21        INT     21
0104 81E9C607    SUB     CX,07C6
0108 88C8        MOV     AL,CL
010A 3C0A        CMP     AL,0A
010C 7D04        JGE     0112
010E B44C        MOV     AH,4C
0110 CD21        INT     21
0112 30E4        XOR     AH,AH
0114 B30A        MOV     BL,0A
0116 F6F3        DIV     BL
0118 2C01        SUB     AL,01
011A B44C        MOV     AH,4C
011C CD21        INT     21
011E 4C          DEC     SP
011F CD21        INT     21
```

The program is, as I have said, identical up to address 118, at which point, as you will recall, the least significant byte of the CX register has been subtracted from 4C, leaving a result which is in the range 0-9 for the years 1990-1999, and 10 plus thereafter.

This time we are interested, not in the result, but the remainder. Perhaps a couple of examples will explain things best. If we change the year to 2067, which in hex is 813, and subtract 7C6, we get 4D. Now we divide 4D by 0A. The result in AH=7 and the remainder in AL=7. Subtract 1 from AL, and you have the tens value for the year: 6.

Alternatively, set the year to 2045, in hex 7FD, and subtracting 7C6 gives 37. Dividing 37 by 0A gives a result of 5 and a remainder of 5. Subtract 1, and you get the tens value of 4 for the year.

Now we can invoke the batch file to do the whole job for us. Do ensure that you have the right number of per cent signs all the way through the file:

```
DIGITS
IF ERRORLEVEL 10 GOTO POSTMILL
FOR %%A IN (0 1 2 3 4 5 6 7 8 9) DO IF ERRORLEVEL %%A SET
     YEAR=199%%A
GOTO OK
:POSTMILL
FOR %%A IN (0 1 2 3 4 5 6 7 8 9) DO IF ERRORLEVEL 1%%A SET
     TEMPA=%%A
TENS
FOR %%A IN (0 1 2 3 4 5 6 7 8 9) DO IF ERRORLEVEL %%A SET
     TEMPB=%%A
REM put a SET command then PAUSE here to see what's happening
REM SET
REM PAUSE
```

```
SET YEAR=20%TEMPB%%TEMPA%
SET TEMPA=
SET TEMPB=
:OK
```

The batch file first runs DIGITS, and if the result returned is 9 or less, we have a year before 2000. Otherwise, we go to the commands labelled POSTMILL, short for post-millenium.

In order to get day of week, date of month, month and year all together, it would make sense to put them all into one operation, and that is how it is done on the disk which comes with this book. Do test the program out on different dates – to that, just type:

DATE

– and fill in new values, remembering that you need all four year digits for 2000 and above, and remembering also to set the date back to its original value when you have finished playing!

Saving and restoring the date

Armed with all these techniques, we are now in a position to write a couple of batch files which save the current date, allow you to play around with different dates, and then restores the current date for you.

First, we need a file to save the current date (called SAVEDATE.BAT):

```
@ECHO OFF
CALL WHATDATE
CALL WHATMONT
CALL WHATYEAR
SET XDATE=%DATE%
SET XMONTH=%MONTH%
SET XYEAR=%YEAR%
```

Note that you must use CALL, otherwise you do not return control back to this file (I stress this because that is precisely what I forgot to do when I first put this together). As you may alter the environment variables DATE, MONTH and YEAR before you restore the old date, I have copied their contents to XDATE, XMONTH and XYEAR.

You should ensure that you have enough environment space for this purpose. You could delete the three main date variables at the end of the file by adding:

```
SET DATE=
SET MONTH=
SET YEAR=
```

To restore the date, you need this file (called OLDDATE.BAT):

```
DATE %XDATE%-%XMONTH%-%XYEAR%
SET XDATE=
SET XMONTH=
SET XYEAR=
```

As a side effect of these two batch files, if you wanted to know whether Christmas Day 1999 is a Sunday or not, type:

```
SAVEDATE
```

– followed by DATE, into which you type when prompted:

```
25-12-99
```

Then type DATE again, pressing Enter twice to retain the value and return to the prompt. The DATE function tells you which day of the week 25/12/99 is, and to return to your proper date, type:

```
OLDDATE
```

That ends a selection of extremely useful and valuable routines built round a not too demanding set of assembler programs. We turn now from dates to strings, and something altogether more demanding.

22

Where's that string? – I

Why not make a program serve two masters? It saves a great deal of time and effort if you can make one of your routines perform two or more different tasks for you, and the little program I have devised here does just that. It is designed to search through files matching a given mask for a specified string and list the result. It will probably give some experts in the field of concordancing a nasty turn, for reasons which will become apparent in a moment, but it does what it is designed to do, and that's all I ask of a program.

First, we need to do a bit of jargon-busting for those not familiar with terms like concordance and KWIC listing. The idea of a concordance is to take all the words in a text, sort them into alphabetical order, and then print them out with page and line references (or whatever), plus the context in which they occur. For poetry, say, a line of verse may be a reasonable context, for prose some other technique is necessary. The concordance was a hugely cumbersome and time-consuming project in the pre-computing days. Some of the early concordances took literally decades to complete, whereas a half-decent computing program can sort the whole thing out – literally – and produce copy ready for the printer in minutes or, at most, an hour or two.

A KWIC listing means a Key Word In Context listing. In other words, the particular word we are searching for appears in the middle of the line with so many characters before and after it – and that is the kind of listing we are after here. Not that we are going for a full-blooded concordance, just typing in a search string and producing a KWIC-type listing of the strings which match the search string.

At the same time, they can be used for quite a different purpose, namely stylistic analysis, for which there are some pretty sophisticated and expensive products in the software market place, in other words, stylistic analysis. It can only deal with one aspect of stylistic analysis, but it does it pretty well, as we shall see later. First, though, let us consider the design of the program itself.

Searching for strings

I often need to search through a number of different files in a given directory in order to find out if I have used a particular word or phrase, or referred to a particular date or individual, and if so in which files and how often.

Writing an assembler program to do this is far less difficult a challenge than it might seem, and it has the added advantage of being very fast indeed at doing its job. The program as it stands has two main limitations: the first is that it will search only in the current directory using ASCII text files, and the second is that the maximum file size is limited to around 60K, but in text files I take the view that it is crazy to work with text files greater than around 40K or so, unless there are very special circumstances.

Both these obstacles can be overcome if you put your mind to it, and later I will give you a few pointers as to how to go about making it a universal search program.

Too many programmers set off on a project without any clear idea of their precise objective. To them, it's not arriving that counts, it's the challenge of writing a program and nailing bugs that excites them. So let us be dull, practical and pragmatic and work backwards from the objective, which is to report on occurrences of a specified string in a number of different files.

Defining the search string

The first question is "What kind of string?" and the answer to that, based on years of examining concordances and similar programs, is: "As simple and unfussy as possible with upper and lower case ignored". In other words, if you ask for occurrences of "program", you are presumably interested in the word at the beginning of a sentence – "Program" – or as part of a subheading – "PROGRAM" – or in its various forms – "programs", "programming", and so on.

On the other side of the coin, it is far easier to allow for "noise" – "programmatic", "radio programmes", and so on – than it is to try and produce "clean" output with no distractions in it. Besides, who is to say what is and what is not a distraction or extraneous material? There is far too great a temptation on the part of programmers to decide what the user wants and to force formatting, layout and printout decisions upon him or her.

Let me offer an example from the listings which we shall be producing, based on the Chapter you are reading:

```
171 vantage of employing this technique.////          The next DEMO
197 ////        How is this possible? The answer lies in ASC DEMO
209 ends///////        This means that there has to be a two DEMO
231 reboot.////        This is the program and how to type i DEMO
360 am go something like this. The CX//      register is 1 DEMO
374 n intruder to bypass this password//       program by p DEMO
376 C or Ctrl+Break, and this is why I//      have used fu DEMO
409 der.////        At this point the program sits and twidd DEMO
439 out, load debug like this:////      DEBUG PW.COM////    DEMO
455        U////        This will unassemble the program, and DEMO
469 more detail later in this book. Suffice it to//       s DEMO
489 As a consequence of the overlap between files and device DEMO
556 reset the system.   At this point, it may occur  to you DEMO
558 you//        that this is precisely what the above aver DEMO
612 e air and despair at this//       point? Not a bit of i DEMO
```

All of which indicates that I tend to be rather too fond of "this". I dread to think what would happen if the string searched for was "now" or "so"!

A word of explanation is called for. The line numbers on the left are based on the number of carriage returns which the program picks up, the slashes stand for carriage return/line feeds, and the excessive spaces are caused by the way in which the word-processor saves ASCII files. This (that word again!) is just raw output to show what is happening. The filename – DEMO in this case – runs down the right-hand side, and is needed as more than one file can be searched.

Some of the programs I have seen will exclude material which is part of the previous or next sentence. So, if there is a full stop in the context, everything before or after it – depending on where it falls – is excluded. That is not a great deal of help if you have requested a listing of occurrences of "this", for example, in order to check on its use at the beginning of a sentence and what it refers back to. This (to coin a phrase) is hardly useful.

What kind of context?

The most important question is "What kind of context is required?" – in other words, once we have picked up an occurrence of the string which we are looking for, we need to see it in context with the maximum chance of that context being meaningful and with the minimum amount of output for the sake of readability, and the world's forests, come to that.

In the case of prose, a single line as a context is hardly appropriate, since it is an arbitrary division dependent on the font size, pitch and width of the page or column in which the text is printed and, unlike poetry, is likely to vary considerably from one version or edition of the text to another. As you can see from this example, a centralised keyword gives a pretty clear idea of the context (note that it has read from two different files):

```
Search string > program
12 se if for developing programs in PowerBASIC and assembler. BOOT.DAT
24 ys develop assembler programs from a RAM drive into which   BOOT.DAT
28 un even the simplest programs.////What is needed, in effec BOOT.DAT
 8 d somewhere that the programming involved in designing com LOGO.DAT
 8 the more complex the programming involved, so it seems, an LOGO.DAT
24 sing all the data or program which I had been working on f LOGO.DAT
46 SUB onechar ()//REM program to draw a logo//DATA 203,201, LOGO.DAT
66 the prompt designing program."//PRINT "Please note that th LOGO.DAT
```

How are we going to search across a number of files?

More than one file

The functions of INT 21 are very numerous and extremely useful to the programmer, and there is one dynamic duo which is of particular value in a program of this kind: the function which finds the first file matching a particular mask – say, *.DAT or *.WP? – and the one which finds the next, and the one after that, and so on until there are no more left which match.

First, though, we need to do a bit of housekeeping. Having powered up DEBUG with a filename like SEARCH.COM, load this message at location 1050 onwards, using E:

E1050 0D,0A,"Which file(s) to search? > $"

The leading carriage return and line feed are necessary to ensure that the message doesn't get overwritten. Remember, in assembler, it's the reverse of BASIC, where PRINT generates a carriage return line feed unless you specifically ask it not to by appending a semi-colon to the PRINT statement.

The first few lines of the program write that message on screen and wait for an answer, using the buffered input function 0A:

```
0100 B409        MOV     AH,09
0102 BA5010      MOV     DX,1050
0105 CD21        INT     21
0107 B410        MOV     AH,10
0109 88260010    MOV     [1000],AH
010D B40A        MOV     AH,0A
010F BA0010      MOV     DX,1000
0112 CD21        INT     21
```

As you will recall, function 0A invites buffered input, with DX holding the first address, into which the hex value 10 has been inserted, more than enough for the buffer. 1001 will hold the actual number of characters typed in, and 1002 and following will contain the text, followed by 0D.

Now to create an ASCII string followed by zero for the MS-DOS file opening

routine, we pick up the number of characters read, add that to 1002, and deposit a
zero at the end of the string:

```
0114 BB0210        MOV     BX,1002
0117 8A260110      MOV     AH,[1001]
011B 00E3          ADD     BL,AH
011D B400          MOV     AH,00
011F 8827          MOV     [BX],AH
```

Now to ask the user for the string which is to be looked for. Again, using E, type this
in (again, note the leading carriage return line feed):

E 1010 0D,0A,"Which string to search for? > $"

The code which handles this string is:

```
0121 B409          MOV     AH,09
0123 BA1010        MOV     DX,1010
0126 CD21          INT     21
0128 BB3010        MOV     BX,1030
012B B00D          MOV     AL,0D
012D 8807          MOV     [BX],AL
012F B40A          MOV     AH,0A
0131 BA3010        MOV     DX,1030
0134 CD21          INT     21
```

This time with function 0A, I've allowed for 0D characters to be typed in. That's
more than enough to look for a unique string in a text, but if you insist on more, that
is up to you.

Moving the PSP

Now we need to perform a little more housekeeping. In the PSP, the program
segment prefix, in other words, the 100 hex bytes which precede address 100 where
the program proper starts, bytes 80-FF are set aside for what is known as the default
DTA (disk transfer area). In other words, that is where information about an open file
is recorded, but in programs like this it is far safer to set up a separate DTA, which
you do with function 1A of INT 21, indicating the start of your own personal DTA
with DX:

```
0136 B41A          MOV     AH,1A
0138 BA0012        MOV     DX,1200
013B CD21          INT     21
```

Now we come to the business of finding the first file to match the information stored
in addresses 1002 and onwards. Remember, 1000 contains the maximum length of the
string that can be typed in, and 1001 the number of bytes actually keyed in:

```
013D B44E        MOV      AH,4E
013F 31C9        XOR      CX,CX
0141 BA0210      MOV      DX,1002
0144 CD21        INT      21
0146 7305        JNB      014D
0148 B8014C      MOV      AX,4C01
014B CD21        INT      21
```

The function which looks for the first matching file is 4E of INT 21. CX is set to zero to match ordinary files, and DX to the first byte of the ASCIIZ string we have set up. JNB – the same as JNE – checks to see if the carry flag has been set. If it is clear, a match has been found and all is well.

If not, I summon up function 4C of INT 21, which closes the program with the exit code in AL set by the programmer (01 in this case), which enables any batch file we shall be designing later to pick this up and offer a message to the effect that no matching files could be found.

Once you have found your file, you have to open it, using function 3D, with AL set to zero for normal access mode:

```
014D B8003D      MOV      AX,3D00
0150 BA1E12      MOV      DX,121E
0153 CD21        INT      21
```

At this point, we wander off to a subroutine at address 400 which starts the searching process:

```
0155 E8A802      CALL     0400
```

Once the first file has been searched from beginning to end, we look for the next matching file, using function 3E (with no other parameters – MS-DOS looks after all that for us), and if a match is found, the program goes round again, opening the file and calling 400. If the matches are exhausted, the program shuts down leaving a return code of 02 to be picked up by the surrounding batch file:

```
0158 B43E        MOV      AH,3E
015A CD21        INT      21
015C B44F        MOV      AH,4F
015E CD21        INT      21
0160 73EB        JNB      014D
0162 B8024C      MOV      AX,4C02
0165 CD21        INT      21
```

Next we turn to the subroutine at 400.

23

Where's that string? – II

The first thing to remember, which often causes errors if it is overlooked, is that the file handle is returned in the AX register, but that file write and read functions require that handle to be in the BX register:

```
0400 89C3            MOV     BX,AX
0402 31ED            XOR     BP,BP
```

The second of the instructions just listed zeroises the BP, or base pointer register. I am using it simply because it is not required for any other purpose, and as you will see soon, the purpose behind it is to count each carriage return character as it appears so that we can give a line number to any matched string when we print it out.

The next thing we have to do is one of those fiddly bits of housekeeping which never occur to me, at least, until the output on screen looks unaccountably scrambled. If we are, as here, creating a KWIC listing, it means that so many characters before the string matched are printed out and so many after it.

In other words, if a match is found in the very first bytes of the file, it is necessary to set a number of bytes before the beginning of the file to spaces, otherwise unpredictable garbage will be printed. We are loading the entire file(s) to be searched at location 1300 onwards, so the next bit very craftily sets the preceding 20 (hex) bytes to zero.

In case any sea lawyers are wondering, yes, it isn't strictly necessary to reset this area before every file that matches is opened, but I prefer to deal with this matter of setting to spaces all at the same time. Clearing spaces at the end of the file comes in a moment or two. It is a piece of programming which is executed in the twinkling of an electronic eye, and it may offend some old-timers for whom saving time and space used to be a top priority:

```
0404 B020          MOV      AL,20
0406 BED012        MOV      SI,12D0
0409 BFD112        MOV      DI,12D1
040C 8804          MOV      [SI],AL
040E B92F00        MOV      CX,002F
0411 F2            REPNZ
0412 A4            MOVSB
```

This is an extremely powerful routine, once you get the hang of it. First, you load a value into AL (or anywhere else that is convenient). Then you set up SI and DI, SI with the first address in the area you want to set to the value in AL, DI to the second address.

Just to recap: At location 040C, we are moving 20 in hex, the space character, into the address pointed to by the SI register, in other words, 12D0. DI is loaded with the value of the next address, 12D01. Now we load the CX register with the number of times we want the transfer of data to take place.

Then come the key instructions of this routine. First, REPNZ, which tells the computer to repeat while not zero. The test is performed, as you may remember, on the CX register.

Now comes the second part of what I believe is called in political circles a double whammy: MOVSB. This instruction means move a single byte from the address pointed to by SI to the address pointed to by DI. Then three things happen automatically: SI is incremented by one, DI is incremented by one, and CX is decremented by one.

If you find that a little difficult to follow, use the tracing facilities of DEBUG to follow it through. The other use of this kind of routine is to move data from one part of memory to another.

Finding the end of the file

Now we have set the area immediately before the beginning of the area where the file is to be loaded to spaces. What about the area after the end of the file? The question to be answered here is: How do we know where the end of the file is? The answer lies in the DTA, the disk transfer area. The file length is found in byte 1A of the DTA, and this is added to the beginning of the buffer – 1300 – to calculate where the end of the file will be in memory.

You will have noticed that we have not yet read in the contents of the file. This can be done either before or after we "top and tail" the file, since the information is sitting there waiting for us. The AL register still contains the space character, so the REPNZ MOVSB instruction swings into action again to space fill the end of the buffer:

```
0413 BE0013        MOV      SI,1300
0416 03361A12      ADD      SI,[121A]
041A 89F7          MOV      DI,SI
041C 83C701        ADD      DI,+01
041F 8804          MOV      [SI],AL
0421 B95000        MOV      CX,0050
0424 F2            REPNZ
0425 A4            MOVSB
```

One advantage of using the Find first file option is that it delivers the file length for us, as we have just seen, which means that we can now load CX with the precise number of bytes to read into memory. So we load the contents of 121A with that byte count and proceed:

```
0426 8B0E1A12      MOV      CX,[121A]
042A B43F          MOV      AH,3F
042C BA0013        MOV      DX,1300
042F CD21          INT      21
```

Now we are about to start the search, loading the beginning of the search address into SI and the file byte count into CX. The technique used is to LOOP back to address 43E. LOOP decrements CX until it is exhausted. The address of the beginning of the string to search for is loaded into DI.

As the search proceeds, AH is checked to see if it is a carriage return character, and if so, the line counter in BP is incremented. The routine at 700 converts the search string byte and the byte from the file to upper case as necessary, and if a match has been found, we go to the routine at 500, otherwise we continue looping until the count is exhausted:

```
0431 BEF412        MOV      SI,12F4
0434 8B0E1A12      MOV      CX,[121A]
0438 83C118        ADD      CX,+18
043B BF3210        MOV      DI,1032
043E 8A05          MOV      AL,[DI]
0440 8A24          MOV      AH,[SI]
0442 80FC0D        CMP      AH,0D
0445 7F01          JG       0448
0447 45            INC      BP
0448 E8B502        CALL     0700
044B 38C4          CMP      AH,AL
044D 7503          JNZ      0452
044F E8AE00        CALL     0500
0452 46            INC      SI
0453 F2            REPNZ
0454 E2E8          LOOP     043E
0456 C3            RET
```

The first requirement in the subroutine at 500 is to PUSH the CX, DI and SI registers so that we can go back to the search at the point at which we left off:

```
0500 51              PUSH    CX
0501 57              PUSH    DI
0502 56              PUSH    SI
```

Remember that the stack is a LIFO stack, last in, first out, so the POP instructions will have to be in reverse order. Do single step through these instructions to see what happens, checking with the address of the SP register each time and using D to examine the stack contents (D FFE0 FFFF should do it).

Now we have found a match for the first letter in the string, we need to see if a complete match for the whole string can be found. To do this, we must know how long the search string is, and its length is a side effect of the fact that it was read in using function 0A of INT 21. The buffer area started at 1030, so the byte count of the string will be in 1031 – and that is why, at address 43B above, the start of the string is at the apparently off-beat address of 1032, which we put into the CX register.

A word of explanation and advice is in order about how this is done. Note that I first zeroise CX and then read the contents of 1031 into CX. Why not simply use the instruction MOV CX,[1031]? The answer is that if you ask for that, you are moving the byte pair 1031 and 1032 into CX, which is not what you are after at all. This is a common cause of bugs in assembler programs.

We continue with the matching process, with the routine at 700 converting alpha characters to upper case, until either the match fails – at which point the instruction at 51A tells the program to jump to 55E – or the count in CX is exhausted, which means that we have found a complete match:

```
0503 31C9            XOR     CX,CX
0505 8A0E3110        MOV     CL,[1031]
0509 49              DEC     CX
050A 83F900          CMP     CX,+00
050D 7410            JZ      051F
050F 46              INC     SI
0510 47              INC     DI
0511 8A24            MOV     AH,[SI]
0513 8A05            MOV     AL,[DI]
0515 E8E801          CALL    0700
0518 38C4            CMP     AH,AL
051A 7542            JNZ     055E
051C F2              REPNZ
051D E2F0            LOOP    050F
```

At this point, a complete match has been found, so the first thing the program does is to print out a carriage return line feed. Then it goes to the routine at 600 for the fiddly business of putting the line number at the beginning of the output line:

```
051F B20D          MOV      DL,0D
0521 B402          MOV      AH,02
0523 CD21          INT      21
0525 B20A          MOV      DL,0A
0527 B402          MOV      AH,02
0529 CD21          INT      21
052B E8D200        CALL     0600
```

Odd instructions

This particular program was actually written some time ago, and when I came to annotate it for this book I was brought up short by the next two instructions. For a long moment, I could not understand what the possible purpose of POP immediately followed by a PUSH was, but it does, in fact, demonstrate the basic principle that every time you POP there must be a matching PUSH.

The contents of SI are popped, because they point to the byte in memory where the beginning of the match was found, and we need to line the text neatly up on screen based on that location. However, having already pushed the trio CX, DI and SI on to the stack it is necessary to PUSH SI back again so that they can all be properly popped at the end of this routine.

If you are still confused – and if not, why? – run the program to this point (by typing P 52E), and then examine the SP (stack pointer) register. It should contain the value FFF4. So type:

D FFF4 FFFF

Note that the stack grows "down" from the top of memory, while programs and data grow "up" from 100 – and if they meet in the middle, as they can occasionally do, disaster can result.

The data you should see should look something like this. Some of the values will differ in your case, depending on the length of the file you are searching, and where the first match has occurred in that file. It seems at first like a random collection of bytes, but examine it carefully and it all makes sense:

16 13 32 10 A5 39 52 04 58 01 00 00

The first point to remember is that, as ever, addresses are saved backwards way on, so the address of the first match, in SI, is in my case 1316. The contents of DI when pushed on the stack were 1032, and they are the fourth and third bytes respectively. The next pair unscramble as the contents of CX, and that comes out here as 39A5.

The next four bytes should be the same in your program. If you look back, you will see that the subroutine 500 was called by the subroutine 400 which, in turn, was called by the main module of the program. The next two bytes are 52 04, unscrambled as 452, and if you glance back at the appropriate point in the listing, you will see that the subroutine at 500 was called from address 44F.

When CALL is executed, the return address is pushed on to the stack, and as you will see, the address of the next instruction is indeed 452. The next two bytes on the stack are 158, and if you look at the main module, you will see that the call of 400 occurs at 155, and that the return address is 158. The last two bytes are 00 00, and a jump to zero returns the program to the command prompt. So our POP and PUSH of SI does make sense after all:

```
052E 5E            POP     SI
052F 56            PUSH    SI
```

Printing out the context

Now the program is going to print out a line of data with the matched string in the middle. You can juggle with the figures in addresses 532 and 541, which determine how far back the string starts and how long it is. Do remember not to ask for something too long for your printer, though, or for the screen. For details of printer and file output see the end of this Chapter.

Note that the byte pair 0D 0A, when encountered, is replaced by a slash (ASCII value 2F). The second increment of BX at 545 jumps over the 0A:

```
0530 89F3          MOV     BX,SI
0532 83EB15        SUB     BX,+15
0535 B93A00        MOV     CX,003A
0538 B402          MOV     AH,02
053A 8A17          MOV     DL,[BX]
053C 80FA0D        CMP     DL,0D
053F 7F02          JG      0543
0541 B22F          MOV     DL,2F
0543 CD21          INT     21
0545 43            INC     BX
0546 F2            REPNZ
0547 E2F1          LOOP    053A
```

Next, a space is output and then the name of the file currently being searched. The start address of the filename is in 121E and following, terminated by a zero:

```
0549 B402          MOV     AH,02
054B B220          MOV     DL,20
054D CD21          INT     21
054F BB1E12        MOV     BX,121E
0552 8A17          MOV     DL,[BX]
0554 80FA00        CMP     DL,00
0557 7405          JZ      055E
0559 CD21          INT     21
055B 43            INC     BX
055C EBF4          JMP     0552
```

Then, to round things off, we POP the trio of byte pairs and return to look for more matches:

```
055E 5E            POP      SI
055F 5F            POP      DI
0560 59            POP      CX
0561 C3            RET
```

Displaying line numbers

One of the things which computing beginners always find difficult to master is the difference between 456 as a numerical value and the string "456", consisting of three ASCII values. High-level languages like BASIC are very kind to us, doing all the messy conversion work when printing out a variable containing a numerical value, but in assembler we have to do our own dirty work.

As you will remember, the BP register pair contains the current line count, and this routine converts the number into bytes. It is a bit complicated, but rewards careful study, because not only does the conversion take place, but the number is neatly right justified with a space before the beginning of the text and leading zeros automatically suppressed.

The first thing we do is to fill six bytes beginning at 1070 with spaces:

```
0600 BA2020        MOV      DX,2020
0603 BE7010        MOV      SI,1070
0606 8914          MOV      [SI],DX
0608 83C602        ADD      SI,+02
060B 8914          MOV      [SI],DX
060D 83C602        ADD      SI,+02
0610 8914          MOV      [SI],DX
```

That could have been done with a loop, but by the time it is set up it is hardly worth doing for just three times. At this point, addresses 1070 to 1075 contain the space character.

Now DX is zeroised – we shall see why in a minute – and the last address in the space-filled buffer is given a dollar sign (again, explanations in a moment):

```
0612 31D2          XOR      DX,DX
0614 B024          MOV      AL,24
0616 BF7510        MOV      DI,1075
0619 8805          MOV      [DI],AL
```

We are now going to divide DX:AX successively by ten (that's why DX was set to zero a moment ago), picking off each digit and converting it to ASCII, starting with the least significant digit and working backwards. The upper limit for line numbers in this program, then, is 999. To make it longer, just stretch the buffer and alter addresses accordingly.

Converting to ASCII

The first stage in the division is to put BP into AX. Let us assume that the line number for conversion from hex is 11F (decimal equivalent 287):

```
061B BE0A00        MOV     SI,000A
061E 89E8          MOV     AX,BP
0620 BF7310        MOV     DI,1073
0623 F7F6          DIV     SI
```

The first location set aside for the conversion is address 1073. You can follow this through at the computer by running the program up to address 600. Then use R BP to change the value of BP to 11F.

Before the division, AX = 011F and DX=0000. After the first division, AX = 001C and DX = 0007. DL has 30 added to it, and hex 37 is placed in DI. DI is decremented in preparation for the next digit, and DX is zeroised. Then the program loops round for the second division:

```
0625 3C00          CMP     AL,00
0627 740A          JZ      0633
0629 80C230        ADD     DL,30
062C 8815          MOV     [DI],DL
062E 4F            DEC     DI
062F 31D2          XOR     DX,DX
0631 EBF0          JMP     0623
```

The second time around, AX = 001C and DX = 0000 before the calculation, and afterwards AX = 0002 and DX = 0008. DX is converted to the ASCII equivalent, deposited in the buffer, and round we go again for the final time.

After the third division, the result in AX is zero and the remainder in DL is 2, so the program jumps to 633, where the final character is deposited in place. If you now examine the buffer beginning at address 1070, you will find that it contains, respectively, space, 2, 8, 7, space, dollar sign.

That string can be printed out without further ado using function 9 of INT 21:

```
0633 80C230        ADD     DL,30
0636 8815          MOV     [DI],DL
0638 B409          MOV     AH,09
063A BA7010        MOV     DX,1070
063D CD21          INT     21
063F C3            RET
```

Finally, a look at the routine at 700, which converts incoming characters from the search string and the searched for string to upper case. You can alter this feature to make the search case sensitive:

```
0700 80FC40          CMP      AH,40
0703 7F01            JG       0706
0705 C3              RET
0706 80E4DF          AND      AH,DF
0709 3C40            CMP      AL,40
070B 7F01            JG       070E
070D C3              RET
070E 24DF            AND      AL,DF
0710 C3              RET
```

To send output to the printer, press Ctrl+P before running the program, Ctrl+P again after the program has run.

An upgraded version of the program which sends the output to the screen and also to the file SEARCHOP will be found on the optional disk which accompanies this book. For details, see the Preface.

Finally, as well as searching for specific strings as a data retrieval exercise, you can – as I suggested at the beginning of the previous Chapter – use this program for a second purpose, namely, stylistic analysis. In the last Chapter, I indicated that I had an over-fondness for "this", "now", and "so".

You can highlight your own stylistic peccadillos by searching your text for words you tend to use to excess. Also, look for vague expressions like: perhaps, some, may, seem, could, might, and so on.

Stylistic analysis

One valuable tip is to make the search string a full stop or other punctuation sign, to check if you tend to use and or but at the beginning of sentences, for example, or for repeated patterns at the beginning of sentences. Here is just part of the listing from this Chapter, which fortunately does not reveal any serious offences against accepted good stylistic practice:

```
 8 d here does just that. It is designed to search through fi DEMO
 8 g and list the result. It will probably give some experts  DEMO
 8 ll I ask of a program.////First, we need to do a bit of ja DEMO
12 ance and KWIC listing. The idea of a concordance is to tak DEMO
12 t in which they occur. For poetry, say, a line of verse ma DEMO
12 echnique is necessary. The concordance was a hugely cumber DEMO
12 he pre-computing days. Some of the early concordances took DEMO
12  most, an hour or two.////A KWIC listing means a Key Word  DEMO
16 rd In Context listing. In other words, the particular word DEMO
16 ing we are after here. Not that we are going for a full-bl DEMO
16 tch the search string.////At the same time, they can be us DEMO
20 s, stylistic analysis. It can only deal with one aspect of DEMO
```

We cannot conclude without a look at "now", which as you see I tend to put at the beginning of sentences. Note also the "noise" caused by "know" and "known", which if it really offends you, you can weed out by adding an option to search for whole words only. I personally do not believe that it is worth the effort to do so:

```
150 mation goes into DX. Now comes the tricky bit. If we start DEMO
162 offending OD and can now turn it into a zero:////0114 BB02 DEMO
178    MOV    [BX],AH////Now to ask the user for the string wh DEMO
210 hat is up to you.////Now we need to perform a little more  DEMO
210 t aside for what is known as the default DTA (disk transfe DEMO
222        INT    21////Now we come to the business of findin DEMO
288        INT    21////Now we are inside the subroutine begi DEMO
288 wondering, I do not know why. It is just one of those fact DEMO
```

One feature I omitted from the program, but which is present in the full version on disk is giving a total of the matches found at the end of the listing. Still, you could go on embellishing this program for ever. I leave the finer points of improvement to you.

24

Out on the border

A little while back, we explored the question of characters, their attributes and the colours you can generate for the foreground and background in text mode. Now we are going to explore a different aspect of colour on the PC.

Quite often you will find a program which produces an attractive coloured border round the screen, and many people wonder how it can be achieved. It is not too difficult, and not just decorative, as I have used it as a visible reminder to the user of which of a number of menu options is currently being run or what kind of activity the program is carrying out.

Call the program EDGE.COM and type in the following:

```
0100    MOV SI,0081
0103    MOV BL,[SI]
0105    CMP BL,0D
0108    JNZ 010C
010A    INT 20
010C    INC SI
010D    MOV BL,[SI]
010F    CMP BL,20
0112    JNZ 0117
0114    INC SI
0115    JMP 010D
0117    SUB BL,30
011A    XOR BH,BH
011C    MOV AH,0B
011E    INT 10
0120    INT 20
```

Then save the program in the usual way, using R CX and W.

If you have typed it all in correctly and summon up the program with:

```
EDGE 1
EDGE 2
```

– and so on, you will find that your colour screen adds a border in one of the PC's range of colours.

How is it achieved? Well, without getting too technical you can work it out by loading the program like this:

```
DEBUG EDGE.COM 3
```

You will find that the "command tail", that is, the space followed by a 3, or whatever other character you choose, is stored in the PSP.

The Program Segment Prefix

The Program Segment Prefix is the area of the program memory before the code starts at hex 100, hence the numbering above begins at that value, and it contains lots of valuable information about the program, the relevant bit as far as we are concerned being at address 80 plus.

If you type:

```
D 80 8F
```

– you'll see – D for Dumped – a line of information which begins something like this:

```
0080 02 20 33 0D
```

The first number, 02, tells you how long the command tail is, not including the carriage return (0D) which terminates it. Then comes the command tail itself: a space (20) plus 33, the hex for the digit 3.

The program's first task is to pick up that value from the PSP, or to halt if none has been located there. If you reload the program like this:

```
DEBUG EDGE.COM
```

– without a command tail, then ask to see a dump of locations 80 plus, you will get this response:

```
0080 00 0D
```

Now to the program to see how this is coped with. The first instruction moves the value 81 into the SI register, and if you use the P for Proceed Debug command, you can watch this happen before your very eyes.

As 81 is the address we are looking to find, if we next load into the BL register (that's the right-hand side of the BX register) the contents of location 81, we shall either get 0D if there isn't a command tail, or a space if there is.

Remember that the square brackets round SI mean "load what's inside the address which is in the SI register". If we come up against a blank, in other words if BL is equal to 0D, then the program is halted using the standard method of calling interrupt 20. If it isn't, we jump to location 10C and carry on with the program.

Extra spaces

Now we have to cope with another little local difficulty. If you typed two or more spaces between EDGE.COM and the command tail, these are faithfully reproduced at locations 81 and following.

That's why I have added a loop next which increments SI, looks at the contents of the next location, and if it is 20, increments it again and keeps going until it finds a non-space character.

At this point I subtract 30 from it, so that if you have typed 5, for example, the value 35-30 – in hex, of course – is generated, since the colours are conjured up from zero (not ASCII 30 zero) onwards. You can type whatever character you like at this point: the machine will convert it as best it can and come up with a colour of some sort for you.

The last part of the program zeroises the BH register, the left-hand half of the BX register by performing an XOR or exclusive OR operation on itself.

The INT 10 interrupt function 0B sets the border colour, so 0B is located in AH, and it requires BH to be zero and the colour number to be in BL, which we have done.

Don't forget to type Q to get out of DEBUG. Apart from rebooting, resetting or even sometimes switching off the computer, that's the only way of extracting yourself from the program.

25

Dealing with low characters

One of the features of the MS-DOS character set which makes it so flexible is that it not only extends upwards beyond the normal ASCII range, with line-drawing, scientific and foreign language characters, but also below it. In other words the characters 0-31, which function as control characters, mostly originally derived from teleprinter transmission codes, also have printable values.

These take the form of musical notes, a smiling and a sad face, the four suit characters of playing cards, and so on. The only problem is that it appears to be impossible to get at them. As we saw in a previous Chapter, if you use INT 21 function 2, with DL set to 7, the bell rings. The character value 7 is studiously ignored. In what follows, I'll show you how to beat the system and come up with a valuable utility to list the characters below the normal lower limit of 20 hex.

The normal function for displaying a character on screen is function 2 of INT 21. What it does is to take the value in the DL register and display it on the screen. At the same time, the cursor hops forward one to the next available position – to the beginning of the next line, if necessary.

There are a few minor wrinkles to function 2, but that is basically it. It works perfectly well with characters above 2F, as this example listing, which prints out the e acute character, demonstrates:

```
0100 B402        MOV     AH,02
0102 B282        MOV     DL,82
0104 CD21        INT     21
0106 CD20        INT     20
```

As you will see if you try this out using DEBUG as I have explained, there are no problems with this or any other character in the range 80 and above in hexadecimal.

But when it comes to characters below 20H, space, it's a different story. Try this with the value set to 7, and you will hear the strangled bleep which passes for a bell on the PC, not the character which has the value 7:

```
0100 B402          MOV     AH,02
0102 B207          MOV     DL,07
0104 CD21          INT     21
0106 CD20          INT     20
```

The actual IBM character number seven is what typesetters call a bullet, a blocked-in circle used to highlight paragraphs or points in a document. The question is, how do we get our hands on it and print it on the screen? The answer lies in one of the BIOS (Basic Input Output System) interrupts, INT 10 (in hex), and in particular functions 9 and 0A.

Printing the bullet

Here is a program which will print out the bullet character number 7 on screen. As you can see, there's a bit more to it than function 2 of INT 21:

```
0100 B40A          MOV     AH,0A
0102 B007          MOV     AL,07
0104 31DB          XOR     BX,BX
0106 B91200        MOV     CX,0012
0109 CD10          INT     10
010B CD20          INT     20
```

As usual, the function number is loaded into the AH register. AL contains the character to be printed, 7 in this case. BH contains the video page number, and as the default is zero, I have XORed the whole BX register. BL is only used on the PCJr machine, but we might as well be safe.

A video page is an area in memory which contains the information on screen, and it is usually page 0 which you are seeing.

The next register to come up for scrutiny is CX. This contains the 'replication factor', as it is known in the trade, in plain English the number of times you want the character printed. I have – for no particular reason – opted for 12 in hex.

Then the interrupt is summoned up and the program terminated with INT 20. Up comes on screen eighteen neat little bullets. There are a couple of points to note here. The first is that, if you ask in the CX register for more characters than there are on a line, it will not line wrap for you, but only print as many as it can get on an individual line.

Point number two is that, unlike function 2 of INT 21, the cursor is not advanced one location to the right (or wrapped to the next line if the end of the line has been reached), so this is something the programmer has to organise.

In the case of the next little program, which displays all the characters in the range 1-1F (zero is a blank character, but if you really must, you can display that as well, if the fancy takes you), another function of INT 10 is used to move the print position along. Let us examine it a bit at a time:

```
0100 B001          MOV     AL,01
0102 B40A          MOV     AH,0A
0104 B90100        MOV     CX,0001
0107 CD10          INT     10
0109 50            PUSH    AX
```

So far, we have printed the IBM character with the value 1, using function 0A.

Now that we are going to summon up another function, AX is pushed to preserve the value of AL, which will be incremented to display all the characters in the range 1-1F.

PUSH and POP save and retrieve two bytes at a time from a special area of memory called the stack. One of the registers you see when you press R is the SP, or stack pointer, register, and you will see it decrement by two when you PUSH a register pair on to it and increment by two when you retrieve it.

Note that you have to push the entire register pair. It is not possible to push a single eight-bit register at a time, but that is no hardship, so long as you remember that when the register pair is popped, both the AH and AL values are changed.

Now we need to move two cursor positions to the right, the first to 'clear' the character printed, the second to generate a space so that the output is not too cluttered up:

```
010A B403          MOV     AH,03
010C 31DB          XOR     BX,BX
010E CD10          INT     10
```

Function 3 of INT 10 obtains the current cursor position. BX is set to zero, as the function needs to know the current video page number from BH. You could just set BH if you wished, but I prefer in general to reset a complete register pair. Habit, I suppose.

The XOR instruction needs a word of explanation. There are various logical instructions in assembler, which deal with each binary bit making up a byte or pair of bytes in different ways. Exclusive OR, as XOR is called, compares two bytes or pairs of bytes, and if it finds a 1 in either or both of them, it sets it to zero. So exclusively OR-ing BX with itself is another way of zeroising the BX register pair.

The default video page is zero, and the number of pages available for the user – allowing instant swapping of screenfuls of information – varies according to whether you are using text mode, graphics mode, and a number of other considerations.

The function offers a wealth of information in the CX and DX register pairs, not all of which we need for our present purpose. The CX register contains the shape of the current cursor: CH offers the starting line and CL the ending line. That's not much use to us here – it's the DX register which contains the coordinates we are after.

DH holds the row number and DL the column number. You may know that the top left-hand corner of the screen is row 0, column 0, and also that the row is also referred to as the x coordinate, the column as the y coordinate.

So what we want to do is to add two to the column number and reset the current cursor position, which is achieved by means of function 2 of INT 10:

```
0110 80C202    ADD   DL,02
0113 B402            MOV   AH,02
0115 CD10            INT   10
```

That moves the cursor two locations to the right (as we are only dealing with 31 characters, there is no danger of falling off the right-hand side of the screen), and now we just pop the AX register, increment the value in AL, and go round again until we have printed all the characters we want:

```
0117 58     POP  AX
0118 FEC0           INC   AL
011A 3C20           CMP   AL,20
011C 7CE4           JL    0102
```

Numbering the characters

You could terminate the program at this point with INT 20, but now we have gone this far, let us make it a little more useful by numbering the characters, so that we have a utility which enables us to work out quickly in decimal what the value of the character is. To achieve this, we first need a carriage return and line feed, using the familiar function 2 of INT 21 with the line feed and carriage return characters 0D and 0A:

```
011E B402    MOV  AH,02
0120 B20D           MOV   DL,0D
0122 CD21           INT   21
0124 B402           MOV   AH,02
0126 B20A           MOV   DL,0A
0128 CD21           INT   21
```

Next, we need to print 1 plus space plus 2 plus space underneath the characters up to 31. From 1 to 29 can be done in a little loop controlled by the contents of the CX register:

```
012A B90300    MOV  CX,0003
```

More about the significance of this in a moment or two. To set the loop off first time round, we load DL with 31 (ASCII equivalent of the character 1) and go round printing 31, 20 (space), 32, 20, and so on, using function 2 of INT 21, until we reach 3A:

```
012D B231        MOV      DL,31
012F B402        MOV      AH,02
0131 CD21        INT      21
0133 52          PUSH     DX
0134 B220        MOV      DL,20
0136 B402        MOV      AH,02
0138 CD21        INT      21
013A 5A          POP      DX
013B FEC2        INC      DL
013D 80FA3A      CMP      DL,3A
0140 75ED        JNZ      012F
```

Note that it is necessary to push the contents of DX after the number is printed in order to preserve it while we are printing the space character in the instructions beginning at address 134. At address 13B, once DX has been popped, the contents of DL are incremented, and if they are not equal to 3A, we go round the loop printing 2, 3, 4 and so on up to 9 (one short of 3A).

At this point in the proceedings, we have printed out 1 to 9, so we need to set DL to 30, so that the next character printed out is 0 (to indicate that we are up to 10). To print the next two lots of ten characters, we use the REPNZ (repeat not zero) instruction in conjunction with the LOOP instruction. This is one of those extremely convenient commands for looping which come with 8080 assembler, and which make life a lot easier for the programmer.

In order to understand what it does, we need to look in a little more detail at the registers. The AX one is the accumulator register pair, in which many calculations take place. The BX register is the 'base' register, which is often used for addresses which are added to in order to move data around in relation to a particular base address. The CX register is the count register pair, and is used by quite a few commands for the purposes of decrementing a value and performing a set of instructions until that value is zero.

In the present case, we set CX to 3, and the REPNZ instruction first decrements CX by one, and then, in conjunction with the LOOP instruction, sends control back to location 12F, until, that is, CX is zero. To watch this happening, use the DEBUG commands G 145, P, G 145, and so on, keeping a stern eye on the contents of the CX register each time. Don't do that, though, until you have keyed in the entire program.

Incidentally, it's worth mentioning here a small point which confuses some people. If you type G 145 to go to the instruction beginning at address 145, you cannot then immediately type G 145 again. I can understand the human logic which says, for example, that this is part of a loop, and I want to proceed from here all the way round to 145 again.

However, we are dealing with computer logic, I'm afraid. DEBUG looks at the number, if any, you type after G, and if you are at that address already, it simply stops there. That is why I add in a P to ensure that you proceed one instruction beyond 145.

Here are the instructions to load DL with zero and decrement and loop:

```
0142 B230          MOV    DL,30
0144 F2            REPNZ
0145 E2E8          LOOP   012F
```

Next, use the E command:

```
E 200 "0 1$"
```

– or, alternatively:

```
E 200 30,20,21,24
```

– which comes to the same thing.

Just to remind you: E means "Enter", and it is used to enter information directly into memory. What I tend to do in a short program is to put data at an address a fair distance away from the program instructions, here at address 200 hex. E can be followed either by hex bytes separated by commas or information inside double quotes, or a mixture of the two.

Note that if you want to save this program, you should insert enough bytes into CX to include the data entered into memory. In the present case, 300 bytes will be more than enough.

Now we use the print string function to put out the last couple of digits under characters 30 (decimal) and 31:

```
0147 BA0002        MOV    DX,0200
014A B409          MOV    AH,09
014C CD21          INT    21
014E CD20          INT    20
```

Function 9 prints out characters starting at the address pointed to by DX until it comes up against the dollar sign (24 in hex). So, whenever you use this function, do ensure that you have a dollar sign – otherwise the function will keep on, and on, and on, printing garbage out on screen.

So it is possible to print out those elusive characters below space in ASCII, but do note first, that you have to use a function of INT 10, not INT 21, secondly, that the function does not move the cursor on for you, and thirdly, that there is no line wrap.

In order to ensure that line wrap occurs, you should check the DX register pair to find out where the cursor is along the current row. Finally, if you intend to use the characters in this lower range a lot, you should have a subroutine at your disposal which does all these things for you.

26

Locking the keys

Security is a bore – until something goes wrong for you, that is, until your bike is stolen, your credit card abused, your computer data destroyed. This is why I have devoted the next couple of Chapters to the topic, ending up with an entertaining exercise in decryption.

The real problem is striking the right balance between leaving the front door of your computer open, so to speak, with a large neon-lit sign above it reading "Come and steal or corrupt all my data", and on the other hand creating the microcomputer equivalent of Fort Knox, in which you erect electric fences, have armed guards at all the entrances, and work in a bomb-proof shelter to which access is gained only by passing through ten different password-controlled steel doors.

All right, I am exaggerating somewhat, but the fact is that most computer users are far too near the open door end of the spectrum and miles away from the Fort Knox extreme. Before I show you some very simple techniques for protecting your precious data, ask yourself these three questions:

If you are in business and use a computer, what would happen to that business if you found that your data was destroyed by fire, theft or some other villainry? Or again, you find yourself outside your front door, and discover you have lost your keys. How would you break in?

Imagine (perish the thought) that you are a car thief. You are after a Jaguar XJ-S, find two identical vehicles in a car park. One has an alarm fitted, the other doesn't. Which would you steal?

You can't beat all the crooks all the time, but you can deter them by some extremely simple techniques which cost absolutely nothing.

Here is a nine-line program which locks up your keyboard and prevents an unauthorised individual from tampering with your machine while you are away from your desk.

Let's explore the technique a step at a time. What we need is a program which causes the computer to hang until you press the appropriate key or key combination.

Selecting a password

The first problem to arise is to choose between a single keypress and a password. The longer the password, the harder it is to break, and the shorter it is, the easier it is to remember.

Let's go down the route of a double bluff, by putting our simple program into a batch file which puts up a message on screen asking for a password to continue. The implication is that you type a line of text in plus Enter.

Having decided on a single keypress, let us make it a little more complicated by making that keypress a combination of characters, let's say Ctrl+F9. There is, as we shall see in a moment, a very special advantage of employing this technique.

The next question to arise is what happens if the wrong key combination or the wrong key is depressed. If you allow the intruder any number of attempts at pressing the right key, then he or she will eventually get there, if they recognise that a single keypress is what is required.

So the obvious step to take is to limit the number of times a key can be depressed before the system locks. If you decide upon a combined keypress, you can actually set off that system lock if the intruder presses just one key.

That is made possible, as you will recall from our discussions in earlier Chapters, by the extended ASCII codes. The function keys, among others, are represented by two values, the first of which is zero.

This means that there has to be a two-stage method of reading and detecting one of these characters. The first stage is to detect zero, and if it isn't a zero, it means that either a normal keyboard key has been pressed, or one of the extended character set accessed by Alt plus keys on the numeric keypad.

In that case, that is, if we detect a non-zero key, we can set off the alarms immediately. Let us allow two attempts before the system ties itself in knots, at which point the only way of unlocking the system is to reset or reboot.

A simple security program

Let us call the program PW.COM, short for password. Using DEBUG in the normal way, type the program in:

```
0100 B90200      MOV      CX,0002
0103 B407        MOV      AH,07
0105 CD21        INT      21
0107 3C00        CMP      AL,00
0109 750D        JNZ      0118
010B B408        MOV      AH,08
010D CD21        INT      21
010F 3C66        CMP      AL,66
0111 7502        JNZ      0115
0113 CD20        INT      20
0115 49          DEC      CX
0116 75EB        JNZ      0103
0118 B43E        MOV      AH,3E
011A 31DB        XOR      BX,BX
011C CD21        INT      21
011E EBF8        JMP      0118
```

The contents of the program go something like this. The CX register is loaded with the value 2 – that's the count for the number of tries allowed. If you want to make it just one try, or more than two, adjust the value accordingly.

Function 7 of interrupt 21, character input without echo on screen, is then invoked. It may well have occurred to you that it might be possible for an intruder to bypass this password program by pressing Ctrl+C or Ctrl+Break, and this is why I have used function 7 instead of the more usual function 8.

With Function 8, the program can be interrupted by Ctrl+C or Ctrl+Break, but function 7 is described as "unfiltered" input, in other words, it ignores the Ctrl plus key combinations which normally bring a program grinding to a halt, thereby cutting off that option for the potential intruder.

At this point the program sits and twiddles its thumbs waiting for a keypress. If the incoming character is non-zero, the program jumps to location 118, at which point the system seizes up, as we shall see in a moment.

If the key is zero, the program checks for hex value 66 (decimal 109), the value of Ctrl+F9, and if it is found, halts with interrupt 20, at which point you are returned to the MS-DOS prompt.

If 66 is not found, CX is decremented and if it is non-zero, you jump back to location 103 at which you get another attempt at keying in the correct combination.

Switching off the keyboard

Now to the technique I've adopted to cause the system to hang. It's linked to the notion of files and devices, which we have already referred to earlier in this book. MS-DOS links the two and in many ways treats them as identical.

We are all familiar with the notion of a file, but let us recap what a device is. It's either one of the standard devices – the keyboard, the screen , for example – or a device which is added using a device driver, like a CD-ROM, a scanner, and so on.

As a consequence of this overlap between files and devices, function 3E of interrupt 21, which is billed in the reference books as 'close file', actually has a different role.

When you open a file, it is given a 'handle', a unique number which is used instead of the filename in all future references to it, including when you close it. That handle starts at 5, and goes on until you come up against the limit of files which the system allows or you have set.

But what about 0-4? These are reserved for the standard devices. So if, instead of putting a handle number of 5 or more into the BX register, where the operating system expects to find it when you call function 3E of interrupt 21, you put a plain zero, the close file function actually closes down the keyboard device, causing the whole system to hang.

If you look back at the program, you will find that this is in fact what happens at the address 11A – the file handle BX is indeed set to zero and the keyboard is effectively closed down.

The only way out of that little blind alley is to reboot or reset the system. At this point, it may have occurred to you that this is precisely what the above-average intruder might do anyway, in order to bypass our password program. However, we have another little surprise in store.

All you have to do in order to protect your system against that kind of assault is to add the name of the program – PW – at the end of your AUTOEXEC.BAT file, using EDIT. However, before you do so, do ensure that there is no chance of you locking yourself out of your own system. That would be taking security too far!

To set the password batch file up for use when you leave your computer unattended, use EDIT to create a file called, say, PASS.BAT, containing the following lines:

```
@ECHO OFF
CLS
ECHO (put next bit in middle of screen)
ECHO System halted. Please type password to continue >
PW
```

That should keep the intruder at bay, or at least puzzled for quite some time, and in security matters time can be important. No potential thief wants to waste time during which he or she could be caught while there are other, less well protected, computer systems waiting to be raided. So this technique offers a good level of support. But what if you want to go further? The next Chapter will explain all.

27

Pass the word
and wipe the file

In this Chapter, we consider two important aspects of security. First, I am going to show you a public key technique for overcoming the perennial problem of forgetting what your password is. Then we will look at a means of deleting files – but really deleting them. It is not so simple as it seems.

One technique for creating a password is to add a program to the beginning of your AUTOEXEC.BAT file which will require you to type in a password before you can access your computer.

As this is a fairly dodgy process if you make a mistake and lock up your machine for ever, it's advisable to test the routine out thoroughly from the MS-DOS prompt before going live, as it were.

At the same time, I offer you a public key cipher which will enable you to pin the password over the computer – which enough people do anyway! – but without anyone being able to make use of it. Now there's an intriguing possibility.

So let's explain and summarise the first objective: we want to put together a program which is added to the AUTOEXEC.BAT file, which asks for a four-letter code (which can be pinned up on the wall for all to see), and which will crash horribly if you fail to provide it.

Let us first of all look at one possible way of designing the code. If it is acceptable to change the code once per day, we can easily print out a grid which looks like this:

0	0	1	2	3	4
0	G	W	R	P	V
1	X	Y	Z	A	B
2	Z	B	C	D	S
3	X	O	B	B	F
4	C	R	F	G	O
5	F	K	L	Z	Y
6	R	L	Q	O	O
7	B	R	M	P	U
8	E	N	A	Z	W
9	J	R	F	E	Q

This is a set of random letters – we'll look later at how to change the public code and print it out. The table contains some irrelevant information, just to put the snooper off the scent.

A unique four-letter code

It offers a unique four-letter code for every day of the month. The best way of demonstrating how this works is by a couple of examples. The code for 14th of the month is RKLR, the code for 21st ZCBF, for the 18th NRRZ, and so on.

To extract the code for a particular day – take 14th as an example – simply look across the columns to column 1, down the rows to row 4, and read vertically the next four letters.

If the date is the 8th, go to column zero, then down to row 8. Read off the next four letters, and if, as here, you run off the end of the column, simply continue on the top of the next column. Column 4 is just there as window dressing.

To achieve this objective, we need a program which finds out what the date is, moves along the data stored in column order to the appropriate starting point, and then try matching it with the user's input. That is an interesting and – as it turns out – not too demanding challenge.

The first problem is to prevent anyone overriding the program by typing Ctrl+C. Normally, input is 'filtered', in other words if you press Ctrl+C the program is abandoned and control passed back to the command prompt. That would defeat the object of the exercise by allowing the intruder access to your MS-DOS prompt.

So we need an interrupt which waits for a keypress, but ignores Ctrl+C. The answer lies in function 7, which we used for the same purpose in the previous Chapter. First, though, we need to set the DI register to the number of attempts you allow yourself (or anyone else, for that matter) before the system hangs up on you. In this case I've allowed two attempts.

Next, we summon up function 2A of INT 21 to access the current system date –

remember, it's the date as the system knows it which it accesses, so it's important that it is set correctly by using the DATE command. Here are the first couple of lines of the program:

```
0100 BF0200        MOV     DI,0002
0103 B42A          MOV     AH,2A
0105 CD21          INT     21
```

Now in this program, we have stored the password data at location 500:

```
E 500  "GXZXCFRBEJWYBORKLRNRRZCBFLQMAFPADBGZOPZE"
```

In order to point at the correct starting point in this string, we take the date, which is returned in the DL register as a hex digit in the range 0-31, and add it to 500 (the starting point of the string). It's necessary to zeroise DH, because you cannot add DL to AX, you have to add like to like, in other words 16 bits to 16 bits, not 8 to 16:

```
0107 B80005        MOV     AX,0500
010A 30F6          XOR     DH,DH
010C 01D0          ADD     AX,DX
010E 89C6          MOV     SI,AX
```

As you can see, I've moved the result into the SI register out of the way. Now we set up a count in the CX register of the number of letters in the code to be typed in and matched, then comes the first call of function 7, the unfiltered input function:

```
0110 B90400        MOV     CX,0004
0113 B407          MOV     AH,07
0115 CD21          INT     21
```

The incoming character ends up in AL. Next in line comes a Boolean instruction, AND, which converts the incoming character to upper case (if necessary). Then we move the character which SI points to (the square brackets, remember, mean 'the contents of') into AH, do a spot of comparison, and if all is well, increment SI, and use REPNZ and LOOP to decrement CX and go back to location 113 for the second character input.

If all is not well, we toddle off to location 150, more of which in a moment:

```
0117 24DF          AND     AL,DF
0119 8A24          MOV     AH,[SI]
011B 38C4          CMP     AH,AL
011D 7531          JNZ     0150
011F 46            INC     SI
0120 F2            REPNZ
0121 E2F0          LOOP    0113
0123 CD20          INT     20
```

If a perfect match is found, the program simply terminates, the AUTOEXEC.BAT file trundles through the rest of its commands, and you gain access to your computer. If not, we end up at location 150:

```
0150 E8AD00        CALL    0200
0153 4F            DEC     DI
0154 83FF00        CMP     DI,+00
0157 7409          JZ      0162
```

The subroutine which starts at location 200 will need some further tinkering, so for the moment at location 200 just put:

```
RET
```

That's as good a way as any to create a dummy subroutine. At location 153, we decrement DI, and if it is zero – if, with an initial value of 2, we are on our third attempt at the password, we jump to 162, of which more in a second. Otherwise, we are allowed a second attempt, but first comes a warning message, set up like this:

```
E 530 "Password incorrect ... Try again $"
```

Then we jump back to 106 for a second try:

```
0159 B409          MOV     AH,09
015B BA3005        MOV     DX,0530
015E CD21          INT     21
0160 EBA4          JMP     0106
```

Illegal access

If the number of attempts allowed is exhausted, we put up a message like this:

```
E 560 " *** Illegal access !! ",07,"$"
```

Character 7 rings the bell just for a bit of dramatic effect. After the message is printed we wait for a keypress, using the unfiltered input function, and when it comes, we loop back to the message:

```
0162 B409          MOV     AH,09
0164 BA6005        MOV     DX,0560
0167 CD21          INT     21
0169 B407          MOV     AH,07
016B CD21          INT     21
016D EBF3          JMP     0162
016F 207661        AND     [BP+61],DH
```

The only way out of this is to reset the machine or press Ctrl+Alt+Del, at which point you will end up at the beginning of the program again!

Now how to we get the table printed? You could go for a hard copy, but that would give the prospective villain a chance to take it away and work out how to get into the system. So perhaps the best approach is to add a routine to the program which would allow you to put the table up on screen. I leave that bit of additional decoration to you.

Really deleting files

When you delete a file, you do not actually delete it. That sounds a bit illogical, but it isn't really. What happens is that the directory entry for the file is marked as clear. The space taken up on disk is also released for subsequent use.

If you delete a file and then undelete it immediately afterwards, or before any material is written to the disk or drive, no harm will be done.

To prove this, if you have Version 5 of MS-DOS or higher, take a blank formatted disk and copy a few files on to it. Then erase them. At this point, assuming you are logged on to Drive A, type:

UNDELETE /LIST

You will find that MS-DOS will tell you that all the files are available for undeletion, but that the only thing which has gone astray is the first letter of the file, which the system overwrites when a file is deleted.

To get the file back, type UNDELETE followed by its name, and then fill in the initial letter when asked to do so. Back comes your file. And that is without either of the other two higher levels of protection against accidental deletion which MS-DOS can offer you. For further details, see the appropriate HELP files.

All of which means that when a file is deleted, the directory entry is marked as free for subsequent use, but that the data is still scattered over the disk and can be recovered. Even if new files are created, bits of the deleted file could still be sitting there on the disk, waiting to be reoccupied by other files.

So if you have sensitive information which you do not want prying eyes to see, you had better do something a little more drastic than simply deleting the file.

Filling a file with gibberish

If your intention is not only to delete the file but to wipe out sensitive contents, here is a simple trick which works for files up to 64K, or at least the first 64K of a file.

First, use EDIT to create a three-line file containing the following called WIPEIT, which I shall explain in a moment:

```
F O FFFF "BLABLABLA"
W
Q
```

Now create a batch file – let's call it WIPEOUT.BAT – containing the following:

```
REM @ECHO OFF
IF "%1" == "" GOTO ERROR
IF NOT EXIST %1 GOTO ERROR
DEBUG %1 < WIPEIT
REM DEL %1
GOTO END
:ERROR
ECHO Sorry, I can't find the file %1
:END
```

The two REM lines are to allow you to see the batch file working. Now make a copy of any file to try out, and call it XXX. Then run the batch file:

```
WIPEOUT XXX
```

To find out what has happened, then type:

```
MORE < XXX
```

You will find that the contents of XXX have been changed to "BLABLABLA...". This means that the file can now be safely deleted and if it is undeleted, it will just contain gibberish.

How has this been achieved? What happens is that DEBUG is invoked, with the dummy parameter %1 replaced by the filename – in this case, XXX. Then the redirection operator tells the batch file to take the input to DEBUG from the file WIPEIT, which first invokes the command:

```
F O FFFF "BLABLABLA"
```

This fills the whole 64K with "BLABLABLA". Then comes the one-character command W, which writes the number of bytes as specified in BX:CX into memory under the name of the file XXX. That value is written into the two register pairs when DEBUG is loaded with the file, so the effect is to fill the file – up to 64K – with garbage.

Then comes the vital Q command, enabling you to quit from DEBUG. Next you delete the file, and the security problem is resolved.

28

Creeping in to encrypt – I

As promised, I approach the end of the book on a lighter note with a BASIC program to allow you to test yourself against the clock and become a codebreaker. It is written in a fairly standard form, with no calls to subroutines with parameters, so you can try this out – with variations, as necessary, in commands like UCASE$/UPPER$, LOCATE, and so forth – even if you do not have access to Version 5 of MS-DOS. You may have to make other minor adjustments to the program.

Have you seen the film HZOA TIDZ EAFB WROC? No, my spell checker hasn't had a nasty turn, this is the serious stuff that spies are made of.

The idea behind the program which produced this conundrum goes something like this: cryptography, the art of encoding and decoding messages, has two basic forms. The first is substitution ciphers, in which you replace one letter of the alphabet with another. The commonest of these is the Caesar cipher which apparently was used by no less a person than Julius himself.

In this particular instance, each letter of the alphabet is shifted by four letters, so A becomes D, C becomes F and so it goes on. However, that's not a particularly difficult kind of code to crack, not least by working out the frequency of the letters in the code and matching them against the known frequency ratings of letters in English, which starts: E T I A O N S R H.

We ought to set ourselves a slightly stiffer challenge. This can be found in the other main brand of cipher, the transposition cipher, as it's known in the trade. The commonest of these goes by the name of "rail fence transcription", which encodes a title like this:

```
G   N   W   T   T   E   I   D
O   E   I   H   H   W   N
```

If you haven't cracked that one, read vertically down the columns from right to left, and if you haven't got it then, well, frankly, my dear, I don't give a damn.

Adding an encryption key

That is still a little on the obvious side, once it has been cracked, so here is a variation on this two-level transcription which uses another important concept in encoding: the key.

The idea here is that you scramble the code up in an additional way which is conditioned by some keyword or other. It's best explained by offering an example, and here come the strange-looking blocks of letters I started this Chapter off with:

P A R T

T	H	E	W
I	Z	A	R
D	O	F	O
Z	A	B	C

Note that the title is padded out with A, B, C to make up an even number of blocks of letters and that spaces between words are omitted.

The key in this case is the word PART, and the trick here is to print out the code in blocks of letters using the alphabetical sequence of letters in the keyword to determine the order.

In plainish English, that means the first letter in alphabetical order in PART is A, so we print out vertically that column first (HZOA), followed by the column under P (TIDZ), then the column under R (EAFB), and finally the one under T (WROC).

This gives the challenge the right amount of spice, especially if we add a time factor into the equation, and that's the program I've come up with. It offers three kinds of help for the weaker brethren, and you can tinker with it to increase the number of film titles and keywords, or if you feel like making the time allowed longer or shorter as the fancy takes you.

The code cracking program

The program gets under way with two lists of DATA, each preceded by a value indicating the number of items in the list. The first is films, the second keywords. If you want to tinker around with these lists, please feel free to do so, but avoid a keyword longer than 10 letters. Note that the DATA lists are headed by a number corresponding to the items in the list:

```
REM Code testing program
DEFINT A-Z
DIM cipher$(1 TO 10, 1 TO 10)
DIM order(10)
score = 0: total = 0
title:
DATA 20,Gone with the Wind,High Noon,Genevieve,A Tale of Two
Cities
DATA The French Connection,The Wizard of Oz,All Quiet on the
Western Front
DATA The Prime of Miss Jean Brodie,The Great Train Robbery,The
Hound of the Baskervilles
DATA White Christmas,Whistle down the Wind,Young at Heart
DATA From Russia with Love,A Man and a Woman,The Guns of Navarone
DATA Gunfight at the OK Corral,Three Coins in a Fountain,The
Dirty Dozen
DATA Rock around the Clock
cipherkey:
DATA 8,film,actor,part,camera,screen,house,cat,room
```

The subroutine SET-UP reads a random title and key, and then uses the
two-dimensional array CIPHER$ in the subroutine ENCODE to set up the code:

```
REM first pick up at random a title and a key
another:
```

```
GOSUB set-up
```

We will consider all the subroutines at the end of the listing, where they belong.

The decode routine is the main question and answer part of the program, and it is
here that I deal with the reader's question about how to type in an answer and deal
with function key calls. I've added a third level of complexity, a countdown which
restricts the time allowed for answering the question:

```
GOSUB encode
test = 0
IF test = 1 THEN
FOR a = 1 TO rows
FOR b = 1 TO tklen
PRINT cipher$(a, b); "+++";
NEXT
PRINT
NEXT
PRINT "The title and key are " + thistitle$ + " - " + thiskey$
FOR a = 1 TO tklen: PRINT order(a), : NEXT
INPUT "Continue....", xxx$
END IF
```

Now we set up the screen for testing the user:

```
REM Ready to set up the test
COLOR 14, 1, 4: REM or whatever colours you want to define, if
any
CLS

GOSUB decode

reask:
a = 12: b = 12: c = 15: d = 60: GOSUB boxdraw
LOCATE 13, 14: PRINT "Your score is "; score; "out of "; total
LOCATE 14, 20: PRINT "Another go (Y/N)?"
x$ = "": WHILE x$ = "": x$ = INKEY$: WEND
x$ = UCASE$(x$)
IF x$ = "Y" THEN GOTO another ELSE IF x$ <> "N" THEN GOTO reask
END
```

Now to consider the subroutines.

The SET-UP subroutine

The set-up routine randomises the choice of title and also that of the key. The quickest way of doing this is to take the number of items in the DATA list, randomise that value and read that number of items from the list.

If you do that, of course, you have to use RESTORE to ensure that you start off each time at the beginning of the list. Note also that both titles and keys are converted to upper case:

```
set-up:
RESTORE title
RANDOMIZE TIMER
READ rnumber
chosen = INT(RND * rnumber) + 1
FOR a = 1 TO chosen: READ thistitle$: NEXT
REM Now set title to upper case and get rid of spaces
REM Next line probably upper$ rather than ucase$ in your Basic
thiscode$ = UCASE$(thistitle$)
a = INSTR(thiscode$, " ")
WHILE a <> 0: thiscode$ = LEFT$(thiscode$, a - 1) + MID$(this-
code$, a + 1, 999)
a = INSTR(thiscode$, " ")
WEND
tclen = LEN(thiscode$)
RESTORE cipherkey
RANDOMIZE TIMER
READ rnumber
chosen = INT(RND * rnumber) + 1
FOR a = 1 TO chosen: READ thiskey$: NEXT
thiskey$ = UCASE$(thiskey$): REM again probably upper$
tklen = LEN(thiskey$)
RETURN
```

The ENCODE subroutine

The routine begins with a fairly hairy piece of programming, so let's walk through it rather gingerly. ENCODE begins with a nested FOR loop that gives B values between 65 and 90. That makes sense if you recognise that those are the ASCII equivalent of the characters A to Z.

What the double loop does is to scan down the keyword (THISKEY$) looking for the letter A, then B, then C and so on to Z until it finds a match and then it puts a pointer for that match into the appropriate element of the array ORDER.

Rather than spell all this out in painful detail, you'll see that in the main part of the program immediately after the GOTO ENCODE instruction I've added a block – which you can leave out altogether if you like – which enables you, if you set TEST to 1, to inspect the contents of the array CIPHER$ and see how the code will be set out depending on the key.

Back to the ENCODE subroutine: the fancy IF statement which compares an integer divide with a normal divide of TKLEN and TCLEN – the length of the key and the code – checks to see if the code can be divided exactly by the key. If not, the letters "ABCDE..." are added to allow the program to pad out the code with the required number of letters, so that each block comes to the same length:

```
encode:
a = 0
FOR b = 65 TO 90
FOR c = 1 TO tklen
IF MID$(thiskey$, c, 1) = CHR$(b) THEN
a = a + 1
order(a) = c
END IF
NEXT
NEXT
```

The rest of the routine fills up the cipher$ array if there are surplus characters required. The test using backslash and slash says: If integer divide equals normal divide, then there is no problem, otherwise we need to put the remaining characters into a new row and pad it out with ABC... and so on:

```
REM Now fill up the cipher$ array
REM First pad out thiscode$ to a multiple of thklen with ABCDE
etc to use if needed
IF tclen / tklen = tclen \ tklen THEN rows = tclen \ tklen ELSE
rows = (tclen \ tklen) + 1
thiscode$ = thiscode$ + LEFT$("ABCDEFGHIJKLM", tklen)
c = 0
FOR a = 1 TO rows
FOR b = 1 TO tklen
c = c + 1
```

```
cipher$(a, b) = MID$(thiscode$, c, 1)
NEXT
NEXT
RETURN
```

At this point, you can make life harder for the potential decoder by scrambling those surplus letters in a random way. At the end of the routine, the array cipher$ is filled with the code.

29

Creeping in to encrypt – II

In looking at our encryption test program, we have got to the point at which we look at the decode subroutine.

The DECODE subroutine

This subroutine puts up the screen with the questions testing the user. Note first that the time allowed the user is in the variable counter, which can be changed, of course, as is the speed at which the counter decrements, which is in the variable whattime.

The speed of the countdown will be conditional on the clock speed of your processor, so experiment until you get the result you are after:

```
decode:
REM The next bit assumes your Basic can't call procedures with
parameters
a = 5: b = 12: c = 7: d = 65: GOSUB boxdraw
LOCATE 6, 25: PRINT " *** CODE CRACKERS PROGRAM ***"
LOCATE 8, 12: PRINT "===> ";
FOR b = 1 TO tklen
FOR a = 1 TO rows
PRINT cipher$(a, order(b));
NEXT
PRINT " ";
NEXT
a = 18: b = 5: c = 24: d = 70: GOSUB boxdraw
a = 10: b = 5: c = 17: d = 70: GOSUB boxdraw
LOCATE 16, 14: PRINT "NOTE - the code may be padded out with
ABCDE... "
counter = 99
LOCATE 19, 7: PRINT "Crack the code! And beat the clock ... 99"
LOCATE 20, 7: PRINT "F1 tells you what the key is"
LOCATE 20, 38: PRINT "F2 shows the solution as xxx's"
LOCATE 21, 7: PRINT "F3 gives the first letter of each word"
```

```
LOCATE 23, 7: PRINT "My answer is ==> ";
whattime = 999
response$ = ""
morechars:
x$ = ""
WHILE x$ = ""
whattime = whattime - 1
IF whattime = 0 THEN
whattime = 999
counter = counter - 1
LOCATE 19, 49: PRINT counter
```

Now we get to the point at which the program looks for an input, using INKEY$, and
we have to set up a means of emulating buffered input as well as for keeping the
countdown going, and checking for input of F1, F2, and F3, the three help buttons:

```
REM You may have to put a goto to skip past the end of the loop
to the label fail
END IF
x$ = INKEY$
IF counter < 0 THEN x$ = "fail"
WEND
IF counter < 0 THEN GOTO fail
REM Here's where you may have to make changes. Power Basic allows
you to
REM have two chars input if it's an ASCIIZ string, so I can test
for
REM function keys. If you can't, use the numeric keys for getting
access to
REM help panels
IF LEN(x$) = 2 THEN
y = ASC(RIGHT$(x$, 1))
IF y = 59 THEN LOCATE 11, 14: PRINT "The key is: "; thiskey$
IF y = 60 THEN
LOCATE 12, 14: PRINT "The title as a pattern of xxx's and spaces
is:"
LOCATE 13, 14
FOR a = 1 TO LEN(thistitle$)
IF MID$(thistitle$, a, 1) = " " THEN PRINT " "; ELSE PRINT "x";
NEXT
END IF
IF y = 61 THEN
LOCATE 14, 14: PRINT "The first letters of each word are:"
LOCATE 15, 14
PRINT LEFT$(thistitle$, 1) + "... ";
FOR a = 2 TO LEN(thistitle$)
REM Next line - you may have to put upper$
IF MID$(thistitle$, a, 1) = " " THEN PRINT UCASE$(MID$(thisti-
tle$, a + 1, 1)) + "... ";
NEXT
END IF
ELSE
IF x$ > CHR$(31) THEN
```

```
response$ = response$ + x$
ELSE
IF x$ = CHR$(8) AND LEN(response$) <> 0 THEN response$ =
LEFT$(response$, LEN(response$) - 1)
END IF
END IF
LOCATE 23, 24: PRINT response$ + " "
IF x$ <> CHR$(13) THEN GOTO morechars

fail:
LOCATE 22, 7
total = total + 1
IF UCASE$(response$) = UCASE$(thistitle$) THEN score = score + 1:
PRINT "Correct!" ELSE PRINT "Wrong! The right answer is: ";
thistitle$
RETURN
```

Checking for a function key

QBASIC allows you to check if the user has pressed a function or similar key which requires an extended ASCII code. The keys F1-F10, Shift+ function key, Alt+ function key, and various others return not one, but two ASCII characters.

The first is a zero, and in the case of the three we are using this time (F1, F2 and F3) the second values are 59, 60 and 61.

This means that if one of those keys is pressed, it can be detected in Power BASIC first by checking to see if the length of X$ is 2, in which case the second character of X$ may be the value we are looking for.

I'll examine what the function keys offer by way of help in a moment. We now need to examine what we have to do to emulate INPUT, because with INKEY$ you are left to your own devices.

INPUT echoes the character on screen for you, allows you to rub out characters, prevents you from backspacing further than the starting point for keying in, and waits patiently for you to type Enter before inserting the string into the variable.

There is no such help with INKEY$. When you type a "normal" keyboard character, as you will see from the latter part of the subroutine, you have to build up in a character variable (in this case RESPONSE$) the characters one by one and print them out at the right location on screen.

But it doesn't end there: if you press the left Delete key to rub out a character, you not only have to remove it from the end of RESPONSE$ and print the reduced string on screen (that's why RESPONSE$ is printed with a trailing space), you also have to check that the user isn't inadvertently asking you to remove a character from an empty string.

That's why there is a double check, not just for the presence of CHR$(8) – left Delete – but also to ensure that the length of RESPONSE$ isn't zero, otherwise we would go on merrily backspacing our way across to the far left of the screen.

Examining the help keys

Now for the function keypresses and what they achieve. F1 tells you what the key to the code is, and that lets you work out how to unscramble the order in which the blocks of characters appear.

The next level of help, F2, prints the answer as a pattern of xxx's on screen, and the highest level of help, F3, prints out the first letter of each word of the answer.

If you fancy tinkering with the program to incorporate difficulty levels, one approach would be to progressively restrict access to the help information – another would be to penalise pressing the F1, F2, and F3 keys by decrementing the variable COUNTER and reducing the time left for typing in the answer.

Boxing clever

At the end of the program is a useful subroutine for drawing a box on screen. It assumes a bog standard BASIC which doesn't allow CALL with parameters, and you can tinker with the program if your version permits that luxury:

```
boxdraw:
REM Note that your Locate function may require semi-colons
between the values
REM a,b = row column top left, c,d = row column bottom right of
box
LOCATE a, b: PRINT CHR$(201); : PRINT STRING$(d - b, CHR$(205));
LOCATE c, b: PRINT CHR$(200); : PRINT STRING$(d - b, CHR$(205));
LOCATE a, d: PRINT CHR$(187);
LOCATE c, d: PRINT CHR$(188);
FOR e = a + 1 TO c - 1
LOCATE e, b: PRINT CHR$(186); STRING$(d - b, " ");
LOCATE e, d: PRINT CHR$(186);
NEXT
RETURN
```

You can change the numbers from double to single lines. Check the ASCII tables in your manual.

Enjoy typing it all in – it looks easy when it's done, but there is some pretty smart footwork in the program, though I say it myself. It's a really addictive teaser of a quiz and even if your randomizer offers you the same title twice, you will almost invariably get a different key to the code.

30

Hints and tips

To round things off, here are some of the various hints and tips which I have picked up along the way as I wrote this book and have not found a real home for in any of the earlier Chapters. You will find a wide variety of information here, which I hope will be as valuable to you as it has been to me, together with a last-minute improvement on a utility designed earlier in the book.

I start with perhaps the best tip of all, which is to ignore the splendid new EDIT program – and instead, go for something much more powerful.

Better editing

Before MS-DOS 5 came along, there was no simple screen editor available for creating batch files and performing other basic tasks. Only the hoary old EDLIN, user-hostile and line-based, was on offer, except for fortunate Amstrad PC users for whom the little screen editor had been copied from the PCW.

Called RPED after its creator Roland Perry, it enabled you to create and edit files in non-document mode. That means that there is no word wrap, and this mode is designed for typing in source code for programs, batch files and the like.

With Version 5, along came EDIT, an excellent full-screen editor which gives you much more power to your elbow. In fact, it is not a stand-alone editor at all, but the edit facility of QBASIC, which is why EDIT cannot be run unless QBASIC.EXE is available.

One very useful tip is that you should not run EDIT at all while editing, but QBASIC. The reason is that EDIT does not give you access to all the powerful features of QBASIC – apart from those specific to BASIC itself, I mean.

One thing you cannot do from EDIT is to press the F4 function key which under

QBASIC in edit mode toggles you back and forth from the screen from which you loaded QBASIC, which gives you an opportunity to relate what you are editing to what may have gone wrong immediately before.

In addition, you can actually split the screen using QBASIC which allows you to see different parts of the file at the same time. You gain access to this via the View split F6 toggle.

The only snag is that QBASIC expects to find files with the BAS extension. Otherwise you have to specify the extension or, if the file has no extension, put a full stop after its name.

Waiting for CHOICE

It might be tempting to use CHOICE to wait for a certain number of seconds at the beginning of a batch file while you put up, say, a screenful of introductory information:

`CHOICE/N/Tn,10`

If ECHO is OFF, this produces no output, and sits waiting for ten seconds. Unless, that is, you press an invalid key, at which point the wait goes on for ever, or until you press Y or N.

There are two ways round this. One is to specify every key on the keyboard with the /C option. The alternative is to be a bit kinder to your users by not assuming that a predetermined number of seconds is right for all of them all of the time.

Where is DOSKEY?

Here is a nice short tip. If you are not sure if DOSKEY is loaded into memory, press the Ins key, and if the cursor shape alters, DOSKEY is loaded, because DOSKEY's command line editor can switch from insert mode to overstrike mode and back.

You should add DOSKEY to the end of your AUTOEXEC.BAT file, unless you have applications programs which cannot abide any TSR programs sitting around in memory.

Hanging around

One of the big problem areas with the PC is that of the printer – what emulations to use, how to ensure that what you send from the computer arrives on the printer in more or less the same condition, and so on.

A difficulty can arise if you press Ctrl+P inadvertently or when the printer is switched off. You receive an error message:

```
Write fault error writing to device PRN
Abort,Retry?
```

The system will hang unless you either switch on the printer, sending an unwanted character to it. The alternative is simple: just press Ctrl+P again, and then A for abort. That will sort the problem out.

A different PAUSE

As you will know, the batch file command PAUSE puts up this message on screen:

```
Strike any key...
```

It would be nice if it were possible to change the PAUSE message and it is not that difficult to achieve, so long as you redirect the message from PAUSE to the NUL device and replace it with an ECHOed message.

Here is an example:

```
ECHO Ensure you have a disk in Drive A then press a key
PAUSE > NUL
```

The PAUSE command means redirect the usual message and send it "nowhere".

Selective erasing

If you want to erase all the files in a directory except for a couple you need to keep, here is a simple technique. For example, if you have a directory with PKUNZIP.EXE in it to expand compressed files, it would be nice to explore compressed files and delete them without having to go through elaborate procedures or actually delete the lot and then try and remember which back-up disk you put PKUNZIP.EXE on.

What you do to the file or files you want to preserve from deletion is change the attribute like this:

```
ATTRIB PKUNZIP.EXE +R
```

– which has the effect of making the file read only, in other words, while that attribute bit is set, the file cannot be erased. Then type:

```
DEL *.*
```

– or, alternatively:

```
DEL .
```

– which has the same effect, and don't panic if you are warned that all the files will be deleted or if you are sure (depending on which version of MS-DOS you have). DEL will not wipe out any file on which the read only attribute is set. Incidentally, I always have the R attribute set on the root directory files of my hard disk, in case I try and erase them by mistake.

Which version?

It is possible, using SETVER, to pretend to a piece of applications software that MS-DOS is running under an earlier version. Some packages will not run under the latest MS-DOS and some, too, it seems, cannot be resuscitated even with the use of SETVER.

If you need to know which version of MS-DOS is currently being emulated on your machine, write a short assembler program using function 30 (hex) of INT21.

This will return the major Version (the bit before the full stop) in the AL register, the minor version in the AH register. Do not use function 3306 (large numbers like these need loading into AX rather than AL), since that returns the actual current Version loaded, regardless of whether SETVER has been invoked.

The old directory

As I was putting the finishing touches to this book, it occurred to me, first, that I had not really done the BP register justice, having just used it because it happened to be there and free and, secondly, that I had missed an opportunity with Chapters 13 and 14 to add an equally valuable feature to the one I had created for you.

In those Chapters, we explored how best to switch instantly to a subdirectory on Drive C, given only that we knew the name of the subdirectory (assuming it was unique) and that we had no idea of the full path name of the subdirectory.

What I had omitted to do was to offer you the opportunity to switch back to your previous directory with just as much ease. This can be done with one tiny change to the SF.BAT batch file described in those Chapters, together with a COM file created by DEBUG in the usual way, which I will talk you through now.

The change to SF.BAT consists in adding the command OLDD as the first line of the batch file – and do note that it must be the very first line, before the @ECHO OFF command. Now power up DEBUG:

```
DEBUG OLDD.COM
```

There is one other assumption made by the utility, and that is that your prompt is in the form PG, in other words, it gives the full path of the current directory and ends with ">". Type SET to check that your PROMPT line does that, and if it does not, add a line to AUTOEXEC.BAT:

PROMPT PG

Here are the instructions to type in, together with an explanation of what is going on, and a demonstration of the potential of the BP register:

```
0100 B403        MOV      AH,03
0102 31DB        XOR      BX,BX
0104 CD10        INT      10
0106 80EE01      SUB      DH,01
0109 B402        MOV      AH,02
010B 31DB        XOR      BX,BX
010D CD10        INT      10
```

We start on unfamiliar territory with function 3 of INT 10. What it does is to read into the DX register the current cursor position on screen. Then DH is decremented, causing DX to point to the line above the current line, and function 3 moves the cursor to that position.

Before I go any further, a word of explanation is clearly in order. Say, for the sake of argument, the current prompt is:

C:\LS.PC\LS.ETC\MSDOSBK>

If at that prompt you type SF (for SF.BAT), and the first command summons up the COM file we are currently working through, the cursor hops down a line when you press SF, as it always does on receipt of a command. The first thing that the program does is to cause the cursor to hop up a line to the prompt line from which you typed SF – and now we come to the crafty bit, where another function of INT 10 actually reads that line off the screen.

Function 8 reads the character and attribute at the point on screen defined by the DX register (where DH = row, DL = column). In what follows, I have allowed for a maximum of 30 (hex) characters to be read – you can make it more if you like or need to – and I have set BP to address 200.

This time I am again using BP just because it happens to be there. The more powerful use of BP comes later. What the next few lines do is to read 30 characters from the screen to addresses 200 and following. Function 8 returns the attribute byte in AH and the character in AL, another example of 8086 reading a word (two bytes) backwards way on.

Hence the AL register contents are stored each time. Note that with this function of INT 10 we have to loop back to address 115 to reload AH with 8. The contents of

AH are always corrupted by this call. Remember that LOOP decrements CX each time and checks for zero:

```
010F B93000        MOV      CX,0030
0112 BD0002        MOV      BP,0200
0115 B408          MOV      AH,08
0117 31DB          XOR      BX,BX
0119 CD10          INT      10
011B 884600        MOV      [BP+00],AL
011E 45            INC      BP
011F FEC2          INC      DL
0121 B402          MOV      AH,02
0123 31DB          XOR      BX,BX
0125 CD10          INT      10
0127 E2EC          LOOP     0115
```

At this point you should insert the following into memory:

```
E 1FD "CD",20
E 400 0D,0A
E 500 "C:\DOS\OLDDIR.BAT",0
```

The next chore is to open the file OLDDIR.BAT, using the create file function, and then move the file handle to BX in the usual way. Note that the file is located in the DOS subdirectory, to which it is assumed that there is a path opened as discussed earlier:

```
0129 B43C          MOV      AH,3C
012B 31C9          XOR      CX,CX
012D BA0005        MOV      DX,0500
0130 CD21          INT      21
0132 89C3          MOV      BX,AX
```

Now BP is about to be used properly. If you type:

```
D 1F0
```

– you will see that, starting at 1FD, you have the beginnings of a CD command, currently terminating with the ">" sign. We need to replace that chevron with carriage return, line feed (currently sitting at address 400, 401) and save that information in the file OLDDIR.BAT. In order to find out where the chevron is in that buffer area, BP is first set to zero, then SI is set to the beginning of the buffer (where the "C" of "CD" is sitting).

Now comes the real use of the base pointer register. At address 139 SI is added to BP, and the contents of the address to which that value points are loaded into AL. First time round the value will be 1FD + 0 = 1FD, second time round 1FE, and so on, until AL matches 3E, the ASCII for the chevron:

```
0134 31ED        XOR    BP,BP
0136 BEFD01      MOV    SI,01FD
0139 8A02        MOV    AL,[BP+SI]
013B 45          INC    BP
013C 3C3E        CMP    AL,3E
013E 75F9        JNZ    0139
```

Now we shave one off BP so that it gives the exact byte count of "CD C:\LS.PC\LS.ETC\MSDOSBK" and write that to the file OLDDIR.BAT:

```
0140 83ED01      SUB    BP,+01
0143 89E9        MOV    CX,BP
0145 B440        MOV    AH,40
0147 BAFD01      MOV    DX,01FD
014A CD21        INT    21
```

Next we add the carriage return and line feed and close the file:

```
014C B440        MOV    AH,40
014E B90200      MOV    CX,0002
0151 BA0004      MOV    DX,0400
0154 CD21        INT    21
0156 B43E        MOV    AH,3E
0158 CD21        INT    21
015A CD20        INT    20
```

Whenever SF.BAT is run, the subdirectory from which the change takes place is saved, and all you need to do to get back there is to type:

OLDDIR

There are a couple of refinements which I leave to you. You could add a line containing @ECHO OFF to the OLDDIR.BAT file, which is simple enough to do. A more complex challenge would be to have a succession of files up to a given total, so that you could move back over, say, five previous subdirectories.

That trick could be managed within the SF.BAT file, using the IF EXIST command.

31

And finally...

That just about finishes this exploration of the nooks and crannies of MS-DOS. One of the key features of a powerful, flexible and expandable system is that there never seems to be an end to the things you can do with it, and this is certainly the case with MS-DOS. I have had to cut out far more from this book than I would like to have done, and I am already beginning to build a nest egg of material for a future book or two or more.

One important lesson from the various projects we have undertaken is to think in terms of horses for courses. In other words, there are certain tasks most easily performed by a batch file, others by BASIC, and others still by assembler. Then, of course, there is a judicious combination of two or even all three of them.

Programming is always a means to an end, not an end in itself, so do not hesitate to grab whatever tools are to hand and exploit them as best you can.

For further information on assembler and DEBUG, see the appendices which follow, and for books on various aspects of MS-DOS, see the bibliography which, given the vast number of books on the topic, many of them duplicating each other, cannot aspire to be any more than selective.

And finally, remember that the best way to learn is to practise and keep on practising. In the end you will be rewarded by a greater knowledge of computers and computing which will not only bring you practical results but also give you the great pleasure which comes with fully understanding the powerful tool which is the modern personal computing machine.

Appendix A

DEBUG

This appendix begins with a simplified checklist of how to enter, edit, run and save a program. Next, there follows a full description of DEBUG commands.

Using DEBUG

If you are experimenting with DEBUG, I strongly recommend that you either run from a disk dedicated to the purpose on Drive A or B, or alternatively from a RAM drive (see Chapter 1 and the HELP facility). The reason for this is that any inadvertent damage you do will be most unlikely to be visited on your precious hard disk. With a RAM drive, remember that its contents are lost when you switch off or reboot, so make frequent backups to a physical drive.

A simple DEBUG session goes like this. First load DEBUG, with or without a filename (but do ensure the filetype is COM):

DEBUG DEMO.COM

Ignore the "File not found" message. The minus sign is DEBUG's prompt. To type in instructions, type (plus Enter each time):

A 100

The 100 is not strictly necessary first time round. Now type in instructions a line at a time. DEBUG will protest if you try an illegal instruction which it cannot understand.

When you have finished, press Enter again. If you have not named the file, do so now:

N DEMO.COM

Then type:

R CX

The BX and CX registers contain the byte count for the file to be saved. Always allow plenty. Assume you have just typed in a few lines, respond to the colon prompt with, say 100. Then type:

W

- which writes the file to disk. Finally, to quit:

Q

Do note that it is very easy to corrupt the contents of a file, so every few sessions, create a new version:

COPY DEMO.COM DEMO1.COM

- and work from that, and so on. Alternatively, use the N facility within DEBUG to give the program another name. Two very important points to remember relate to running and saving programs.

The first is never to try and run a program twice. When you get to the "Program terminated normally" message, or you have worked your way as far as you want through a program, save your work so far if necessary, type Q to quit and then press F3, which should still contain your DEBUG loading command.

The second point is that BX and CX are, of course, often changed as a program runs, so when you save after running or partially running a program, check by typing:

R

- what the register values are, and use R BX to zeroise the BX register first if necessary.

If you save zero bytes, for example, or if you get a message about insufficient disk space, you have effectively destroyed the current contents of the file on disk, and you must - repeat must - ensure that you save what you have done properly before quitting.

An alternative approach is to use what are called script files, but I find this more longwinded and lacking in directness. Files of instructions are created using EDIT or a similar program and loaded into DEBUG using a redirection operator. For all but the simplest files, I find this approach fraught with difficulties. And for the simplest files - you might as well type them directly into DEBUG.

Finally, a reminder about moving program instructions around. As pointed out in Chapter 15 in the section Mysterious moving bytes, you have to use M with some care.

The DEBUG commands

This is an account of the features of the MS-DOS DEBUG program for reference purposes. In general terms, each DEBUG command consists of a single letter which may have one or more numbers associated with it, or the letter L. In each case, you should type Enter after each command. As elsewhere in this book, I have put all commands in upper case for purposes of legibility - you can use either upper or lower in your own work with the computer, DEBUG doesn't mind.

The commands are given in alphabetical order with notes as appropriate and indications of problems that may arise. Note that the segment number preceding the colon will almost inevitably be different on your machine - I'm just using the value which my AT coughs up at me.

? - Help

This gives a list of DEBUG commands and their functions.

A - Assemble

Type A followed by a number to assemble instructions into DEBUG. If you type:

A100

- you will be greeted with a similar message to this and invited to type:

33C0:0100

If you make a mistake, DEBUG will pinpoint it and invite you to retype the line. If you press Enter twice, you will be returned to the DEBUG minus prompt.

If you type:

REPNZ MOVSB

- or a similar command on a single line, DEBUG will place them on succeeding lines, and the instructions:

JC
JNC

- will be listed as JB and JNB, to which they are functionally identical.

Do be careful to ensure, when changing an instruction, both that you are starting at the correct address, since inserting in the middle of an instruction will have totally unpredictable and probably disastrous results, and also ensure that you are replacing like with like, byte-wise.

In other words, if you want to replace an instruction which occupies three bytes, like:

`MOV BX,1234`

- with one occupying one byte, like:

`POP AX`

- you should fill the unused bytes with the NOP instruction, otherwise the whole of the rest of the program may be gibberish.

Working the other way round is more difficult. If you wanted to replace this instruction:

`MOV BX,1234`

- with this one:

`MOV BX, [1234]`

- you would be in hot water, since the second takes up four bytes, one more than the first.

There are two ways round this problem, short of retyping everything that follows. The first is to use M for move, which is described later, but which has its pitfalls. The second is always to include plenty of NOP instructions when you are typing in a program using DEBUG, so that it is less tricky adding instructions at a later stage. I have avoided this practice in the programs listed in the book, simply to prevent you typing in reams of NOPs, but it is by far the safest approach in designing your own material.

Although I have used a different approach in the body of the book, you can also use A to assemble DB and DW pseudo-instructions into memory.

C - Compare

Not used in this book, this command allows you to compare two chunks of memory, and reports where differences occur. The command is typed in like this:

`C 250 L 30 550`

That compares the 30 hex bytes starting at 250 with those at 550.

D - Dump

This dumps information from memory on to the screen. Examples are given in

Chapter 11 of the form of the layout of the dump. The command can be invoked in one of three ways:

```
D
D 100 11F
D 150 L 20
```

The first default call takes the first 80 bytes starting either from address 100 or from the last address specified. This can easily cause material you require to scroll off the top of the screen, so the next two variations are extremely useful. Number two tells DEBUG to list from address 100 to 11F inclusive, and the third variation tells DEBUG to start at 150 and list the next 20 bytes.

E - Enter

This allows you to inspect and/or alter information in memory, and works in one of two ways. The simpler method is the one I use in the body of the book for data byte (DB) areas of memory, such as:

```
E 1000 "This is a message",0D,0A,"$"
```

That inserts bytes starting at address 1000. Do watch that you are not overwriting information you require further up the memory. It's easily done, especially when you are altering messages.

Approach number two is more complicated. Type:

```
E 100
```

- and the contents of 100 will be displayed. You can either press Enter to return to the prompt, minus to go back one memory location (to FF), space bar to go forwards one location, in both cases with the contents of the new location being displayed, or you can type in a two byte value to replace the current value.

F - Fill

Fills an area of memory with a given value. If, for example, you are unhappy with the spurious code that an area of memory filled with spaces generates, you can change it to NOPs:

```
F 100 500 90
```

Fill from 100 to 500 with the value 90, which is the machine code for NOP. You can mix hex values and ASCII typed in double quotes, that is, if you can think of a reason for wanting to do such a thing.

G - Go

Tells DEBUG to execute the program which you have either loaded into memory or typed in. The first important point to note is that when a program has run through DEBUG with a message like Program terminated successfully, or you have run part way through a program, never try and run it again, otherwise the machine will almost certainly hang.

The most frequent use of G is in conjunction with an address you want to stop at, like:

G 504

- but ensure that the address marks the beginning of an instruction, not the middle of one, otherwise it will never stop. It is possible to put more than one breakpoint, as it's called, after G.

If, as often happens, you want to inspect the changing contents of registers and addresses in a loop, use G to go to the instruction you want to halt at, then T (unless the next instruction is an INT, in which case use P) to single step past that instruction, then issue G with the same address as before. You can't type:

G 546

- and then, when you are at 546, type the same again. DEBUG will just sit there muttering to itself something about silly programmers not realising that I am at address 546 already.

H - Hex arithmetic

Follow H by two values:

H 120 445

- and DEBUG will tell you their sum and their difference, but will get confused if you put, as here, a smaller value before a larger one, and also if you exceed the maximum permitted value of FFFF.

I - Input

This is unlikely to be used by you as it refers to inputting a byte from a numbered port.

L - Load

This enables you to load a file or program into DEBUG:

```
L
```

It requires that the file has already been made known to DEBUG by the N = name command. Alternatively, L can be used to load sectors direct from disk:

```
L 1000 0 12 02
```

This will load into addresses 1000 and following the contents of sector 12 and 13 from the A drive (drives are numbered from zero).

M - Move

Moves bytes around the memory. Say you are trying to add an instruction to a program at location 145. You might take the rest of the program typed so far and move it well out of the way to, say, location 800:

```
M 145 1B0 800
```

Alternatively, you can use L as in the case of the D command. Then at 145 you add in your new instructions, which, say, finish at 14A. So:

```
M 800 850 14A
```

- to allow for plenty of characters left over. And all is fine. Only it isn't. What no one tells you is that DEBUG always works in terms of relative jumps to specific addresses. That is usually well and good, since it renumbers them again when you return the rest of the program to its new starting address, but unfortunately it insists on renumbering CALL instructions, sometimes with catastrophic results.

The moral of the tale is, first, practise with M until you understand what it does, and second, always check on JMP, JNC, CALL and similar instructions to check that the addresses are valid still.

N - Name

An alternative to typing:

```
DEBUG MYFILE.COM
```

- is to type DEBUG without parameters and then:

```
N MYFILE.COM
L
```

Note that naming the file does not, repeat not, load it. You have to do that as well, since you might be naming a file to write to it.

O - Output

The opposite of I for Input.

P - Proceed

Similar to T for trace, used in single-stepping, but it carries out an interrupt, or a subroutine, or a repeat string, then halts at the next instruction. So, in this sequence:

```
MOV AH,09
MOV DX,1000
INT 21
XOR CX,CX
```

- if you are single-stepping, use T for the first two instructions and P for the interrupt. Similarly, if you want to hop over the CALL:

```
MOV DX,[1234]
CALL 600
CMP AL,FF
```

- use P to move directly from the second instruction to the CMP.

Q - Quit

Immediately abandons DEBUG and causes the memory contents to be lost. It is essential to save your program first using W, and possibly also the R for Register command, which comes next in the list.

R - Register

This command is executed automatically with P and T. If you type it without parameters, the result is a full list of registers. Alternatively you can inspect and alter, if you wish, the contents of an individual register.

When determining the size of the file you wish to save, first ensure that the BX register is zero and then set CX to the value you require. Only then should you Write the file and Quit to MS-DOS.

If you wish to display the flags, type:

R F

You can change the flags at this point by typing the appropriate two-character code, DN instead of UP, for example, to change the direction flag.

S - Search

To search an area of memory, type:

`S 1000 2000 "DIR"`

- or:

`S 2000 4000 0B`

- or a mixture of hex and values in strings. Note that the values in strings are case sensitive. The result will either be nothing, if no match has been found, or a list of addresses which indicate where the match begins. This is a powerful tool, useful in patching programs as demonstrated in the body of the book with COMMAND.COM.

T - Trace

Single-steps through a program. If you put a number after the trace, it will execute that number of instructions, putting up the register contents and flag states after each instruction.

Do remember that any number you put after T is in hex, so 20 means 32 decimal instructions, quite a few screenfuls of information.

U - Unassemble

Tries to convert the contents of memory locations into valid assembler code. Again, it can be followed by values exactly like D. Note that if you try and unassemble in the middle of an instruction, you will get either garbage, or an implausible but wrong instruction, or a subtle blend of the two.

If you want to see instructions around address 14B but you aren't sure whether 14B is the beginning of an instruction, try:

`U14B`
`U14C`

- and so on, until the instructions make sense to you.

W - Write

Takes the contents of memory as specified in the BX and CX registers and saves them to a file named either as a parameter to DEBUG when you called it, or with the N command.

A note on segments

If you change the segment, or if you inadvertently stroll into the middle of an interrupt, you can issue an R command to inspect the segment values, so that you can find out where you are. To override the current segment to find out where an INT finishes, type:

`U DS:100`

- to unassemble instructions starting at 100 in the segment specified in DS.

Appendix B

8086 Assembler

This is a list of the commonest 8086 instructions, together with comments, most of which have been used in the course of this book. For a complete list, see the book by Wyatt recommended in the bibliography. His book also includes the enhanced instruction sets for the 80286 and 80386, together with those of the numeric coprocessors.

If you're not sure how these instructions operate, experiment using DEBUG, watching particularly for any change in the state of the registers and flags. Here is a list of the flags:

OV DN EI NG ZR AC PE CY
NV UP DI PL NZ NA PO NC

In the first line they are set, in the second clear. They mean, in order:

Overflow
Direction
Interrupt
Sign
Zero
Auxiliary carry
Parity
Carry

In what follows, there are many references to bytes and words. As a reminder, a byte is an 8-bit value and a word is two bytes. So the AH register is an example of an address which can hold a byte, and the AX register of a word. Another reminder:

MOV AX, 1234

refers to an actual value, whereas:

MOV AX, [1234]

refers to the contents of address number 1234.

References to the source and destination operands have the following meaning:

MOV AL, 99

- means move from the source operand 99 to the destination operand AL.

Please note again that my aim has been to introduce you to a subset of 8086 assembler to enable you to write programs using DEBUG and to get a general feel for assembler. If you decide to go further and use a full-blooded symbolic assembler, which enables you to give names to labels and addresses, I recommend the shareware product called A86 assembler which, with its parallel debugger D86, is the product I use to develop commercial software. It is widely advertised and readily available via shareware marketing companies.

The MASM assembler which forms the basis of the books by Norton and Miller is less user-friendly and far more bureaucratic. Norton's book is none the less recommended for its description of 8086 programming instructions and techniques. Here now is a description of the main assembler instructions in alphabetical order.

ADD

Can be used with either an 8-bit or a 16-bit register. Here are a couple of examples:

ADD AX, DX
ADD AL, [1080]

To take the first example: It means add the contents of AX and DX and put the result in AX.

AND

Compares bit by bit, and sets bits in the destination operand only when both are set. Example:

AX = 4C56
BX = 00FF
AND AX, BX

The result in AX is 0056, since the lower four bits of BX are set and the rest is zero.

CALL

Loads the IP register with the address after CALL, saves the return address on the stack. The subroutine is executed until a RET instruction is encountered, then we return to the calling code.

CLD

Clears the direction flag so that instructions like REPZ MOVSB will work in increasing memory addresses. This is the default state of the flag, and appears on the register list as UP. (The opposite is DN - see STD).

CMP

Compares bytes or words, and sets the flags accordingly. Example:

```
CMP BX, DX
JE 500
```

If the two are equal, jump to the instruction starting at address 500.

DEC

Decrement a byte or a word by one.

DIV

Divide. If you are dividing a byte, the assumption is that the contents of the AX register are divided by whatever you specify as an operand:

```
MOV AX, 1234
MOV BL, 2
DIV BL
```

The result is stored in AL, the remainder in AH.

If you are dividing by a word, on the other hand, it's assumed that DX:AX is being divided. The result is held in AX, the remainder in DX.

INC

Increments the value of a byte or word by one. It can also be applied to an address:

```
INC BX
INC [1234]
```

JC and JNC

Jump if carry, or if not carry. The first instruction is functionally identical to JB or JNAE, and you will find that DEBUG alters any JC you type to JB.

JNC is functionally identical to JAE and JNB, and DEBUG puts up JNB if you type JNC.

JE, JG, JGE, JL, JLE, JNG, JNGE, JNZ

That's a selection from the "jump if" set of instructions, some of which duplicate each other. JNZ, for example, is the same as JNE in function.

They should cover just about every contingency. Reading from left to right they are: Jump if equal, jump if greater, jump if greater or equal, jump if less, jump if less or equal, jump if not greater, jump if not greater or equal, and jump if not zero.

All the jumps should of course be followed by an address which points to the beginning of an instruction.

JMP

Jump whatever, again to a specified address.

LOOP

LOOP to the given address, decrementing CX each time until CX is zero. It's up to you to ensure that CX has a sensible starting value and that you do not interfere with the value during the loop, otherwise it could go on for some time. One way of protecting yourself is to PUSH and POP CX if you are designing a long loop, and certainly if you want to create an inner loop.

MOV

Move from source operand to destination operand. Note that it doesn't make sense to try and move a byte to a word, and vice versa. DEBUG will not approve if you try. If you want, say, to put a value in AL into the CX register to set up a count, use this technique:

```
XOR CX, CX
MOV CL, AL
```

That first instruction zeroises the whole of the CX register for you.

MOVSB and MOVSW

Powerful commands which need to be set up carefully. The first moves a single byte, the second a word. You first put into SI the source address for the move, and into SI the destination address. Then you put the number of bytes into CX. Take a deep breath and type:

REPNZ MOVSB

- to move the number of bytes specified in CX. A technique to clear an area of memory to, say, spaces, is to put the value 20 into the first address (let's say it's 1050), and move it like this:

```
MOV SI,1050
MOV AL,20
MOV [SI],AL
MOV DI,1051
MOV CX,100
REPNZ MOVSB
```

Whether you are working up through the memory or down depends on the state of the destination flag. See CLD and STD.

MUL

Like DIV, it depends on whether you are dealing with bytes or words. In the case of bytes, AL is multiplied by the operand and the result goes into AX. If it's a word, the contents of the whole of AX are multiplied by the operand and the result goes into DX:AX.

Note that this implies you should not have a value lurking in DX that you may want later, and this kind of consideration is important in arithmetical operations.

NOP

Does nothing. Use it as a filler when writing code, and for leaving spaces to enable you to add in instructions.

OR

A logical bitwise OR. If bits in both operands are set to one, the destination operand has the corresponding bit set to one.

PUSH and POP, PUSHF and POPF

Put a register or the flags on to the stack, and remove them. Remember, it's last in, first out. The stack is located by default at the top of the code segment.

REPNZ

Repeat while the contents of CX are not zero. Usually linked with an instruction like MOVSB (move a single byte). The opposite and equivalent instruction is REPZ.

RET

Return from a subroutine.

ROL and SAL

Two of the rotate instructions, moving bits left and right. The difference is that the rotate instructions move bits round in a circle, so to speak, whereas the arithmetic ones lose bits off whichever end you are moving to.

Note that DEBUG is not happy with all these instructions, and will only let you rotate one bit at a time. Multiplying and dividing by powers of two are another way of arithmetic shifting.

STD

Makes the direction flag point downwards.

SUB

Subtracts source from destination and stores result in destination operand.

Appendix C

Hex and binary

The object of the exercise in this appendix is to explain the significance of decimal, hexadecimal and binary on your PC, and to demonstrate why this range of number systems is not only necessary but very desirable in aiding the advanced user to get the best out of his or her machine.

Let's begin by getting one myth out of the way, and that is, that decimal is the "normal" system since, after all, we have ten fingers (thumb included) on each hand, and ten toes on each foot. That, however, could equally be an argument for working from the base 20, or even 40. There's nothing sacred about decimal, nor is it necessarily the most straightforward system to function in.

Take oldfashioned pounds and ounces, for example. There are 16 ounces in a pound, as every schoolboy used to know before the world went mad for grammes and kilogrammes. Take the decimal 10 and divide it by 2. Answer = 5. Divide that by 2, and you are already into decimal points with 2.5. By contrast, you can divided good old 16 right down to 1 and not have a single fraction in sight, since it's a power of two.

So there is no truth in the rumour that there is some preordained reason why we should either think in decimal or, indeed, work to a regular number base at all. Going back to ounces: 16 in a pound, 4 in a quarter, and on to stones, hundredweights, and the rest. If you are still not convinced, ask yourself how many seconds there are in a minute, minutes in an hour, hours in a day, and so on. And then go on to inches, feet, yards, chains, furlongs, and the rest.

But, if we are to stray from familiar systems to oddities like binary and hex, then we at least deserve to know what the reasoning is behind them. Why are they so necessary and why is the decimal system so inappropriate?

Let's start with binary. Computer systems work with electronic states which are either "on" or "off". That's a choice between two, so it makes sense to describe them in terms of a number system which functions in two's. It requires just two digits, a "0" and a "1", to describe the numbers in the system. That makes it very simple, but there's a huge drawback to it, as we'll see in a moment, which positively invites the introduction of hex.

Let us try a bit of binary first. Here are the numbers 1 to 7 in binary:

binary	decimal
0	0
1	1
10	2
11	3
100	4
101	5
110	6
111	7

I hope you can see the pattern emerging in binary. If you work onwards, 8 will be 1000, 9 1001, 10 1010, and so on. The main pattern to spot, though, is obviously that at every power of two, we have the equivalent of 10 in decimal, in other words, a number followed by a string of zeroes:

$10 = 2$

$100 = 4$

$1000 = 8$

$10000 = 16$

- and so on and so forth. On the other side of the coin, though, there is no really convenient, easy-to-remember pattern at all between the decimal numbers and their binary equivalents, and it is important that there should be some human-friendly correspondence when it gets to reasonably large numbers, since I would be totally lost trying to work out a way of pinpointing or remembering a number like:

11010011

- or of converting a decimal value like:

3256

- into binary.

To the rescue comes hex, or hexadecimal, to give it its full name. Instead of working to the base ten, hex works - like oldfashioned ounces - to the base 16. First, here are the hex values between 0-15 with their binary and decimal counterparts:

hex	decimal	binary
0	0	0000
1	1	0001
2	2	0010
3	3	0011
4	4	0100
5	5	0101
6	6	0110
7	7	0111
8	8	1000
9	9	1001
A	10	1010
B	11	1011
C	12	1100
D	13	1101
E	14	1110
F	15	1111

Now you can see that there is a correspondence between hex and binary, and that is that all the different possibilities in four bits (binary digits) can be represented by a unique hex value. C is 1100, 2 is 0010, and so on. The letters A-F have been imported into the number system simply because we have run out of digits.

The PC works in units of storage called bytes, each of which hold 16 bits, which means very conveniently that they can be described in terms of two hex digits. Here is an example:

11011111 = DF

01000001 = 41

And this means that it is pretty straightforward to convert back and forth, a task that would be almost impossible in decimal.

Let's take the idea a stage further. If you have a byte containing this information:

4142

- which happens to be the values corresponding to the characters A and B, and you wanted to pick out just the second character and find out what it was, you could use a technique called masking, which you will find explained in detail in the chapters on DEBUG, and you will also see that the character sets are created in such a way that it is simple, using a bit mask, to convert from upper to lower case and back again.

Hex, then, is an ideal means of taking all those strings of ones and zeroes which look so confusing and converting them into a form which we poor humans can just about understand. So hex looks difficult and obscure, but once mastered, it will enable you to work more closely and effectively with your computer, especially when you are dealing with DEBUG and assembler.

Appendix D

Bibliography

This is an expanded list of the books which I have found most useful in delving into MS-DOS during the time I've been writing about it. It's not intended to be an exhaustive account of every last title on the subject - far from it, since there are far too many works around which duplicate material found in others or where there is a great deal of overlapping.

Alongside the details of each book, I offer a brief account of what you might expect to find inside. In some cases, I would advise you to take a wealthy friend or a rich aunt to the bookshop with you. The going rate for a computing paperback, even though it is large format and runs to several hundred pages, is over twenty pounds, and one book on the list that follows - DOS Power Tools - weighs in at just under forty pounds, and that's money, not pounds and ounces. One word of advice before you purchase: ensure that the book you are after covers your version of the operating system, if that's the kind of information you are after. I've tried to indicate where appropriate which versions are considered.

You may notice that I recommend more than one book for many of the aspects of MS-DOS, like batch files or DEBUG, for example. This is simply because each book approaches the subject in a different way, and that there is no "last word" on any aspect of the system.

The omission of a book from the following list may mean that it duplicates other similar books, that it is too general to be of value to the more advanced user, or that I have simply not come across it in the flood of literature on this wide and ever-expanding subject. Some of the titles which refer to earlier versions of DOS may have been more recently upgraded to 6.2, so do check with your bookseller before purchasing.

Angermeyer, J., Fahringer, R., Jaeger, K, and Shafer, D. *Tricks of the MS-DOS Masters*, The Waite Group, 1987. (Ver.1-3.1)

Silly title for a super book for anyone keen to get the best out of MS-DOS. Particularly good on batch files and redirection, pipes and files. Large sections of the book are given over to add-on software and add-on boards, so check that the contents are really what you are after. I found it worth buying for the chapter on batch files alone.

Ainsbury, R., *DOS 6 Secrets*, IDG Books, 1993.

Don't be put off by the gaudy cover - this book is the best I have found among the many which claim to tell you "secrets" of the MS-DOS operating system. Very comprehensive and comes with disks.

Angermeyer, J., Fahringer, R. (and others too numerous to mention). *The Wait Group's MS-DOS Developer's Guide*, Second Edition, The Waite Group, 1989.

This is a book for the advanced user, including topics such as TSR programs, real-time programming, devices, recovering lost data, and a technical description of the differences between the various versions of MS-DOS. The latest edition I have seen covers up to DOS 4.0.

DeVoney, C. *MS-DOS User's Guide*, Second Edition, Que Corporation, 1987. (Ver. 1-3.1)

A clear and detailed introduction to the MS-DOS commands and to the system generally. Recommended if you can't make sense of your manual, or if you would like a readable account of what MS-DOS has to offer.

Duncan, Ray. *MS-DOS Functions*, Microsoft, 1988.

One of my constant companions when programming, this quick reference guide covers the INT 21 functions.

Duncan, Ray. *BM ROM BIOS*, Microsoft, 1988.

Another constant companion, this time detailing interrupts 10 to 1A.

Duncan, Ray. *Advanced MS-DOS Programming*. Second Edition, Microsoft Press, 1988. (Ver. 1-4)

Here you will find a detailed account of all aspects of the operating system, from the video display to file management, and from interrupt handlers to installable device drivers. I find it most useful of all, though, for its clear account of all the INT 20, INT 10 and other interrupts which make MS-DOS the powerful and portable operating system it is.

Goodman, and Socha, *DOS 6.0 Power Tools*, Bantam 1993.

A wealth of information on MS-DOS, together with disks.

Goodwin, M. *Power of QBASIC*, MIS Press, 1991.

If you need an additional guide to QBASIC other than the manual, this is it.

Hogan, T. *The Programmer's PC Source Book*, Microsoft Press, 1988.

Hardly a compulsive read, this is a compilation of tables about every last aspect of the PC, from CPU chip pinouts, the video adapters, the complete DEBUG and EDLIN command sets, to hex tables and Microsoft Windows.

Jamsa, K. *DOS Batch File Power*, Sams, 1991.

Covers a wide range of batch file options. Some of the batch files seem unnecessarily long-winded. Comes with disks.

Lai, R. *Writing MS-DOS Device Drivers*, Waite Group, 1987.

This is a one-topic very advanced account of device drivers which covers every last gory detail of the subject. Well written and lucid, but you really have to be a committed and knowledgeable user to get the best out of it.

Microsoft MS-DOS Programmer's Reference, Microsoft, 1993.

Covers up to Version 6. More or less indispensable if you are seriously interested in assembler programming. Among other things, details the PSP, file system, character handling, program management, and interrupts.

Miller, A. R. *Assembly Language Techniques for the IBM PC*, Sybex Corporation, 1986.

Written for MASM assembler, this book offers a good introduction to the registers, interrupts and other aspects of the PC which you need to master before you can write your own code. The main programming part of the book shows how you can write macros in MASM.

Norton, P., and Socha, J. *Peter Norton's Assembly Language Book for the IBM PC*, Brady Books, 1986.

Describes the MASM assembler. A readable introduction, but obviously biased towards the proprietary assembler.

Norton, P., and Wilton, R. *The New Peter Norton Programmer's Guide to the IBM PC and PS/2*, Microsoft Press, 1988.

Peter Norton is one of the gurus of the PC, and his Utilities for examining, modifying and rescuing disks are known throughout the PC world. This is a comprehensive introduction to all aspect of the operating system. More than most of the books on this list, it can be read from beginning to end out of interest, but I have found it also contains a great deal of detailed information not printed in other supposedly exhaustive guides.

Norton P., Ashley, R. and Fernandez, J. *Peter Norton's Advanced DOS 6*, Bradley Publications, 1993.

A useful guide to this version of MS-DOS.

Norton, P. and Jourdain, R. *Peter Norton's PC Problem Solver*, Brady Publishing, 1990.

Not too advanced, but a comprehensive explanation of MS-DOS facilities. The 1990 edition covers up to 4.0.

Schulman, A., et al., *Undocumented DOS*, Addison-Wesley, 1990.

A must for inveterate tinkerers who like to know what is going on behind the scenes.

Somerson, P. *DOS Power Tools. Techniques, Tricks and Utilities*, Bantam Books, 1988. (Comes complete with a 5.25 inch disk of utilities.) (Ver. 1-3)

Put together by the editor of PC Magazine, it runs to a massive 1275 pages and covers every aspect of MS-DOS from the user's point of view. Especially recommended are the chapters on the keyboard; EDLIN; DEBUG; batch file techniques; and different screen video modes. Sometimes repetitive and wordy, not always exhaustive, but certainly the best encyclopedia-type book on MS-DOS around, even if it doesn't cover MS-DOS 4.

Stitt, M. Debugging. *Creative Techniques and Tools for Software Repair*, Wiley, 1992.

A specialised investigation of the techniques for good program design.

Uffenbeck, J. *The 8086/8088 Family. Design, Programming and Interfacing*, Prentice Hall, 1987.

An advanced technical reference manual to all aspects of using the 8086. Advised only for the experienced user, particularly if you are interested in interfacing the 8086 with external devices.

Wilton, R. *Programmer's Guide to PC and PS/2 Video Systems*, Microsoft Press, 1987.

Just about every last detail on the video systems of the PC. Assumes a knowledge of assembly language programming.

Wolverton, V. *Supercharging MS-DOS*, Microsoft Press, 1986. (Comes with a 5.25 inch disk) (Ver. 1-3.2)

This is a well-written "post beginner's" manual which you might find useful to reinforce some of the material in this book. Don't expect any advanced stuff on assembler or video systems, though.

Wyatt, A. L. *Assembly Language Quick Reference*, Que Corporation, 1989.

This is an almost indispensable work of reference for the assembly language programmer. It lists and briefly explains all the instruction sets for the 8086 family of processors, including the 80386. In addition, there are sections on the mathematical coprocessors.

Young, M. J. *MS-DOS Advanced Programming*, Sybex Corporation, 1988. (Ver. 1-4)

For this book, a knowledge of the programming language C or of assembler is assumed. It's an in-depth analysis of topics like the BIOS, interrupts, device drivers, and memory management. More of a reference work than a gripping read.

Index